THE
GAME

ON RON SIMON AND
THE GAME BEHIND THE GAME:

"*The Game Behind the Game* tells it like it really is. An awesome chance to be the fly on the wall during heavy-duty dealmaking. When it comes to sports, Ron Simon writes the *real* rules. Read it and win!"

—HARVEY MACKAY, AUTHOR OF *SWIM WITH THE SHARKS WITHOUT BEING EATEN ALIVE* AND *SHARKPROOF*

"Ron Simon knows that in sports, often there is more action off the field than on. Ron is a master at making things happen."

—SPARKY ANDERSON, MANAGER, DETROIT TIGERS

"Every season, I'm glad that we don't have to face an equivalent of Ron Simon. He is a winner, and he does it with class!"

—LOU HOLTZ, HEAD FOOTBALL COACH, UNIVERSITY OF NOTRE DAME

"The strategies Ron Simon uses would look good on anyone's blackboard. He's got the moves and know-how that really set him apart."

—BOB KNIGHT, HEAD BASKETBALL COACH, INDIANA UNIVERSITY

"Ron Simon offers us an inside view at the modern business of sports. But he is also an agent who understands that there is more to sports than just winning, losing, and making money. His is a thoughtful, experienced, and—above all—a caring voice."

—WALTER F. MONDALE

"Simon was such an effective negotiator that I once offered a player a $5,000 bonus to get rid of him. I got him to do it, too."

—LOU NANNE, FORMER GENERAL MANAGER, MINNESOTA NORTH STARS

"On a scale of 1 to 10, I'd rank him a 10. He is the type of person that if my son were to turn professional, I'd hire him on the spot."

—MIKE LYNN, FORMER GENERAL MANAGER, MINNESOTA VIKINGS

"He does a good job. He does his homework, understands the market, and keeps the bigger picture in mind when he conducts the negotiations."

—ANDY MACPHAIL, GENERAL MANAGER, MINNESOTA TWINS

BEHIND THE
GAME

MORE ON RON SIMON AND THE GAME BEHIND THE GAME:

"Without Ron Simon, I wouldn't be where I am today."

—KENT HRBEK, MINNESOTA TWINS

"Ron Simon has not only given me 16 years of fabulous representation, but he has also given me a very special friendship."

—PAUL MOLITOR, TORONTO BLUE JAYS

"Talk about color commentary. Ron Simon reports what you never hear on the networks. He's behind the scenes, in the clubhouse, across the desk, on the phone—and his book tells it all."

—JIM KAAT, CBS TV BASEBALL ANALYST

"If there was a Hall of Fame for agents, Ron Simon would be in it. His book is a fascinating, no-holds-barred look at the big business of the big leagues."

—AHMAD RASHAD, NBC SPORTS ANALYST

"In *The Game Behind the Game* Ron Simon reveals how to skillfully negotiate big league contracts while remaining a class act. He is a master at making negotiations non-antagonistic."

—PAUL BEESTON, PRESIDENT, TORONTO BLUE JAYS

"*The Game Behind the Game* is a winner! A rare chance to experience Simon's playing field . . . the negotiating table. His inside moves, grasp of the real life issues, and keen business instincts are unrivaled in the major leagues."

—KEN BLANCHARD, COAUTHOR OF *THE ONE MINUTE MANAGER*

"Any sports fan will appreciate this insider's look at pro athletes. The stories Ron Simon has to tell are the kind that never make it into the sports pages."

—HERB BROOKS, COACH OF THE 1980 U.S. OLYMPIC HOCKEY CHAMPIONS

The
Game Behind the Game

NEGOTIATING IN THE BIG LEAGUES

RON SIMON

Foreword by
HARVEY B. MACKAY

Voyageur Press

Edited by Jane McHughen
Printed in the United States of America
93   95   96   97   5   4   3   2   1

Library of Congress Cataloging-in-Publication Data
Simon, Ron.
The game behind the game : negotiating in the big leagues / Ron Simon.
        p.   cm.
        ISBN 0-89658-197-7
1. Simon, Ron. 2. Sports agents—United States—Biography.
3. Professional sports contracts—Case studies. I. Title
        GV734.5.S59   1993
        338.4'7796'092—dc20
        [B]   93-17730
                                           CIP

Published by
VOYAGEUR PRESS, INC.
P.O. Box 338, 123 North Second Street
Stillwater, MN 55082 U.S.A.
612-430-2210

Please write or call, or stop by, for our free catalog of publications.
Our TOLL-FREE number to place an order or to obtain a free catalog is 800-888-9653.

Educators, fundraisers, premium and gift buyers, publicists, and marketing managers:
Looking for creative products and new sales ideas? Voyageur Press books are available at
special discounts when purchased in quantities, and special editions can be created to
your specifications. For details contact the marketing department.

To my wife Schatzi, my son Stephen, and my daughter Andrea.
I wrote the book for them.

CONTENTS

FOREWORD

STOP. RIGHT HERE. NOW. DON'T SKIP TO THE MAIN story until you have read this introduction.

I am shocked, yes, shocked, to have to report to you that the autobiographical material herein contains several glaring omissions that render this manuscript almost totally unreliable as an historical record.

The man about whom *Sports Illustrated* wrote, "If there was an MVA [Most Valuable Agent] for the [baseball] meetings, it was probably Ron Simon," has not told you the true story of his own athletic career.

Yes, he was on the University of Minnesota tennis team.

Yes, he earned his "M" and he deserved it.

And yes, he was elected by the 1,900-member University "M" Club to head that organization, and he did an admirable job in that capacity.

But, how did Ron Simon get on the tennis team in the first place? What were the real origins of his interest in sports?

He never tells you.

I'm here to set the record straight. My credentials: I have known Ron Simon for nearly 50 years. It was 1942, the year of the unforgettable "Clash of the Titans," when Horace Mann met Groveland for the St. Paul sixth-grade city softball championship. It's the bottom of the fourth in a tight game. I hit a scratch single to right. The right fielder, a kid so skinny he made Lou Holtz look like Arnold Schwarzenegger, let the ball scoot between his legs. I rounded first, certain the ball would carry to the fence. I eased up a tad on my way to second, with visions of home plate and immortality dancing in my head. The ball beat me to the bag by ten feet. The right fielder had more than compensated for his shaky glove work with a clothesline throw to second. I had been victimized by the erratic but amazing athletic skills of one Ron Simon for the first time.

Over the years, when I have needed the services of a skilled negotiator, I have never had to look further than my playground buddy. Ron has all the qualities that make up the standard for a first-rate negotiator, plus one that seldom gets mentioned but belongs at the top of my list: an obsession for confidentiality.

Protecting your client's interests, particularly in the rumor-filled world of sports negotiating, means protecting your client's privacy. Though confidentiality is one of the cornerstones of every professional canon of ethics, I cannot count the times I have been in an elevator or at a restaurant and overheard the most prominent attorneys in our community casually discuss their clients' most private affairs. Ron is a fanatic on the subject. If his hotel room is next to that of his opposite number, he'll move or place his phone calls from the lobby. If you've got Ron Simon on your side, you won't have to worry that your cards are face up on the table.

As my attorney, Ron established a great track record on my behalf, just as he has with athletes like Paul Molitor, Kent Hrbek, and Steve Jordan. Ron has been one of only two or three sports agents who have represented first-round draft choices in all four major sports: baseball, basketball, football, and hockey. While a lot of the fun of this book is reading about the famous sports personalities Ron has represented, his insights into the psychology of negotiating will be just as fascinating to anyone who has ever had to strike a bargain as it will to sports nuts. Ron's concepts are to the art of scoring a deal what the head fake is to the art of scoring a goal.

Yet behind all of those sports headlines, psych jobs, 30-page contracts, "end run" negotiations, and multi-million-dollar deals, is a guy for whom an orthodox backhand is still pretty much of a mystery.

Ron tried out for the University of Minnesota tennis team as a freshman. He didn't make it.

He tried out as a sophomore. He didn't make it, but the burning desire to make the team was still there as he approached graduation. So, to preserve his eligibility, he purposely remained two credits shy of an undergraduate degree. Although the degree he didn't have was a prerequisite for admission to law school, he persuaded the dean to let him in anyway.

Ron tried out for the tennis team as a first-year law student. He didn't make it.

It takes three years to graduate from law school, and no doubt about it, Ron was going to graduate. In fact, he was on the *Law Review*, and only three people in the entire class had a higher grade-point average. It was now evident that, after three unsuccessful tries, there were but two chances left for Ron to make the team.

In his second year of law school, on his fourth try, Ron Simon made the University of Minnesota tennis team.

While there is no way I can prove that Ron was the cause, shortly after he finally succeeded in winning the number-six slot on the university's six-man tennis team, the NCAA adopted what I call the "Simon rule." Under that rule, no one has more than five years of eligibility, whether they make the team or not. The clock starts to run from the date of their admission. If that rule had been in effect in Ron's college days, the Ron Simon tennis story would have ended after his first year in law school.

It didn't because Ron's courage and determination were in effect then, and now, as a result, he has lived a remarkable life.

Despite his lowly status on the tennis team, Ron went on to compile a very respectable record and in later years won some major tournaments. He'll never win points for style with his grip on a ping pong paddle, yet he captured the state doubles championship. The only basketball player to use the two-handed jump shot, Ron was deadly on the hardwood. Ron's competitive nature and incredible tenacity are traits that have served him well in the no-holds-barred world of sports negotiations. He never quits. He knows how to win. I have no bias against natural, God-given physical talent, but if someday someone were to do a survey on the post-athletic careers of star athletes and those of the benchwarmers, I'd be surprised if the second-stringers didn't hold their own or even surpass their athletic superiors once the cheering stopped.

Walter Alston, Tom Kelly, and Earl Weaver were all cup-of-coffee guys as major league ballplayers, and went on to become superstars as managers; while many more gifted players, like Ted Williams, never cut it. Williams just could not understand why his players did not simply perform to the Williams standard on command. When you're the greatest left-handed batter of all time and you're managing one of the weakest teams in baseball, the Washington Senators, as Williams was, the leadership gap yawns wide.

Fortunately, most of us are not Williams. We realize that athletic shortcomings are not character flaws. The man in the arena, trying hard despite repeated failure, is our role model. Adversity, not easy victory, is our annealing agent. Those, like Ron, who combine natural intelligence with the will to overcome every obstacle, have helped teach us that brains and guts are the qualities that define real winners.

Ron may never challenge Bjorn Borg on the tennis courts, but clients have been able to count on Ron Simon to carry the day in other courts, where year after year, he has performed the many miracles you will read about here.

HARVEY B. MACKAY
MAY 1993

1
BEGINNINGS

ON NOVEMBER 27, 1989, LINDA MOLITOR LEFT this message with my secretary, Gail Hyster: "Pigs end up being slaughtered."

I am a sports attorney. Paul Molitor is one of my best clients. Linda Molitor is Paul's wife and her message says a lot about my profession, sports in America, and the pressures of big-league negotiations. In the fall of 1989, Molitor was eager to sign a new contract with the Milwaukee Brewers. After a couple of years of free agent freeze-outs, we were experiencing a great thaw. Baseball club owners were celebrating the holiday season and a lucrative new TV contract with a flurry of spending, and Molitor was in line for a nice Christmas package. My client was sitting on a three-year, $6-million contract offer that had been on the table since before the season started, and he was ready to sign.

I understood Linda's frustration and anxiety, and admired her concern for her husband's peace of mind. Nevertheless, I still wasn't in a rush. I'd been busting my butt for eight months persuading Paul not to accept the Brewers' offer and reassuring him that we would end up with a much better contract. I had already won the gamble: The 1989 season was history; Paul had had a very good year and had ended the season healthy; and players' salaries were beginning to take off. I knew waiting was in our best interests.

I am a very deliberate person with infinite patience when it comes to the decision-making process. This may well have come from my dad's warning that I should always think before I speak. He pointed out, "Once you have spoken, you can't take the words back." My standard response to any idea or proposal is, "Let me think about it and I'll get back to you." My slow methodical style in negotiations is as displeasing to some of my own clients as it is to the people who sit across from me at the negotiating table. However, I have found that my "batting average" is much higher if I reflect on the matter for some time and give myself a chance to sleep on things. Often, my final judgment is different from and better than my first reaction.

There is one case in particular where this approach served me well. My client, a businessman whom I shall call Arnold Everett, owned 20 percent of a cellular telephone company that won a government lottery to sell cellular telephones in ten midsized cities in the U.S. The license for each city had a market value based in large part on the population of the community. A major rift developed between Arnold and his partner. Arnold was in desperate financial straits and wanted out in the worst way. Messrs. Glass and Murphy, representatives of the partner company, were downright nasty during the protracted unsuccessful negotiations for the purchase of Arnold's interest.

I calculated the value of Arnold's share in the company to be $187,500. On August 3, 1987, I was surprised when Murphy offered $170,000, threatening litigation if the offer was not accepted. By letter of August 6, I made a counterproposal for $200,000.

On August 17, Murphy and Glass contacted me by telephone, and after a brief but cordial discussion they quickly increased the offer to $187,500. No arguments, no broadsides, no haggling. Arnold was turning cartwheels while I was growing suspicious. Although my goal had been met, I gave the callers my usual line: "Let me think about it and get back to you." Arnold was stunned when I told him I wanted to sleep on it.

Next morning, a light went on. I instructed my secretary to send a wire withdrawing my offer and told Arnold to check the company out. He did and found the company's value to have increased considerably because of a license dispute they were set to win. In February of 1989 we settled for $819,000. For me, it pays to be a good listener and to sleep on things before making a final decision.

In the Molitor case, I was getting heat from both sides of the table. The Brewers wanted to get the contract signed, and Molitor and his wife also were eager to get it done. I was the only person who wanted to wait.

In my business, you come to expect rhetoric and emotion from sports fans and members of management. Handsomely paid professional athletes are easy targets. We all play ball when we are kids, and it's difficult for most people to accept the notion that people deserve to be highly paid to do something that many of us did for fun when we were children. My job as a sports attorney is to cut through the emotion and see that my clients are paid what they are worth.

Worth is a difficult word to define. When pro athletes are paid large sums, it often inspires a barrage of columns and sound bites about how players are not as important as schoolteachers or medical researchers. I agree. In a perfect world, the teachers and scientists would be wealthy because they are doing things to better mankind. But we live in a country of disposable dollars and leisure time. Americans want to be entertained and they will pay lofty prices to those who fulfill this need. Nobody wants to pay a $23 cable-television bill to watch a man in a lab coat attempting to discover the cure for cancer. Sad, but true. We pay top dollar to watch the best entertainers—and that includes athletes.

My experience has been that employers almost never pay employees more than they are worth. If a player is making $2 or $3 million a year, it is because the owner thinks he's worth it. Owners of pro sports franchises are captains of industry and do not rise to their positions by making bad investments. A star player means more television dollars, more fannies in seats, and maybe a championship. Some sports franchises are worth more than $100 million and most every owner who has sold a team has ended up with a much higher price than the price he paid for the franchise.

These protestations were voiced long before baseball salaries began to escalate dramatically in the mid-70s. In 1930, Babe Ruth was reminded that President Hoover made less than the $80,000 he was asking from the Yankees. "I had a better year than he did," the Babe said. He eventually got his money, a salary 80 times greater than the average American worker earned at the time.

I recommended that Molitor wait because I thought he would do better if he waited. But it isn't easy to wait when you've got a loyal client's wife telling you that you are being greedy and ought to take what's being offered.

That's okay. Make me the bad guy. I can take it. I'm a sports attorney. It's my job.

Our team was not on the same wavelength. I called time out. We needed to regroup. Molitor came to my house two days after Christmas and we talked for two and a half hours. I did most of the talking.

I told him, "Paul, both you and Linda have been sending the wrong signals to the ball club. I can't get you what you're worth if we're not working together. Somehow, [Bud] Selig [principal owner] and [Harry] Dalton [general manager] must be getting a message from you that you are calling the shots and are willing to accept a much smaller contract than I am. Also, you and Bud Selig are good friends. This makes it difficult for you to refuse to discuss the matter with him, and when you do talk to him, you feel guilty about holding out for a larger contract. We have to immediately send them new signals that we are all united, that I'm calling the shots, and that you will go along with my decision. I don't want you to see Bud, or talk to him or anyone else in management. You and Linda shouldn't discuss the contract with anyone or do anything that will tip your hand. The reactions you've been showing have hurt our cause, but it's not too late to reverse the signals and land a great contract."

Paul didn't say much. He seemed to recognize the problem. He agreed with my strategy. We were back on track. Less than two months later, Molitor agreed to a three-year, $9.1-million contract. The meeting was the turning point in the negotiations.

What qualifies Ron Simon to negotiate multi-million-dollar deals with some of America's most prominent businessmen? That's a hard question to answer. Being a sports attorney is not something little boys set out to do. When was the last time you heard a ten-year-old kid say, "I'm going to negotiate contract extensions when I grow up"?

There is no university for sports agents, and little has been written about the field. There are approximately 190 registered baseball agents, almost 100 registered hockey agents, slightly over 200 registered basketball agents, and just under 700 registered football agents. Most of these agents specialize in one sport. The field is so crowded that nearly 700 agents are battling for the 336 college football players drafted each year. I've always found it interesting that while lawyers, doctors, accountants, architects, real estate agents, stock brokers, and insurance agents are regulated by the states, there are no specific qualifications required of sports agents. Although at least 21 states require agent registration and each of the players' associations requires certification, these requirements are primarily formalities. Any jock-sniffer, alumni booster, family member, or barstool patron can hang a shingle and say he's a sports agent.

There is nothing specific that prepares you for this kind of work, but looking back I can see where I got some of the skills and values that serve me well today.

I was born in the teeth of the Great Depression on November 16, 1933. My mother, Gertrude, and my father, I. E. Simon, were Minnesota natives. All four of my grandparents came to this country in the 1880s from Lithuania. Both of my parents had degrees from the University of Minnesota, and my father was the principal partner in a very successful family business in St. Paul. The company manufactured and sold children's play clothes to retail stores throughout the country. In those days, if you were fortunate enough to be a member of a family that had a successful family business, all the sons were expected to go into the business. You were happy to do it.

Even though my father was successful, he was tough with a buck. When my brothers and I were ready for bicycles, he bought us used Silver Kings. After my freshman year in college, I wanted to go to New York with a friend for a couple of weeks.

We had been invited to stay with his relatives there. My dad refused my request to pay for the transportation, but he had no objection to my plan to hitchhike both ways. When we were in college, my dad purchased a Chevy for me and one of my brothers to share. It was stripped down and didn't have a radio. He wanted to make sure that we were unspoiled and that we developed an understanding of and appreciation for money.

My dad encouraged hard work and emphasized the importance of being able to get along well with people of all types. Above all he wanted us to learn what the real world was like. In business, he placed a high premium on people's sales ability.

My first job was selling magazines on commission door-to-door. It was a tough sell with lots of rejection. I learned the value of a dollar and about dealing with the public. I was 14. At age 16, I worked a summer in the shipping room of the family business. My dad told the foreman to treat me the same way as any other employee, and the foreman happily complied.

During our college summer break, my brother Howie and I were slow to get jobs. Finally, my father announced if we didn't get jobs within a week he would throw us out of the house. The only work we could get was being door-to-door Watkins salesmen, selling everything from spot remover to shampoo to vanilla extract. We met all kinds of people, learned how to communicate with them, and improved our sales skills. It was a fascinating challenge, and we did very well financially. I firmly believe that if you can sell door-to-door, you can sell anything.

The next summer my dad lined up a construction job for me. The pay was great, but wrecking buildings and building roads was back-breaking labor. My dad made it clear at the outset that he did not expect me to quit before the job was completed. I stayed with it.

My father and grandfather fostered in us an interest in sports. My grandfather loved baseball and took his grandchildren to the St. Paul Saints' games, minor league but Triple A. I am the youngest of three boys and my older brothers, Jerry (five years older) and Howie (18 months my senior), got to go first. When my grandfather first took Howie to a baseball game at age seven, I was five and a half and wanted to tag along, but he wouldn't allow it. I waited a year and a half for that day, really appreciated that first game, and have been an avid sports' fan ever since.

My dad encouraged us to play sports. Although I was smaller than most of my peers, I played basketball, football, and tennis with the rest of them. Tennis was my best sport because I was quick and had good reflexes. My dad used to tell us all the time that playing sports is great for sublimation. I didn't know what he meant at the time, but I do now. He figured sports would help keep us steer clear of teenage mischief. Nice try, Dad!

I liked sports because I was competitive by nature. At our house, everything was a competition between the brothers. At about age 10, I began consistently beating my older brothers in ping pong. Usually after I won the final point, the ping pong paddle came flying at me from the opposite end of the table. Endless skirmishes would follow if I didn't get out of there quickly enough. I continued to play and beat them, even though I knew what the consequences would be.

Combined with my competitive nature and love of sports, I had a natural ability with numbers. Before I went to school I could add, subtract, and multiply. I don't know how that happened. That was the only sign I had that I was a little more advanced. When I was eight years old, I skipped third grade. Since I had already been pushed ahead one-half year, and since I was born in November, I graduated from high school two years early. I ended up starting at the University of Minnesota at age 16. I wouldn't recommend this kind of accelerated school career. I didn't have any problems academically, but I found it very difficult to compete socially and in athletics. Life can be tough when you're 12 years old and some of the other people in your high school home room are 18 and already shaving. It's no fun when the 14-year-old girls are half a head taller than you are, either.

I graduated from high school in 1950 with a B-minus average and went to the University of Minnesota. My major activities in college were social ones: fraternity, intramural sports, and beer drinking. My approach to college was that if you didn't make much effort and managed to get by you could never be considered stupid. You could not fail. I figured that if you tried your hardest and still got mediocre grades, then you did fail and everyone knew you were stupid. The fallacy, of course, was that if you don't try, you don't risk failure and never reach the top.

Graduation night for me was meaningless because I didn't feel I deserved a degree. I didn't even bother to go to the ceremony. I hadn't really done anything, and for the first time in my life, it bothered me. I talked to my father about my future. My father was moving the family business to Alabama and I wanted to go with him. He raised the question of my attending law school. He pointed out that, at age 20, I was too young to be in business. He said business people would not take me seriously, not only because of my age but also because of my youthful appearance. He noted that the business had no family member with a legal background and that this kind of expertise would be an invaluable asset. He persuaded me to go to law school.

At that time, almost anyone could get into the University of Minnesota's law school, but once you got there the weeding-out process was underway. The first day, a professor told us to look to our left and to look to our right because two-thirds of us would not be there at the end of three years. He was right. I decided that once and for all I was going to find out if I could be a top student. I told my parents that I would drop out of law school and move with them unless I was in the top 10 percent of my class after the first year.

The first year of law school was more difficult for me than for most of the students because I had a limited vocabulary. I simply hadn't done very much reading, and I found myself running to the dictionary every five minutes to find out what all these words were in the cases. Many nights I burned the midnight oil, discovering strength and discipline. I ended up in the top 10 percent of my class and said good-bye to my southbound family.

When I was 23 and in my third year of law school, I worked part-time as a legal assistant to a nationally known law professor at the University of Minnesota, Kenneth C. Davis. When I told him I planned to move to Birmingham, Alabama, to use my legal background for the family business, he almost shamed me into trying to practice law. He pointed out that I was a good law student, I had spent three hard years in law school, and that it would be a waste not to at least attempt to use what I had learned in the practice of law.

The family business offered security, while the practice of law suggested a struggle and possible failure. I graduated fourth in my class and the decision was put off for a year while I served six months of active duty with the Army in South Carolina. After returning from the service, I recalled our conversation and decided to explore the possibilities of private practice in Minnesota. My father was disappointed, but I assured him that I merely wanted to try it for two or three years to see how it went.

I began knocking on the doors of law offices. I assumed because of my high college ranking and because my family was well known and of good standing in the community, I would be in great demand. Wrong. None of the law firms was interested in adding lawyers, and I was rejected at every turn.

I decided to call a St. Paul attorney named Solly Robins. Our families had many mutual friends, so we weren't complete strangers, and I had met him once briefly at the Hillcrest Country Club in St. Paul, where he and my father were members. Robins was a senior partner of the third largest law firm in the Upper Midwest, with offices in St. Paul and Minneapolis. He was regarded as perhaps the top trial lawyer in the state. I had been talking with lower level lawyers in some of the other law firms and was getting nowhere. I figured I'd change my strategy and go to the top.

At that time, the market rate for a beginning lawyer of my ranking was about $500 a month. I called Robins several times, but naturally without any success. Finally, I talked with his secretary and explained the purpose of my call. She said that Robins didn't usually do the hiring, but if I wanted to take a chance, I could come to his office on a specific day at 5:00 P.M. She said she could not predict when he would finish work, but when he was done, maybe he would consent to see me for a few minutes.

I reported at 5:00 P.M., as suggested, and camped out in the waiting room until 7:15, when Robins cordially invited me into his office. I was pleasantly surprised that he would give me a hearing. When he told me that the firm was not hiring, I told Robins I could make him an attractive proposal: I would work for $300 a month, 40 percent below market, so long as I got substantial experience as a trial lawyer. Courtroom work appealed to me because it was a competition that involved a clear-cut winner and loser. I wanted him to promise me the opportunity to be able to try my own lawsuits with juries, frequently, and as soon as possible. He agreed. It was my first successful negotiation. I was 24.

I worked 11 months with the Robins firm, flying solo through seven jury cases, then joined Michael Robins and William Fine in our own law partnership. They originally invited me to join them as an associate, but I proposed that I receive no salary and instead be awarded a one-sixth or 16 2/3-percent partnership interest. They warned me that the first year or two, because the law firm was just starting up, they would be incurring substantial expenses and there could be losses. But they accepted my proposal. I had no salary, but I was single, had very few expenses, and was in a good position to take a reasonable gamble. And I was a partner. The law partnership, Fine, Robins, and Simon, was formed in 1960, and several months later Fine and Robins earned a fee of 150,000 shares of a local stock for promoting and organizing the company and raising some additional capital. Several years later I sold my shares for $70,000—the gamble had paid off.

These were busy years, professionally and personally. In 1968 I married Marlen "Schatzi" Loew, a native of Austria. At my stag party, speakers emphasized my tenacity and competitiveness. The last speaker recounted that although I wasn't good enough to initially make the University of Minnesota tennis team, I persevered, and when I finally tried out again when I was in law school, I made the team but didn't play. The following year I became a regular as the sixth man on the six-man team and finally earned a letter. My friend concluded by saying, "I call this a tenacious guy and a fantastic competitor." The master of ceremonies, a local judge with a keen wit, immediately stepped up to the podium and said, "I call that a horseshit tennis player." It all depends on how you look at it.

Our first child, Stephen, was born in late 1969 and our daughter, Andrea, was born in 1972. In between these events, I lost my father. He passed away suddenly at the age of 69. At the time of his death, he was still hoping I would join the family business.

It was shortly after my father died that I first got involved in the legal end of sports. In 1971, I was a successful trial lawyer with a modest background in the Twin Cities sports scene. I became a director of the "M" Club, an organization of past letter winners (I had lettered in tennis) in all University of Minnesota sports. As the club's president, I was well acquainted with most of the university's head coaches, who routinely joined us at monthly board meetings to update us and to discuss ways in which we could help their programs.

When I returned from an out-of-town Thanksgiving weekend with family in 1971, one of a number of telephone messages awaiting me was from the hockey coach, Glen Sonmor. I returned his call and the conversation proved to be the beginning of a new career. Sonmor asked me to represent him in his contract negotiations with the new Minnesota Fighting Saints hockey club to be located in St. Paul. The franchise was to be part of a newly formed World Hockey Association (WHA), which was to compete with the established National Hockey League (NHL). Sonmor had been offered the job as coach and general manager. I negotiated with club officials, and Sonmor came away with a two-year deal worth $65,000, guaranteed. (Sonmor had been earning $17,500 at the University of Minnesota, and in those days $65,000 was big money.) I was paid $500 for my services.

In the course of my work for Sonmor, I became familiar with the WHA, its plans and operations. As an avid sports fan, I had observed the skyrocketing salaries in the 1960s in football and basketball—raises triggered by the upstart American Football League and American Basketball Association. I concluded that the WHA would do the same thing for hockey, escalating hockey salaries that, in the early seventies, averaged only $25,000 per year.

My friend Lou Nanne at this time was playing professional hockey for the Minnesota North Stars. Nanne hailed from Sault Ste. Marie, Ontario, where he grew up playing hockey with Phil and Tony Esposito. After making his way to the University of Minnesota, he became an All American in 1963 and the only defenseman ever to lead the Western Collegiate Hockey Association in scoring. A naturalized U.S. citizen, Nanne captained the 1968 U.S. Olympic Team. When the NHL expanded from six to 12 teams in 1967, Nanne joined the baby North Stars.

In January 1972, after I had concluded the Sonmor matter, I called Nanne to share my thoughts regarding what I perceived was a great opportunity for big pay raises for NHL players. I asked Nanne if he could gather his teammates together for a meeting with me, and at considerable risk to himself, Nanne obliged: Club officials would not look kindly upon the organizer of such a gathering. Nanne took great precautions to keep the meeting at his house as quiet as possible. Since Nanne was a team leader, many of the North Stars' players attended.

This was a different era. In 1972, few NHL players had agents. The players were easily bullied by owners and most were not willing to take a firm stand in contract negotiations. They were always told that they could quickly be replaced.

I delivered my presentation, promising to negotiate substantial salary increases for a fee of 5 percent. Three of the team's top younger players—Tom Reid, Danny Grant, and Jude Drouin—signed up with me on the spot. It was almost like taking orders at a Tupperware party.

The rest of the players were skeptical, and I knew why. There was doubt about the stability and security of the new league, and many feared what might happen if they told General Manager Wren Blair that they had an agent.

Wren Blair is the man who discovered Bobby Orr and signed the Parry Sound youngster to his first professional hockey contract. He was picked as the North Stars' general manager when the team was formed as an NHL member in 1967. Blair was loud and animated. He was famous for flapping his arms and unleashing a steady stream of profanities. He would get so excited during games that the team trainer would ice him down between periods. This was unsettling for Blair's players, but it was also a form of motivation. Walter Bush, an original part-owner and president of the North Stars, described Blair as "an actor and a good psychologist." He liked to challenge, threaten, and belittle his players—he thought it made them tougher. He also believed that a player worried about job security played harder.

I wasn't worried about Blair in the hours after my big score. I was delighted with my new-found clients, all of them solid young professional hockey players with great futures. They would form the nucleus for my entree into the new, exciting, and glamorous field of representation of professional athletes. I proceeded to write Mr. Blair (whom I had never met) a formal, lawyerlike letter informing him of my representation of the players. I asked him to contact me to discuss the matter and awaited his response.

Blair, also known as the "Bird Man" because of his first name, telephoned me from Detroit two days later. After identifying himself, he went into a tirade, sprinkling his speech with four-letter words. He told me to go to hell. He said he would not talk with me, but would deal directly with his players as he had in the past. He said that if this arrangement was unacceptable to his players, they would be traded or sent back home to the tin mines of Canada.

Several days later when Blair returned to Minneapolis, I received calls from Grant and Drouin terminating me without explanation. Blair called Reid at his home on the day of a game, calling him every four-letter word in the book. Blair made it clear that a player with an agent was a player who might not be with the club very long.

Finally Reid, too, succumbed to the intimidation, fearing that he would be sent to the minors or released. Blair had bullied each of the players into terminating their agent—me. Simultaneously he had begun negotiations for new contracts. The modest raises that were agreed upon did not reflect the players' improved bargaining position.

There wasn't much I could do. I was angry, frustrated, and embarrassed, but I was also powerless. I couldn't force Blair to talk to me and I couldn't force the players to stick with me. The bully had kicked sand in my face and gotten away with it. I was reminded of the story of Green Bay Packer All Pro center Jim Ringo. In the early '60s, Ringo went into Vince Lombardi's office to talk contract and informed the crusty coach that he would like Lombardi to talk to his agent about his contract. Lombardi politely excused himself, saying he'd return in five minutes. When Lombardi came back, he told Ringo, "Jim, congratulations. You've just been traded to the New York Giants."

A few months later, in April 1972, the North Stars' highest paid and most valuable player, 33-year-old goalie Cesare Maniago, who had earned $50,000 the previous year, walked into my office at Nanne's suggestion merely to have a document notarized in connection with his off-season USO summer trip to the Far East. Maniago had been Minnesota's first draft pick in the 1967 expansion draft when Minnesota was added to the league. He had played the previous five years for the club and had just completed his best year, winning 20 games.

Maniago is a tall, lanky guy with an easy-going disposition. He is quick to laugh and has a noticeable Canadian accent. Feeling comfortable around him, I asked about the status of his contract negotiations. He told me that he and Mr. Blair had agreed on all the terms of an agreement, including the amount, which was quite satisfactory to him, but they had not been able to agree on the deferment payments. Blair wanted the payments on the three-year contract spread out over a number of years. Maniago was willing to have the money paid out over a period longer than the three years of the contract, but not over as long a period as Blair wanted. Although he was reluctant, I persuaded Maniago to permit me (without charge) to find out if there was any interest in him from clubs in the new WHA before he signed the contract. I made the appropriate inquiries, and soon discovered that the Los Angeles Sharks owned his rights and were, in fact, interested in exploring the matter.

A short time later, Steve Arnold, a representative of the WHA, met with me in Minneapolis on behalf of the L.A. Sharks franchise. We hit it off very well. After some negotiation, I had a four-year contract offer totaling $600,000. Hockey players were just not accustomed to these kinds of numbers. The offer was three times what Maniago had made the previous year, and substantially more than the amount he and Blair had agreed upon. It was also guaranteed, meaning Maniago would get paid even if he was released or couldn't play because of injury. When I informed Maniago about the huge offer, he was impressed enough to retain me as his first agent, although he was still skeptical about the new league, its chances for survival, and the quality of its play.

It was now time for me to inform Mr. Blair of my representation of Cesare Maniago. I was looking forward to it. This time, however, I prepared my client for the Bird Man's reaction. I warned Cesare of the inevitable intimidation tactics and advised him how to respond.

Well prepared for Blair's anticipated attack and armed with the strong offer from Los Angeles of the WHA, I made another run at the North Stars' GM. I informed him of my involvement and hit him with the L.A. offer. Predictably, Blair was furious. He contacted Maniago and peppered his goalie with some verbal slapshots. Maniago didn't flinch. He was much older and more secure than my first clients, and would not be intimidated. Since Maniago would not be bullied and the North Stars had no suitable replacement for the goalie, Blair realized he would be forced to deal with me or run the risk that Maniago would defect to Los Angeles. I was thrilled. I not only wanted a big contract for Maniago, but I wanted to make a name for myself and exact my pound of flesh from Blair. Agents are not without competitive fire.

When intimidation didn't work, Blair took another tack. He issued a statement to the media declaring that he and Maniago had reached a binding verbal agreement, and he threatened legal action if Maniago signed with the WHA. I countered with my own formal statement claiming that, although the parties had reached agreement on almost all the terms, including the amount and term of the contract, the question of when the payments would be made remained open and thus there was no legal contract.

I negotiated directly with Blair and a representative of the Los Angeles Sharks, and ultimately we reached agreement with the North Stars on a new three-year contract that was almost twice the amount of the one Blair and Maniago had previously agreed upon. None of the payments was deferred to later years and the contract was guaranteed. Maniago was extremely happy; I had a big fee and a second shot at a new career.

It felt good. On one level, I was happy to have made progress in my new career, but I also realized that I was elated because I'd gotten even with the Bird Man. Blair had embarrassed and humbled me in my first attempt at representing players, but I'd come back and put myself in a position where he had to deal with me on my terms. All my life, I've been competitive and tenacious. These traits don't necessarily make you the most popular guy, but America was built by hungry, competitive people, and the system still serves those who work the hardest to get ahead. In law school and sports, my competitive nature enabled me to go beyond where my natural ability would have taken me. I hated losing to Wren Blair, but it made me better for subsequent bouts of negotiation.

There is no formula or prescription for wannabe agents. In fact, anybody can say he is an agent, and a lot of underqualified and unscrupulous people have invaded the field of sports representation. "Agent" is a dirty word in many circles and I understand why. Although solicitation is a way of life for sports representatives, the sleaze-bag image comes from the aggressive and unethical manner in which some agents seek out athletes as clients. It's amazing that so many agents are lawyers because solicitation of clients in most states is barred by the lawyers' Canon of Ethics. Yet usually, if there is no solicitation, there is no client. Some agents offer payoffs in the form of cash or other benefits; others arrange loans for new clients. In recent years, agents have been convicted of crimes involving illegal payments to college athletes, and misappropriation of large amounts of players' funds that have never been recouped. This is why when I see my name in print, I prefer to be described as a "sports attorney."

In the ensuing chapters you will learn that a final offer is sometimes not a final offer. You will see what can happen when a player gets impatient, or caves in to pressures imposed by family and friends. You will learn when the time is ripe for negotiation and when it is not. You will see the dangers of long-term contracts for young players. You will understand that, while many people have the brain power to be effective negotiators, sometimes the most important body part is the stomach. You will see that great athletes who are idolized for their prowess, fame, and fortune have their ups and downs, too. They shed tears when they're moved, saddened, and disappointed, just like the rest of us. You will learn when a gamble is worth taking, when it's time to hold, and when it's time to fold, and how to renegotiate without really renegotiating. You will see that it's okay to take advice from people who know more about a particular subject than you do, to find leverage through alternatives, and to avoid personal contact when the subject at hand is strictly business. Above all, you will understand why you don't show your happiness when you are happy with a deal.

Most of these chapters deal with successes, but let's state up front that sometimes you roll the dice and you lose. In the late '70s I was representing Wilbur Jackson, the star San Francisco 49er running back. I was in the middle of negotiations with the 49ers' then-GM, the late Joe Thomas, while Jackson was in training camp in the option year of his contract. Thomas's offer "on the table" was substantially higher than the salary Jackson would earn in his option year and included two additional years. I rejected the offer. While the negotiations were in progress, Jackson tore up his knee during a preseason game and was out for the season. He ended up stuck with the lower option-year salary. Fortunately, Jackson recovered from the knee injury and returned to play football, but we were never in the same bargaining position again and were never able to fully recoup the loss.

Today I am one of the few sports lawyers who has personally represented clients in all four major sports, and I am among only a couple who have represented first-round draft choices in each of the four major sports. My practice is almost exclusively devoted to representing professional athletes and radio and television personalities. I have about 35 clients and count several among my closest friends.

Lou Nanne, recently retired senior vice-president and general manager of the North Stars, is somebody I have known from both sides of the negotiating table. It was Nanne in 1972 who called the meeting in his home that gave me my start, but later he fought management's battles with me and others. He once offered a player a $5,000 bonus if the player would dump me as his agent. "I got him to do it, too," gloated Nanne.

I won't try to kid anybody: This is one great way to make a living. I've traveled to Italy with Kevin McHale and celebrated the Celtics' Eastern Conference Championship in their locker room with him; I've been Paul Molitor's guest when he played in the World Series for Milwaukee, and in turn, he was my guest when Jim and Keith Fahnhorst provided 50-yard-line Super Bowl tickets when they played for the 49ers. I've traveled to Czechoslovakia with Kent Hrbek, and we embraced in the Twins' locker room while he was still in his champagne-soaked uniform shortly after the Twins won the 1991 World Series. I've guzzled beer with Neal Broten at a sidewalk café in Berlin. I've been fishing with Jon Casey, and water-skiing with Reed Larson and Don Beaupre. I've played tennis with Steve Jordan and Ahmad Rashad, and croquet with Ahmad's wife, Phylicia of "Cosby" fame. I've been in a TV booth with Jim Kaat. I've walked the French Quarter with Steve Walsh and provided advice to Lou Holtz on a Notre Dame practice field. I have been physically threatened by George Foreman in a Houston courtroom when he was the heavyweight champion of the world, berated and verbally abused by Wren Blair, bullied by Red Auerbach, sweet-talked by George Allen, misled by Bud Selig, praised by Sparky Anderson, conned by Mike Lynn, persuaded by Carl Pohlad, defamed by Norm Green, and charmed by Pat Gillick. I've stolen clients and had other agents steal clients from me. I've been misled and I've done some calculated misleading when it served my clients' purposes. This was not the career I planned, but everything I've seen and done for 59 years has prepared me for my life's work in contract sports.

2
SPORTS AND
THE COURTS

NOWHERE IS IT WRITTEN THAT A PLAYER'S representative must have a law degree, but it helps. I was a lawyer for 12 years before representing my first sports personalities. I feel that my law background gives me a huge advantage in negotiations with general managers. As we near the turn of the century, with the money getting bigger and the contracts more complex, there is no substitute for a strong grounding in law.

In the early 1970s, after my first sports contract negotiations—at a time when I was seriously thinking about making a move from the courts to sports—I argued three trial cases that involved celebrated sports figures. These cases were an important part of my training for my new career and served as a bridge to take me from trial law to a career as a player representative.

CORKY TAYLOR

On January 26, 1972, basketball players from the University of Minnesota and Ohio State engaged in an ugly brawl that forever changed the lives of the young men involved. *Sports Illustrated* photographs permanently etched the incident into the consciousness of America's basketball fans. I didn't need to see any pictures because I was there, and I later represented one of the principal combatants, Corky Taylor.

On the night of the Minnesota–Ohio State game, my wife and I were in our usual seats, ten rows back from courtside, near midcourt, surrounded by 17,000 other Gopher partisans in the cavernous gym we know as "The Old Barn." We tapped our feet to the strains of "Sweet Georgia Brown" as the Gopher players conducted Globetrotter-like ball-handling warm-up drills. The innovation was part of an unusual pregame warm-up instilled by Minnesota's rookie head coach, Bill Musselman, to stir up the crowd into a frenzy. As the players were introduced, The Old Barn rocked.

In his book, *Winfield: A Player's Life*, Dave Winfield, a member of the 1971–72 Gopher basketball team, describes what it was like:

"Back on the court, it's suddenly lights out! The arena goes completely black. A split second later a single spotlight picks out an enormous cutout of a gopher dribbling a giant basketball. The critter is sitting at the edge of the court and there is an open circle in the basketball big enough for a man to run through, which is precisely what you do—poised, ready and waiting until they call your name, until 17,000 Minnesota fans cheer for you and each of your teammates, a cheer that builds to a crescendo when you are finally all standing there together on the court."

Minnesota went into the game with a 4–0 Big Ten record. Ohio State was 3–0 and held the title of defending conference champion. This was to be the only game pitting Minnesota against Ohio State.

The Gophers hadn't won a Big Ten title outright since 1919, but the controversial Musselman had brought new life to the program. He was 31 years old, and extremely intense and competitive. During his first year at Minnesota he hung a sign over the locker room shower door that read, "Defeat is worse than death because you have to live with defeat." Musselman boldly predicted a conference championship.

I was part of the six-person search committee that had brought Musselman to Minnesota. A year earlier, when Bill Fitch departed for the NBA, a search committee followed Fitch's recommendation and chose George Hanson over Bobby Knight. During Hanson's one-year tenure, the Gophers had 11 wins and 13 losses, with a 5–9 conference record as attendance fell to fewer than 8,000 per game. In our search to replace Hanson, Musselman was third on our list of four candidates. We offered the job to Cal Luther, but he changed his mind after originally accepting the position. Our runner-up, Dick Harter, was angry about being passed over and no longer wanted the job. By default, we hired Musselman.

Coaches and athletic directors from the other Big Ten schools strongly resented young Musselman because he broke an unwritten code among Big Ten coaches when he recruited two junior college players. JUCOs are stereotyped as poor students and mercenaries. Most are black. The Big Ten considered itself above them. In addition, Musselman had an "in your face" attitude toward the other coaches, best reflected by the pregame routines and his brash prediction of a Big Ten championship.

There was suspicion that Musselman's prime recruit, Ron Behagen, had been bought by Minnesota. Behagen was one of the top prospects in the country, a junior college All American from southern Idaho via the ghettos of New York City. Behagen had an agent, Lewis Schaffel, who negotiated for Behagen's services with representatives of interested colleges. Bob Knight found out about this and informed all the head coaches in the Big Ten. There was a gentlemen's agreement, ignored by Musselman, that none would recruit Behagen.

Musselman inherited Jim Brewer (6'8"), who later became the first player picked in the 1973 NBA draft, Keith Young (6'5"), and Marvin "Corky" Taylor (6'9"). Taylor had led his high school team to the Detroit City Championship, where for three years he had played competitively against the likes of George Gervin, Campy Russell, and Spencer Haywood. While leading his team in scoring and rebounds, Taylor was named the Most Valuable Player in the City of Detroit. He came from a middle-class neighborhood and was recruited by a number of college powers, but settled on Minnesota because he liked Fitch and the area. Musselman added Bob Nix, and Clyde Turner, other JUCO players, and Dave Winfield, whom he plucked from the ranks of intramural basketball. All of the players except Nix were black.

Ohio State's predominantly white team was coached by Fred Taylor, recognized as one of the best college basketball coaches in the country. Taylor had led his Buckeyes to the NCAA finals in three consecutive seasons (1960–62), winning it all once. He was twice named Coach of the Year and was the Dean of the Big Ten coaches. Musselman had never coached a season of Division One basketball and had a reputation as a loose cannon.

When the first half of this intense duel came to an end, the Buckeyes missed their last shot and Minnesota's Bob Nix raised his fist in triumph. Running off the floor with his hands raised, Ohio State's seven-foot center, Luke Witte, crossed in front of Nix and threw an elbow to his head. The blow stunned Nix but escaped detection by the officials.

Minnesota's frustrations mounted. With 36 seconds left in the game, the Gophers trailed 50–44, when Witte broke loose on a fast break for what appeared to be an easy lay-up. Witte was simultaneously fouled by Turner and Taylor. Witte fell to the floor, and Turner was called for a flagrant foul and ejected. Taylor extended his hand to help Witte to his feet, and as Witte was rising, Taylor kneed him in the groin. Taylor later claimed he did this because Witte spat at him. Witte denied it and the game films were not revealing. Witte fell back to the floor in pain. A melee ensued. Taylor retreated and was no longer involved in the skirmish. Behagen came off the bench and attempted to stomp on the prostrate Witte. Pictures depicted Behagen about to come down on Witte, but fortunately Behagen didn't land squarely on him. Witte's teammates Mark Minor and Mark Wagar were on the receiving end of punches thrown by Gopher players. Ohio State's only two black players, Wardell Jackson and Benny Allison, both on the floor at the time, were untouched. Some fans spilled onto the floor and joined in the brawl. The game was halted and Ohio State was awarded the victory.

The eruption occurred so quickly that no one could recall who hit whom; however, game films in possession of the University of Minnesota, which I reviewed with the other attorneys and several Minnesota officials, revealed that many of the blows were struck by a berserk Dave Winfield. A nervous Paul Giel, the newly appointed athletic director (a Heisman runner-up and Hall of Famer) opted for damage control. He ordered Wendell Vandersluis, the university's photographer, to "bury" the game films. (Richard Nixon could have used advice like this.) Vandersluis obediently trashed the evidence. No other film exposed Winfield's full involvement in the altercation. Many weeks later, Big Ten officials learned for the first time of Winfield's deeds but decided it was too late to take any action, so he went unpunished.

Witte, Wagar, and Miner were taken to University Hospital. Miner was treated and released that night; while Wagar, who suffered a concussion, and Witte, who suffered facial bruises and lacerations and a scratched cornea of the right eye, were released the next day. All were back playing basketball within a week and none suffered significant permanent injuries. Dr. John Najarian, the treating doctor and now a world-renowned surgeon, later testified in court that Witte's injuries were not serious.

The day after the brawl, Big Ten Commissioner Wayne Duke, who was at the game, talked with players, coaches, and referees and reviewed some of the films (but did not see the one depicting Winfield's involvement). Duke's first question to Taylor was revealing: "Which junior college did you come from?" He was under the mistaken impression that Taylor was a dreaded JUCO. Duke had only been commissioner for a few months after stepping down as the Big Eight commissioner, where he started in 1963 at the age of 34. This was a major test for Duke and he elected to rule by "consensus." He polled the Big Ten athletic directors, and the consensus was that the players should be suspended for the entire season. Several of the athletic directors publicly ripped into Behagen and Taylor for their part in the brawl.

There was nonstop fracas fallout. The brawl was seen on evening network news programs. The governor of Ohio described the incident as a "public mugging." *Sports Illustrated* weighed in with a lead article entitled "An Ugly Affair in Minneapolis." The article blasted Musselman and the Minnesota players, and included pictures depicting Taylor kneeing Witte and Behagen about to stomp on Witte. The writer described it as "an ugly, cowardly display of violence" and "a cold, brutal attack governed by the law of the jungle." The writer also ripped Musselman apart, suggesting that the coach's attitude and techniques had incited the players to a violence for which Musselman showed no remorse.

The article prompted Musselman to consult with me regarding a possible libel suit. After reviewing the matter I concluded that, although certain false statements in the article injured his reputation, it would be difficult to win a libel suit because it was necessary but almost impossible to prove the writer's statements were not only untrue but also written with malicious intent.

In the midst of this lynch-mob atmosphere, Taylor and Behagen were suspended for the balance of the 1971–72 season. Both players viewed the penalty as excessive. Taylor's mother came to town immediately to support her son and consulted with me regarding legal action to get Corky reinstated. The players and their families had no money, but I was sympathetic to Taylor's plight, so I agreed to represent him with no charge for my services. Behagen found Minneapolis attorneys Reed McKenzie and Frank Brixius willing to take his case without charge. We knew that the players' only chance to obtain a reduction in the penalty would be to seek relief in the courts, but not the hardwood variety.

We had only one straw to grasp. Although Duke had conducted an investigation of the matter and consulted with all of the Big Ten athletic directors, the players had never received a hearing. We sued the Big Ten Conference, claiming that the players' constitutional rights had been violated because they had been suspended without a hearing.

In the Twin Cities area, I found little support for Taylor and Behagen. I learned that another local attorney, a staunch alumnus athletic booster, had declined the case and said, "Those niggers got exactly what they deserved."

The first step in the legal process was a hearing, which we demanded and received, before the university committee that regulated intercollegiate athletics. This committee, which had approved a temporary suspension, was composed primarily of faculty members, but also included two student and two alumni representatives. One of the student representatives was Dave Winfield. After hearing the evidence, the committee determined that because of significant omissions regarding "due process," the players' constitutional rights had been violated, and for these and other reasons the suspension was removed.

During a break in the hearings, Winfield and I became acquainted while making small talk as we stood side by side at a urinal in the men's room. The introduction marked the beginning of a friendship. Having known Dave for many years, my lasting impression is that his actions on the night of January 26, 1972, were totally out of character.

The Big Ten was not moved by the university committee's decision. Duke refused to modify the suspension. We filed suit against the Big Ten and ended up in federal court before Judge Earl J. Larson.

For me, this wasn't the usual personal injury case. It was a legal dispute that attracted widespread national media coverage and was characterized as a "landmark case." It was the first time I played in front of a packed house.

Taylor testified he turned hostile when Witte spat at him. Duke testified that Witte denied spitting. Films were inconclusive. Witte admitted years later that he couldn't recall anything about the incident because he had amnesia, not unusual for a person who suffers a head injury.

The evidence indicated that no other college or pro athlete had ever been punished this severely for participating in a brawl, and evidence was offered to illustrate other reprehensible conduct that had gone unpunished or less severely punished. Film clips were shown of an irate Woody Hayes, the legendary Ohio State football coach, running amok on the sidelines, swearing like a drunken sailor and flinging yard markers. Hayes not only went unpunished, but there wasn't even a murmur from the Big Ten office. Another example offered was an attack by an Indiana University football player, sidelined with a broken leg, who intentionally struck a helmetless Gopher player over the head with his crutch during a brawl at Bloomington. No penalty. The court was advised that the maximum penalty for fighting in a college hockey game, regardless of the extent of the brawl or the nature of the injuries, was a two-game suspension the following weekend.

As an aside, we also pointed out to the court that although there were a substantial and growing number of black athletes competing in Big Ten football and basketball, there was only one black football and one black basketball official.

In a precedent-setting ruling, the court determined for the first time that the student's right to engage in intercollegiate athletics is a protected right under the 14th Amendment of the Constitution. Therefore, any student deprived of that right must be afforded "due process," or in layman's terms "procedural fairness," which includes the right to a hearing and other procedural safeguards. The players would be entitled to a hearing. The courts of some other states have followed this view, but a majority has ruled otherwise.

We urged the court to appoint an impartial tribunal to determine the players' fate, but the judge inexplicably referred the matter for hearing by the very same Big Ten athletic directors who had already unanimously recommended a season-long suspension. We knew we didn't have a chance before the "kangaroo" court.

The one-day hearing held before the Big Ten athletic directors in Minneapolis was a farce. Most of the ADs were annoyed that they had to come to Minneapolis, and predictably, the athletic directors voted quickly and unanimously to affirm the suspension. A later appeal to the Big Ten faculty representatives also failed. The court's decision was a first. We had lost the battle but won the war—no consolation to Corky Taylor.

Duke, retired since 1989, recently called the case "a landmark for sports litigation" and said it "triggered an influx of sports litigation initiated by amateur and professional athletes." He also said the court decision served as a catalyst for change. A Special Advisory Commission was established to deal with race relations, and the Big Ten's rules on disciplinary procedures were changed to include the right of a student athlete to a full hearing.

Why was Taylor's punishment so severe?

First, politics came into play. There was animosity toward Musselman and Behagen before the brawl, and Ohio State was one of the political powers in the Big Ten. Most importantly, I believe that racial prejudice was a factor. Judge Larson's office was flooded with mail, much of it with racial overtones. I also received some hate mail. I'm convinced that Corky Taylor would never have been suspended for the remainder of the season if he had been white and Luke Witte had been black.

Unfortunately, my hunch about the racial double standard that existed in the Corky Taylor case continues to be validated. Two incidents in recent years involving former Duke basketballer Christian Laettner, who is white, seem to support my conclusion. During the 1991 NCAA basketball tournament, in the Midwest regional semifinal game, Laettner's head was pushed to the floor by Connecticut's Rod Sellers. Sellers, who is black, was suspended from the first game of the tournament the following year. During the 1992 NCAA tournament Laettner was involved in a similar incident, but this time he was the aggressor. In the East Regional final, he deliberately stepped on the chest of Kentucky player Aminu Timberlake, who is black. Laettner received only a technical foul. The Black Coaches Association, outraged at the difference in treatment, formally questioned the NCAA's inequity in treatment. Still, the NCAA refused to intervene. That is the kind of attitude that Corky Taylor had faced.

Despite the loss of Taylor and Behagen, Musselman's brash prediction came true. Minnesota defied the odds and won its first Big Ten title outright in 53 years. Musselman remained a basketball coach after leaving Minnesota in the mid-70s amidst

NCAA allegations of widespread rules violations. In 1989 he returned to the Twin Cities as head coach of the NBA expansion Minnesota Timberwolves. He was fired after two seasons.

Ohio State's Fred Taylor is still bitter about the incident and has said, "Behagen and Taylor should never have been allowed to play in the Big Ten again." Taylor retired a few years after the incident and said, "The brawl was definitely a factor in my decision. It was hard to get rid of the bitterness. It was no longer any fun." He still lives in Columbus, Ohio, where he manages a men's-only golf club.

Corky Taylor played sparingly in his final year of eligibility. He was a late-round draft choice of the Boston Celtics but never played in the NBA. He played a year of pro basketball in Germany, a year in Mexico, and then returned to Minneapolis, where today he works for a community agency's affirmative action program and is also a freelance photographer. He says, "I couldn't go out in public for a long time. I was ostracized because of the extensive negative publicity."

In 1989, 17 years after the episode, Taylor was sitting in a nightclub in Louisville, Kentucky, when a stranger approached him and said kiddingly, "Luke Witte was on his way to the bar until he heard you were here. He decided to go the bar across the street."

Witte played four seasons in the NBA with the Cleveland Cavaliers, where one of his teammates was Jim Brewer. He is now attending a seminary in Wilmore, Kentucky, and eventually hopes to have his own congregation in a small college town. He says the subject of the fight still comes up frequently.

Ron Behagen was the third overall pick in the NBA draft and played pro basketball for seven years for several different teams, averaging 10.3 points per game. He lives in Atlanta with his wife, Pam, a native of St. Paul whom he met while at the University of Minnesota.

Dave Winfield went directly from the University of Minnesota to the San Diego Padres, one of the few players in the history of baseball who didn't need to stop in the minor leagues for some seasoning. Winfield has been a superstar and is a probable future Hall of Famer. After 20 years, he has returned to his home town to play for the Minnesota Twins. He says that from time to time he hears a heckler call out from the stands: "Hey, Winfield. Luke Witte is up here."

In the summer of 1991, Winfield wrote a commentary published in USA Today entitled, "Spectator Decorum Needed." The article was critical of spectator behavior at ball games. Three weeks later, the newspaper printed two letters from readers responding to the article. One from Illinois wrote: "Your Dave Winfield commentary on heckling was as sickening as Winfield's participation in the Ron Behagen stomp of former Ohio State center Luke Witte during a Minnesota–Ohio State basketball game." The other letter read: "Dave Winfield's concern about spectator decorum is the epitome of blatant hypocrisy. This is the same Dave Winfield who participated in a brutal attack on the Ohio State University basketball team during a game in Minnesota when Winfield played for the Gophers."

I continue to be amazed by the number of people from around the country who remember the incident, and how their feelings about it remain so intense.

For my own part, I remember the deluge of calls—day and night—from the media, lawyers, friends, Taylor, and other interested parties. The private and public pressures associated with handling this emotionally charged case exhausted me and my wife. I assured her that never again would I be involved in a stressful matter involving such extensive public interest and media scrutiny. Happily, my assurances proved to be wrong.

GEORGE FOREMAN

I sat across the table from George Foreman, the Heavyweight Champion of the World. It was 1974 and I was in a conference room in Houston, representing Foreman's wife, Adrienne, in a bitter divorce. The champ and I were alone, and he knew I was there to take his money.

He refused to shake my hand. He glowered at me, a look that revealed deep hostility and anger. He was not the cuddly bear we see today. Foreman at this time was 6'3", weighed 220 lbs., and his body looked as if it had been chiseled out of granite. Adrienne had warned me about his uncontrollable rage, and I feared that at some point his anger could erupt in a physical fury directed toward me.

My discussions with Foreman were brief. It was clear that we could not reach agreement. He told me he wanted to pay his wife almost nothing, because he had earned the money with his blood and sweat and she had never entered the ring once. When I disagreed, he threatened to punch me out. I knew that if he sensed he was intimidating me, he would believe I was too frightened to stand up to him in court or at the negotiating table, and I had to gather up all the courage I could muster to eliminate the fear and continue the discussions. But I did wonder what would happen to me if I was struck by the toughest, meanest man in the world.

My mind wandered back to a time six years earlier—I was on my honeymoon in Florida—when I watched an excited 19-year-old George Foreman celebrate his Olympic gold medal victory, waving a miniature U.S. flag in his taped right fist. His actions had been in sharp contrast to the clenched-fist "Black Power" salute of two fellow U.S. Olympic track medalists, John Carlos and Tommy Smith. From that distance on that special day, Foreman struck me as the embodiment of the American Dream. Now, as we stared at one another in a courthouse conference room, he was my worst nightmare, and I was his.

Foreman was raised in a black ghetto in the Fifth Ward of Houston, Texas. His parents, J.D. and Nancy, were separated, but J.D.—when he was drinking—often returned home to physically abuse Nancy. When George was 16, he went looking for his father to give him a beating. J.D. was not found that night, but he got the word and never again laid a hand on Nancy.

George dropped out of school in the eighth grade and roamed the streets for a couple of years before joining the Job Corps. It was at this time that a man named Doc Broadus took a fatherly interest in him and got him involved in Golden Gloves boxing. Foreman was a natural puncher and left a trail of young men on the canvas in his climb to the pinnacle of amateur boxing.

After Foreman won the gold at Mexico City, he turned professional and came under the management of Dick Sadler, a handler of world champions Sandy Saddler, Archie Moore, and Sonny Liston. Foreman became one of Liston's sparring mates. Liston was an illiterate ex-convict and former heavyweight champ. His trademark was a piercing stare. It's unfortunate that Foreman was exposed to a man like Liston at such a young age. Liston died from an apparent drug overdose in 1971. Adrienne later said, "George was so enamored with the fighter that pretty soon he was Sonny."

Sadler moved Foreman to his hometown of Hayward, California. Sadler was from the old school of fight managers who believed that a fighter should concentrate only on improving his boxing skills and preparing for fights. Relationships with women were considered distractions. Prostitutes were periodically provided to Foreman to satisfy his sexual drives, but his handler discouraged him from forming a relationship with a woman.

Foreman met Adrienne on a blind date in Minneapolis in 1970. At that time, he was the number-three ranked heavyweight contender in the world and had come to Minneapolis with Sadler, who was looking into a business matter for Foreman. She knew little about boxing and was unimpressed. Adrienne was 22, while George was only 20 and apparently had never had a serious relationship with a woman. Adrienne observed that he was shy, inexperienced, and "square."

The relationship blossomed, and Adrienne became more impressed with George and the boxing life. She accompanied George to the Muhammad Ali–Jimmy Ellis bout in Houston in 1971. Before the fight at the Astro World Hotel, George introduced Adrienne to Ali in the presence of the news media. Adrienne was dumbstruck. Always "The Greatest" at promoting a future fight, Ali turned to Adrienne and said loudly, "What do you want with him when you can have the real Champ?"

In December 1971, George wanted Adrienne to come to Texas to spend time with him and his family over the Christmas holidays. Adrienne wanted to marry George and was concerned that if the relationship continued without a commitment on George's part he would soon discard her. At the time, she was working for IBM and had used up almost all of her vacation time. She decided to make her move. She told George that she wouldn't be able to get any additional vacation time to come to Texas for the holidays unless it was for something unique or special, like getting married. George went for it and said, "Okay, I'll marry you."

They married on December 23, 1971, at a small neighborhood church in Houston. George's family members were told the day before the wedding. Adrienne's family was represented by an aunt and a couple of other relatives who lived in Houston. There were about 10 people at the wedding.

It was not your typical marriage. After the wedding they continued to live separately—she in Minneapolis and he in either California or Texas. Although they were often together, it was never for more than a month. She didn't want to interfere with his boxing, and she was sentimentally attached to the Minneapolis home she had inherited from her mother.

Foreman wasn't ready to settle down. He had an extramarital affair less than a month after the wedding. When he was with Adrienne, he became chauvinistic and domineering. He wouldn't allow her to wear pants, didn't want her to smoke, and except in unusual circumstances, didn't want her using makeup. He also forbade her from watching him fight. Adrienne was surprised and uneasy.

In late 1972, Foreman's people were finally able to get a championship fight with Smokin' Joe Frazier, scheduled in Jamaica for January 22, 1973. Muhammad Ali still reigned as the world's premier boxer, but he had lost the championship to Frazier in the "Thrilla in Manila." Meanwhile, Adrienne was expecting her first child, and she discouraged George from fighting Frazier because she was concerned that he would be seriously hurt. She didn't care if he was the champion. He last visited her before the fight in Minneapolis on her birthday, December 12, 1972.

On January 6, 1973, their daughter was born. George was in Jamaica training for the fight, but national press obtained photos of Adrienne and the baby and wired them to George in Jamaica. Their newborn daughter was named Michi—after a member of an Amerasian family in California that had befriended George. In Japanese, the name means "beautiful and intelligent." George was afraid to hold or touch the baby for fear that he would hurt her, but he was very happy to be a father and has remained a devoted father to Michi over the years.

Sixteen days after the birth of his daughter, Foreman won the Heavyweight Championship when he upset Frazier in a second-round TKO. Adrienne did not watch or listen to the fight. She got the news via telephone when a hysterical friend called and screamed that George was the new champion. Adrienne was in shock—she couldn't believe a girl from the Minneapolis ghetto was married to the Heavyweight Champion of the World. When she went to the Minneapolis airport to pick up George three days after the fight, he was mobbed by well-wishers and media. She couldn't get close to him.

Adrienne was bewildered by the changes that accompanied George's success. She also was having difficulty coping with the experience of being a mother, especially when the father was not there. Meanwhile, George and his entourage went on a boxing expedition in western Europe. They made lots of new friends in Europe and several members of Foreman's traveling party, including George, came home with venereal disease.

In the summer of 1973, Adrienne did some nifty detective work and learned of George's affairs. Snooping around California, she tracked down Irma Compton, a very high-class, black call girl from the island of St. Lucia. George had met her in London on his European expedition. She was getting women for George and occasionally sleeping with him herself. Adrienne called Irma on the telephone and confronted her. Irma became angry and confessed that she had met George in a whorehouse. Adrienne taped the conversation.

(George's relationship with Irma ended several years later, when he beat her so badly that he almost killed her. When Foreman's business manager, LeRoy Jackson, saw Irma after the beating, he vomited. Compton later received a substantial settlement from George.)

Adrienne confronted her husband, the world champ. They got into a fight, and according to Adrienne, he "beat the crap out" of her. She said she was so scared that she called out for her deceased mother and wet her pants. Her face was swollen and she had bruises on her legs. LeRoy Jackson made arrangements to take her to a doctor after office hours. She wore sunglasses to avoid detection, and he spirited her in and out of the doctor's office without being discovered. The disgusted doctor told her that she had a concussion. When she got home, George told her he wanted a divorce.

Adrienne's world fell apart. To make matters worse, many of her friends and relatives blamed her for the breakup, assuming it must have been her fault. Several told her, "You must have been cheating." She was so distraught she refused to accept service of the divorce papers by the sheriff. During a short period of time, she lost 21 pounds.

The primary issue in this divorce trial was the amount of the property settlement to be awarded to Adrienne. Although Foreman was represented by lawyers from both Houston and California (where he was living most of the time), he insisted on negotiating this issue alone with Adrienne. Why not? He knew he could intimidate her. When we rejected that request, he ignored the advice of his lawyers and angrily elected to talk alone with me.

His lawyers decided to start the action in Houston. Houston was a preferable site for the proceedings (although both California and Texas were "community property" states in which the property of the parties is divided equally) because of Foreman's status as a local hero.

As the trial neared, Foreman was looking ahead to his first big payday. He had earned relatively little in the Frazier fight and had made only $200,000 when he defended the title by knocking out a tomato can named Joe Roman in Japan. But now he was scheduled to defend his title against Ken Norton in Caracas, Venezuela, on March 26, 1974. His take figured to be in excess of half a million dollars.

Foreman faced a dilemma. He could ill-afford to languish in a Houston courtroom when he should be training for the biggest fight of his life six weeks later. On the other hand, if the trial was postponed until after the Norton fight, Foreman likely would have to share the pot equally with Adrienne. He wanted either a quick, small settlement or a speedy trial with a favorable decision. I was blocking Foreman's path to both. We wanted to stall the final divorce until after the Norton fight.

The dispute was complicated. Foreman and his lawyers refused to disclose some financial records, and Foreman claimed that Adrienne was entitled to no part of the proceeds from the Norton fight because by that time the parties would be divorced. We pursued the then-untested legal theory that our client was entitled to some portion of the Norton proceeds because the parties were still married when the fight contract was signed. The Norton purse was available because Foreman was the champion, a status acquired when the parties were married. The big payday was not merely for the one hour in the ring after the divorce, but also for all the preparation and training before the divorce was final. To further complicate matters, we argued that Foreman was not entitled to a divorce in Texas because he was a resident of California. If we were correct, George would have to start over and finalize the divorce action again later in California, with no hope of a divorce until after the Norton fight. Adrienne would then be entitled to half of the Norton fight proceeds.

The presiding Family Court judge was Wells Stewart, a relatively young and inexperienced judge from a wealthy and prestigious Houston family. He looked and dressed the part of an "Ivy Leaguer." He was well mannered and articulate, but carried the airs of a spoiled rich kid. He was a member of the exclusive River Oaks Country Club, a playground for John Connolly and a number of oil-soaked millionaires. The judge mentioned that a couple of months earlier he had attended a banquet at which Foreman had been honored. We gulped. It sounded as though Judge Stewart, like many other Houstonians, was impressed with the celebrated Mr. Foreman.

Several days earlier, my partner, Charles Zimmerman, and I had completed our review of the incomplete financial records provided to us by the Foreman people. We were stunned. The boxer had agreed to pay his manager, Sadler, 25 percent of all of his revenues. An entourage of hangers-on, relatives, and "go-fers" sapped up additional amounts of money. Foreman had expensive tastes, including Irma Compton and her "friends," cars, exotic dogs, and other luxury items. There wasn't much left.

The trial started on Wednesday, February 13. The trial judge dismissed our objection that Foreman was not truly a resident of Texas. We preserved our right to appeal. He also granted Foreman time each day to train for his upcoming fight. We had no objection.

During my cross-examination of Foreman, he became impatient and said, "If this Court continues to Monday or Tuesday, I won't fight. I would have to break training." As Foreman uttered the words, the boxing writers scurried out of the courtroom to the nearest telephones. The next day, newspapers around the country reported that Foreman might cancel the Norton fight.

Meanwhile, the judge had discovered that both Zimmerman and I had played tennis competitively at the University of Minnesota. After the first day of trial, his clerk passed on the message that the judge would like to set up a doubles' game with us at his country club on Sunday morning. We found ourselves in a serious dilemma. If we rejected the invitation we ran the risk of offending the judge; if we accepted, there would be an appearance of impropriety. After discussing the matter with our Houston co-counsel, Huey O'Toole, we decided that the better of bad alternatives was to accept the invitation. Zimmerman and I enjoyed the morning of tennis on the clay courts of Houston's most exclusive country club. Afterwards, the judge insisted we have lunch together. I'm sure Foreman's lawyers would have loved a photograph.

Fortunately, the court never had to make a decision. The case was settled a few days later.

Our breakthrough came through sheer good fortune. O'Toole was tipped off by a New York City friend that Foreman had secretly agreed to fight Muhammad Ali for the championship for $5 million if he defeated Ken Norton. Foreman's people had taken great precautions to try to keep this development secret until the divorce was final. This information was invaluable to us, because if we were able to convince a Texas appellate court that Foreman was not really a resident of Texas, and thus not entitled to a divorce in Texas, he would perhaps still be married to Adrienne at the time of the Ali fight. Adrienne would then share in the proceeds of both the Norton and Ali fights. Our chances of success were not great, but created an uncomfortable risk for George.

The outcome of any negotiation depends, in good part, on your degree of leverage. The knowledge of another big purse in which Adrienne could possibly share if an appellate court set aside the divorce created an additional risk for Foreman. It was not enough for us to merely know about a future Ali fight; it was important to let the other side know we knew.

In the Saturday, February 16, court session, I elicited testimony from a surprised Dick Sadler confirming the new arrangement with Ali. On the same day, Foreman took a complete about-face and testified he was ready to stay in trial as long as it took to work out a property settlement. He said: "Athletes have all been taken advantage of because they wanted to get out of court and go back into training. I'm willing to sit here every day until everything is right. I don't want to go through the problem of someone sharing an interest in my earnings. I just prefer to stay here and take a chance of losing the Norton fight."

Nevertheless, the court ordered a continuance and ordered additional financial records to be produced by Foreman in California. It appeared that Foreman had not accumulated much money, had spent lavishly, and had debts. After reviewing the income tax returns, we were also concerned about possible future IRS claims for back taxes. The main goal of Foreman's advisors now was to finalize the divorce quickly to eliminate any possibility that Adrienne could share in the Norton or Ali fight proceeds. Foreman's lawyers improved their offer of settlement, and we finally cut a deal for $235,000 plus $40,000 in attorneys' fees. On a couple of occasions since, George admitted to Adrienne "that's about the only fight I didn't win."

Foreman defeated Norton in Caracas, then lost his title when Ali rope-a-doped him in Zaire. In late 1974, after the fight, Adrienne resumed her relationship with George after he came to Minneapolis to visit his daughter. They were lovers on and off until the end of 1976. In December 1976, George told Adrienne, "If I knew in 1974 what I now know, I would never have divorced you." He asked her to remarry him but she refused. She couldn't tolerate his infidelities.

Foreman retired from boxing in 1977 after he was upset by Jimmy Young. He became an unordained lay minister, traveling throughout the country and speaking the Gospel at various churches for the next ten years. During this period, he had his ups and downs but he was always on time with his monthly support payments for Michi. After being out of the ring for ten years, in 1987 at age 38 he became the idol of every middle-aged couch potato when he began his gravity-defying ring comeback. This George Foreman did not appear to be angry and sullen. He poked fun at himself and his age, and joked about his flabby 260-lb. frame with protruding gut. He spoke of eating legs of lamb and roasts of beef. But he kept knocking out opponents until he earned a title fight with Evander Holyfield in April 1991. Foreman was 43 when he lost to Holyfield, but he went the distance and took home $12.5 million. At age 45, Foreman will fight Tommy Morrison, age 24, for the vacant World Boxing Organization heavyweight title in June 1993 in Las Vegas. Foreman is guaranteed $7 million and could earn as much as $15 million.

Adrienne Foreman still lives in Minneapolis and has not remarried. George Foreman is married to his fifth wife, and he has nine children, five of whom are boys named George. He continues to capitalize on his amazing comeback. In late 1991, he and his five sons (ages one to 17) did a Doritos commercial that netted each son $25,000. Foreman is making guest appearances on TV shows and will also star in "George," a television sitcom about an ex-boxer who starts an after-school program for inner-city kids. He continues to box professionally.

What happened to the mean George Foreman, the one who wanted to beat up his wife's divorce attorney? Adrienne says, "George hasn't changed much—he is just a lot smarter."

REED LARSON

What is an amateur? What is a professional? For more than a century sports officials and participants have wrestled with these questions. Decathlon and pentathlon champion Jim Thorpe in 1913 had to give back his Olympic medals when it was discovered he'd played some professional baseball in 1909. Today, we have NBA players making millions of dollars who are allowed to represent the USA in the Olympic games. Track stars make hundreds of thousands of dollars, yet continue to compete as amateurs.

Our colleges have their own set of guidelines. You can play professionally in one sport and remain eligible for National Collegiate Athletic Association (NCAA) competition in another. You can be drafted by a professional team and negotiate with that team. Just don't hire an agent. The NCAA will declare you ineligible.

My introduction to the amateur-professional debate came in March of 1974, at a time when I was beginning my conversion from trial law to representation of sports personalities. Wes Larson, father of local hockey player Reed Larson, made an appoint-ment to inquire about the legal consequences of a contract he and his son had signed.

Born and raised in Minneapolis, Reed Larson grew up playing hockey on outdoor rinks. In 1974 he was a senior at Minneapolis Roosevelt High School. A defenseman with a booming slapshot, Reed had just been honored as an All State hockey player. He never went to a hockey school. The summer before his senior season, he played hockey at the Golden Valley Ice Center in a competitive league that included college players. During that summer Reed became acquainted with the two operators of the ice center, Harry Brown and Robert "Red" Kairies. These men owned an amateur hockey team in the Midwest Junior A league, and Brown was an area scout for the Boston Bruins. Brown and Kairies urged Reed to drop out of high school hockey to play Junior A. They also proposed that they serve as his agents in the event he had an opportunity to play professional hockey. On August 11, 1973, Reed (then age 17) and his father signed an agreement with Brown and Kairies authorizing them to act as Reed's agents for negotiating any professional hockey contracts. Reed also agreed to play hockey for their amateur Junior A hockey club. Brown and Kairies promised Reed a job at their ice center and a $3,000 college scholarship two years later if Reed did not play profes-sional hockey. Reed received no money when he signed the agreement.

About five days after Reed had signed the agreement, he changed his mind. He decided he wanted to return to high school to complete his senior year and to play high school hockey. Brown and Kairies voiced no objection. Reed and his father sent letters to Brown and Kairies confirming their conversation. Months later, the Larsons con-tacted me to determine what legal obligations, if any, Reed and his father had under the contract.

Under Minnesota law, minors are not obligated to honor contracts signed by them, and such contracts cannot be enforced against the minor, even if a parent also signs the contract. I advised the Larsons that in my opinion, neither Reed nor his father would have any legal obligation under the contract because Reed was underage when he signed it. I innocently added that the signing of the contract could run afoul of a rule of the NCAA providing that student athletes who agreed to hire agents forfeited their college eligibility. None of the Larsons had previously been aware of this regulation. I later second-guessed myself for volunteering this information.

Most intercollegiate sports are governed and regulated by the NCAA. Over 800 U.S. colleges and universities are members. Each member school is represented by a faculty representative, and these faculty representatives elect 44 of their peers to serve on the NCAA Council. The day-to-day operations are run by the executive director and his staff. In 1974 Walter Byers was the executive director, and Warren Brown was the assistant executive director. Both had been entrenched in power for a lengthy period of time.

The NCAA has a rule stipulating that any individual who agrees to be represented by a sports agent for the purpose of negotiating a professional contract is ineligible to play that intercollegiate sport. Another rule provides that any individual who agrees to accept a promise of money for athletic participation is also ineligible.

The agent rule makes no sense. An agreement to hire a sports agent provides the amateur athlete with no money or other benefits. An agent merely provides a student-athlete with professional advice regarding when and whether the athlete should turn pro. An agent's work may include talks with interested professional clubs and ultimately the negotiation of the terms of the pro contract. The agent rule harms the student-athlete and benefits the professional sports clubs by forcing the student-athlete who turns pro to negotiate his own contract.

College hockey and baseball players can be drafted, whether or not they have requested to be included in a draft, before or during the time they are attending a university. At this point, they may wish to engage in contract negotiations to determine if they should turn pro. In 1990, the National Football League announced a policy allowing college juniors to be drafted and turn professional. The National Basketball Association allows non-seniors to be drafted at their election under certain circumstances. Many of these draftees sign professional contracts before they have used up their college eligibility in their sport, and they may wish to employ agents to discuss the advantages and disadvantages of turning pro early. Unlike baseball and hockey, in basketball and football the player becomes automatically ineligible for college sports when he requests inclusion in the draft. If an athlete in any of these sports hires an agent, he loses his eligibility to play his sport in college. He immediately places himself in a disadvantageous bargaining position with the club, because the club knows he no longer has the alternative of returning to school to play his sport. The club holds all the leverage.

The agent rule encourages the athlete to violate NCAA regulations—in other words, to hire an agent to guide him through the negotiation process while the agent remains in the background. It's not legal, but it's prudent. Unfortunately, an agent's hands are tied when he cannot speak directly to the club's representative. There is also risk that the agent will be detected. The player will then lose his college eligibility and will have no alternative but to sign the pro contract.

I know a baseball agent who claims to have represented 22 first-round draft picks from 1983 to 1989, even though each of them had college eligibility remaining. In each instance, the representation was concealed. In at least one instance, the player didn't come to terms and returned to school to play another year of college baseball. The NCAA never discovered the rule violation.

The agent rule allows a "legal advisor," but does not permit the legal advisor to negotiate with the pro club. This is the loophole most lawyers use in representing college hockey and baseball players with eligibility remaining.

Reed Larson was heavily recruited by many colleges, but for years it had been his dream to play for the University of Minnesota because it had such an outstanding hockey program, a great coach in Herb Brooks, and a winning tradition. When I informed the Larsons about the agent rule and Reed's possible loss of his college eligibility, they were stunned. They could not imagine that Reed would be deprived of a college education and college hockey because of an agreement that paid him nothing, signed when he was 17.

Reed and his parents faced a dilemma. Almost no one knew of the agreement. It would be easy for Reed to accept the scholarship, play for Minnesota, and ignore the NCAA rule. On the other hand, if the agreement was discovered, not only could Reed immediately be declared ineligible, but the team would possibly have to forfeit any games in which he had participated. Reed wanted to avoid possible personal embarrassment or embarrassment to the university.

In 1974, only about 4 percent of all of the players in the National Hockey League were Americans. The odds of a top American high school player developing sufficiently to compete in the National Hockey League were extremely slim, and Larson realized that if he wasn't able to play big-time college hockey, his pro career would be in jeopardy.

I recommended that the University of Minnesota be notified of the circumstances. It was my opinion that there would be no eligibility problem with the Big Ten or NCAA if we were forthright and volunteered the information.

Wes and Ruth Larson were honest, decent people. He was a truck driver and she was a housewife raising four children. For them, the decision was easy.

I had known Brooks for several years, so I notified him of the circumstances. On April 12, the university officials sent letters to both the Big Ten Conference and the NCAA briefly outlining the undisputed facts and simply asking if Reed Larson was ineligible for collegiate athletics. On June 6, 1974, Wayne Duke, the Big Ten commissioner, wrote to the university approving Larson's eligibility and indicating the reason his eligibility was approved was because the contracts were signed by Reed Larson when he was under the age of 18 and he had received no benefits from these contracts. The answer was simple and straightforward. The decision made sense and was not unexpected, but we were relieved nevertheless.

Two weeks later, Warren Brown, assistant executive director of the NCAA, wrote to the university that in his opinion, the rules applied to Reed Larson, that the University of Minnesota not the NCAA had an obligation to apply the rule to Reed—to declare him ineligible—and that the university had the right to appeal to an NCAA eligibility committee but that the appeal only would be entertained when and if Reed Larson became a full-time student.

Come again?

I interpreted this response to mean that Reed would not be eligible to play college hockey until he became a full-time student and the university could appeal to the NCAA. University representatives had indicated to Reed that the offer of financial aid would not be forthcoming unless his problem of eligibility was cleared up because the university could not offer a scholarship to a player who was not eligible to play. Reed could not enroll because neither Reed nor his family had the funds. The university could never appeal the NCAA determination if Reed did not enroll there as an ineligible player first.

I felt responsible for this disaster, and I was outraged at the NCAA, who I felt were acting like an arrogant group of pompous asses with no conception or concern for what was fair or decent.

Since the response from the NCAA was unclear, I requested clarification of Reed's eligibility. Warren Brown replied in writing again. He stated that on August 23 the NCAA Council had met to discuss the matter and had "concluded that Mr. Larson was ineligible for intercollegiate hockey at the NCAA member institution under the provisions of the NCAA Constitution." The letter stated, "This information clearly indicated that the young man, by his own voluntary actions, had definitely professionalized himself under the NCAA professional rulings noted."

The university's fall quarter was to start in about three weeks, and the Larsons had no funds with which to finance Reed's education or a legal battle with the NCAA. I offered to represent Reed without any charge. This gesture itself created yet another obstacle, however, as the NCAA had ruled that the acceptance of gratuitous legal services by a student-athlete constituted a violation of NCAA rules if the services were provided by a "representative of the university's athletic interests." That definition encompassed boosters and contributors to university athletic funds like me. Under the "extra benefit" rules, student-athletes were not permitted to receive anything of value without charge that was not available to non-student-athletes. The NCAA considered free legal services from someone with a connection to the university to be a violation of the rule. In other words, the NCAA enacted a rule that permitted it to trample on a student-athlete's rights, and then as a practical matter to deprive the impoverished soul of the ability to legally fight back. However, at this point, Larson had nothing to lose. I began to prepare for the battle.

Negotiation can be a powerful tool in a dispute if all sides agree that going to court should be the absolutely last resort. I was a civil trial lawyer for many years and unfortunately found that the judicial system was often woefully inadequate for resolving disputes. The judges' decisions are too often unfair and unpredictable, the lengthy delays are intolerable, and the legal fees are astronomical. Many trial lawyers agree with me, but they can't speak out for fear of reprisal by the judges who will sit in judgment on their cases. It is usually preferable to take command of your own situation at the negotiating table rather than abandon yourself to the vagaries of the justice system.

Despite my doubts about the system, I could see that the only chance Reed had was a lawsuit against the NCAA to restore his eligibility. I had to devise a legal theory upon which to base a lawsuit. From a legal standpoint, our case was very weak. Our claim would have to be based upon the grounds that the NCAA had violated one of Reed's constitutional rights, and in cases of this nature the NCAA won in court almost every time. On the other hand, if the matter was to be determined solely on the basis of fairness, we had a good case. Unfortunately, I knew that justice and fairness often placed second to "the rule of law." Supreme Court Justice Oliver Wendell Holmes expressed it best when he said, "The law is an ass."

I filed the lawsuit on Reed's behalf seeking a judgment from the court that Larson be declared eligible to participate in intercollegiate athletics. Our theory was that the NCAA agent rule had violated the "equal protection" clause of the 14th Amendment (equal treatment) of the Constitution, on the grounds that minors generally were not legally bound by their contracts but under the NCAA regulation in question even minors were held accountable for imprudent contracts with an agent. Thus, the argument was that Larson was treated differently from other minors under this rule. The theory was weak, but at least it would get me into court.

The NCAA was a formidable opponent. The courts indicated a reluctance to interfere with the decisions of the NCAA because the schools themselves were voluntary members of the organization who agreed to be policed by its rules. If the rule was unfair, the courts reasoned, the schools should vote to change it. The majority of courts also ruled that a student's right to participate in intercollegiate competition was not a constitutionally protected right.

The case was assigned to Federal Judge Miles Lord in Minneapolis. He initially issued an order on September 17, 1974, restraining the NCAA and the university from declaring Larson ineligible. This order was only to be effective for a few days until the judge could hold a hearing to determine whether the court should preliminarily enjoin the NCAA from declaring Larson ineligible until a full trial approximately a year later. If the judge ruled in our favor, Larson would be entitled to enroll with a scholarship immediately. The NCAA had the right to appeal to the 8th Circuit Court of Appeals, which would take about nine months. During that period, Larson would be eligible to play hockey. If the judge ruled against us, as a practical matter, Larson would no longer be able to play college hockey or attend the university.

During the hearings, Judge Lord continually pressed counsel for the NCAA to explain why Larson would "have a better slapshot" or other competitive edge as a hockey player, or would be any less of an amateur than competing players by virtue of his agreement to hire an agent. In other words, how did the signing of that agreement, which was only in effect for five days, "professionalize" Larson? Fortunately we had a sympathetic judge.

After Judge Lord had heard all of the evidence, he shared some of his thoughts and impressions with the attorneys for the parties. "Maybe the intent of the rule is right," he observed, "but it seems overprotective. The NCAA doesn't seem to make leeway, and there are a lot of circumstances in this case that the organization should consider." It was clear that we had won round number one of the legal battle—he was going to grant our request for a preliminary injunction against the NCAA.

It seemed to me that the timing was ripe to negotiate a conclusion to this sense-less dispute. The NCAA lawyers threatened to appeal the decision and expressed confidence of success, but nevertheless I sensed that the NCAA desperately wanted to avoid an unfavorable trial-court decision, which would embarrass the organization, establish a bad precedent, and encourage other student-athletes to fight NCAA decisions in the courts. My ego did not require a court victory. Sometimes a trial lawyer is tempted to go for a court victory rather than a settlement in a highly publicized case to enhance his own reputation. I didn't want to "press my luck." I wanted Larson's eligibility to be permanently resolved with no appeals hanging over his head to cloud his future. If it could be resolved by agreement, so much the better.

After the hearings were concluded, but before Judge Lord formally issued his decision, an agreement was negotiated by us providing that Reed would receive financial aid from the University of Minnesota for only the fall quarter and not for the usual year. Reed would then be able to become a full-time student, which would enable the university to appeal the question of eligibility to the NCAA. The NCAA Council or an eligibility committee would rule on the matter within ten days after receipt of the appeal. I was essentially promised that the NCAA would rule in Reed's favor. Reed would then be permanently eligible and would receive a full scholarship for the balance of the year. The NCAA would "save face." In the unlikely event the NCAA did not rule in Reed's favor on the question of eligibility, I could march back into Judge Lord's courtroom and collect our favorable order against the NCAA. The NCAA would then have the right to appeal. Reed had everything to gain and nothing to lose.

After the settlement was concluded, Reed Larson, Herb Brooks, and I walked jubilantly out of the courtroom together. As we walked down the street together, Brooks turned to Larson and said: "Now all you have to do is make the team."

Within a few days, an NCAA subcommittee reviewed the information, arranged for a conference telephone conversation with the interested parties (including Larson), asked a few brief questions about the facts and circumstances, and ruled that Larson's eligibility would be restored.

Larson not only made the team but became a standout in his first year. Minnesota advanced to the finals of the NCAA Championship in St. Louis before losing to Michigan Tech, and Larson was named to the All NCAA Team. In his second year, Larson helped lead the Gophers to the National Championship in Denver over the same favored Michigan Tech club. I was fortunate enough to see both championship games. They had a special meaning for me because of my relationship with Reed and the knowledge that I had personally contributed toward the attaining of this NCAA Championship. The unique feeling and satisfaction I had in Denver could never have been matched by any fee for my services.

In 1978, Reed Larson and I were both called to testify before a U.S. Congressional subcommittee conducting an investigation of the enforcement program of the NCAA. At the end of the investigation, Congressman John E. Moss of California, chairman of the subcommittee, concluded: "The unbiased observer sees a very clear picture as he observes the current NCAA enforcement apparatus. The picture is that of a sanctioning body with an incredible power that may effect the careers and ambitions of coaches and student-athletes, as well as the stature of virtually every institution of higher education in this country. This power is exercised by the NCAA without observance to what we all assume are the minimal standards of fairness."

In mid-1991, the human outcry regarding the lack of "due process" or fairness in the NCAA enforcement procedures resulted in yet another Congressional subcommittee hearing on reform. Typical at the hearing was the testimony of Dale Brown, Louisiana State University basketball coach. "I've said for years, the NCAA has legislated against human dignity—they function out of control like the Gestapo." Don Jaeger, author of *Undue Process: The NCAA's Injustice for All*, testified, "It is so one-sided that the NCAA in 40 years has a 100 percent conviction rate." University of Denver law professor Burton Brody ventured the opinion that "the NCAA's practices are unfair, unjust, heavy-handed, and vindictive." In response, several states have passed or are in the process of passing legislation requiring the NCAA to observe the rules of due process in enforcing its regulations.

Finally, in late 1991, under threat of state and federal intervention, the NCAA released a plan changing its enforcement process to be submitted to a vote of the full membership of the organization. The plan included the use of an impartial judge to decide major disputes and a suggestion to open to the public the previously closed hearings on infractions. What emerged from the NCAA's deliberations in January of 1993, however, was less than revolutionary. The NCAA did allow cross-examination of witnesses for the first time, but rejected the calls for public hearings. Their idea of enhanced impartiality was to add two members from "the general public" to the six-member infractions committee, which does little to offset the group's biases.

Reed Larson went on to be the second highest ever American draft pick in the NHL in the June 1976 draft. I was unable to negotiate a satisfactory contract offer with the Detroit Red Wings' general manager Alex Delveccio, and on my advice Reed reluctantly returned to school. A threatened suspension in early 1977, after he pushed an official during a game, precipitated his move to Detroit that year. The club was still not willing to chance a substantial contract over the long term, so we settled for a one-year contract with a player's option to renew for a second year at the same figure. More often than not, I prefer the shortest contract possible for a rookie with good potential. If he turns out to be a player, he ends up making a lot more money than he would have made under a longer rookie contract.

Larson had a sensational rookie season during which he scored 19 goals and had 41 assists for 60 points. At age 22 he was selected to play in the NHL All Star Game. He became a free agent after playing out his option year, and in 1979 I negotiated a three-year contract plus an option year for Reed that averaged almost $200,000 a year, making Reed easily the highest paid American-born hockey player ever. My short contract had worked out well.

Larson played with Detroit until 1986 when he was traded to Boston. Since the fall of 1988, he's played professionally in Italy. As of 1992, Larson ranked fifth in all-time scoring among American players, and thirteenth in scoring on the NHL's all-time scoring list for defensemen.

After Brooks coached the U.S. Olympic team to the gold medal in 1980, he became the head coach of the New York Rangers, where he was voted Coach of the Year by his NHL peers. Later he coached the Minnesota North Stars, was a hockey analyst for NHL games on a major cable television network, was inducted into the U.S. Hockey Hall of Fame, and now is back in the NHL as the head coach of the New Jersey

Devils.

Several years ago, Judge Lord retired as a federal judge and is now practicing law in Minneapolis. Lord recently likened the NCAA action against Larson to "throwing the baby out with the bath water."

Walter Byers retired as executive director of the NCAA in 1987 after 40 years. He severed all ties with the organization in September 1990.

Warren Brown remained assistant executive director of the NCAA until his voluntary retirement in 1977, after having served 11 years.

Neither Henry Brown nor Red Kairies ever acted as an agent for any professional athlete.

After Larson turned pro, Kairies hired an attorney who threatened to commence a lawsuit against Larson for agent fees provided under their contract, but I threatened to counterclaim for damages for legal fees and other expenses incurred in connection with the NCAA lawsuit. Their claim was never pursued.

Ron Simon hung up his trial hat and went to work as a sports attorney.

3
DENNIS HEXTALL'S TALE OF TWO CITIES

HEXTALL IS A HOCKEY NAME, RIGHT UP THERE with Howe (Gordie and sons Marty and Mark), Hull (Bobby and son Brett), and Sutter (five NHL brothers). Three generations of Hextalls have skated in the National Hockey League. Brian Hextall Sr. is an NHL Hall of Famer who led the Rangers in scoring in 1941. Brian's sons Brian Jr. and Dennis were NHL standouts, and his grandson Ron Hextall today is an outstanding goalie in the National Hockey League with the Quebec Nordiques.

I first met Dennis Hextall in a Minneapolis restaurant in May 1973. He was the reigning MVP of the Minnesota North Stars. A fiery redhead from Poplar Point, Manitoba, he'd scored 30 goals with 52 assists, and ranked 17th among NHL scorers in 1972–73. Fans loved him because he'd drop his gloves and fight at the slightest provocation. Management loved him because he played defense and did the little things that win games.

In May of '73, Hextall was 30 years old and had one year remaining on a $38,000 contract with the North Stars. He had been in the NHL for five seasons. His agent was recommending he accept a three-year, $205,000 contract offer from the North Stars. Hextall had some doubts about the contract but was reasonably satisfied. He was receiving a substantial raise.

Hextall knew of my work on behalf of Cesare Maniago, so he struck up a conversation with me about his proposed contract. I expressed no opinion regarding the merits of the contract, but I suggested that he find out if there was a competing offer available from the new World Hockey Association. The WHA had just completed its first season and the league had a team in St. Paul. Dennis said his agent had no interest in exploring the WHA.

I was convinced that Hextall could get a substantial offer from St. Paul. The North Stars were getting some competition from across the river, and Hextall would be a big draw for the upstart team. I was in a good position to work effectively with the St. Paul club because I was friendly with Glen Sonmor, the club's GM and head coach.

Most established NHL players were not interested in moving to the WHA because the quality of play was not as good, the league did not have nearly the prestige or attendance of the NHL, and there was substantial risk of non-payment or failure of the club or league. But a competing offer always helps in negotiations.

I'm not too proud of my actions on this one. I wanted Hextall as a client, and I wanted to get even with Wren Blair, the man who made life so difficult when I first broke into the business of representing professional athletes. I contacted Hextall on several occasions in an attempt to persuade him to replace his agent with me.

This was wrong. It's different if a player is dissatisfied with his agent, but that was not the case here. I've been on both sides of it and it's no fun when another agent takes a client from you. Many athletes are easy prey because they see teammates getting great deals and they think their agent might be missing something. Athletes are less secure than you'd think.

I was pretty persistent with Hextall. I told him I was so convinced that I could better his contract offer that I would charge him no fee if I could not get him a larger contract by September 15, one day before the start of training camp. He could terminate me on that date and then accept the present offer, hire a new agent, negotiate a new contract himself, or complete the season under the old contract at $38,000. On the other hand, if he agreed to an improved contract before September 15, it was agreed that my fee would be 25 percent of the amount by which his actual contract exceeded the $205,000 offer.

Sometimes a creative fee arrangement providing no fee unless the amount of the contract negotiated exceeds the expectations of the client is attractive to the client. Under my proposal, Hextall was in a position where he had nothing to lose. He and his agent were prepared to accept a contract for $205,000. If I couldn't improve upon that offer by the start of training camp, he could always accept the $205,000 contract offer, and he would owe me nothing. I was comfortable with the arrangement because I was more optimistic than Hextall or his agent about the value of the contract I could negotiate for him.

There was one major hitch: Hextall insisted that his present agent continue the negotiations with the North Stars, and he did not want his agent to know of my involvement. My role was restricted to negotiating a contract offer with a club in the WHA. This arrangement was highly unusual, quite awkward, and ultimately unworkable. Despite all of this, I agreed to it because I knew I could get an offer from St. Paul.

In early June, several days before Hextall was due to leave for a tour of the Far East with a group of top NHL players, I advised him to write to his other agent indicating he did not want to sign the contract offered by the North Stars because he needed more time to consider a matter of such great importance to his career. The agent immediately informed Blair, who was in Chicago on business. Blair insisted that the agent and Hextall meet with him immediately in Chicago to conclude the matter. I advised Hextall against doing this, and Blair then threatened to fly to San Francisco to meet Hextall at the airport before his departure to the Far East.

At this point, Hextall told his agent of my involvement. The agent turned around and told Blair, and Blair immediately increased his offer from $205,000 over three years to $337,000 over four. I was not informed of this new contract offer. My prediction that the North Star offer would increase if there was a competing offer from the WHA had already come true—but I didn't know about it.

Blair threatened to withdraw the offer if the contract was not signed immediately. The agent urged Hextall to sign. Hextall did sign on June 3, but all parties agreed to postdate the contract to September 16, one day after Hextall's contract with me would have expired. It was agreed the agent would hold the papers and Blair would sign on September 16.

During late June and July of 1973, I spent a great deal of time negotiating with Glen Sonmor of the Minnesota Fighting Saints. The negotiations were complicated for a number of reasons, but especially because Hextall was under contract to play the next (1973–74) season for the North Stars. When I concluded that St. Paul was ready to make a substantial offer, I called Hextall in San Francisco to tell him the good news, and to suggest that it would be best for me to become involved in negotiations with both the North Stars and the St. Paul club. His response was cool and indifferent, and he rejected my idea that I take over the negotiations with Blair. I was puzzled. I knew something was wrong, but had no idea what it was. I could tell that Hextall didn't want to discuss it with me.

The only way to revive Hextall's interest would be to obtain a formal written contract offer from the St. Paul club. I got it. St. Paul offered a three-year contract (starting after Hextall completed the 1973–74 season for the North Stars) with a signing bonus of $34,000 and additional compensation of $375,000. This was an average of $137,000 a year, more than 50 percent greater than the North Stars' offer when I first became involved and much higher than the contract Hextall had signed. Since there was a risk of non-payment from the fledgling club, I had the pact guaranteed by the WHA.

I called Hextall again, under the pretext that I had to be in San Francisco for other business, and I suggested that he meet me for a drink at the Fairmont Hotel. If I had told him the true purpose of the visit, I suspected he would be unavailable. It was a strange situation. Hextall's other agent and I were competing. The arrangement was not in Hextall's best interests because neither of us could take full advantage of the existence of the competing bidders. The other agent had no interest in talking with the St. Paul bidder and I was not allowed to communicate with the North Stars. Moreover, my objectivity was compromised because I would only get paid if Hextall signed with St. Paul.

When Hextall saw the WHA offer, he blushed. He was impressed and interested. He casually informed me that he had signed a contract with the North Stars in June, that it was not signed by the club and was in his agent's possession. His agent had been instructed not to deliver it to the club until he authorized it. Hextall inquired about the contract's legality, but he did not mention that it was dated one day after my contract with him expired. I told him my gut reaction was that such a contract would not be binding. I had no idea why a contract would be signed by him and not Blair, but I did not question him further because I did not want to embarrass him.

We mapped out our strategy. He agreed that hereafter I would act as his sole agent, and that his other agent would be advised that he should not deliver the contract to the North Stars for signing. I would contact Blair immediately to attempt to negotiate a new contract, and if unsuccessful, we would seriously consider accepting the St. Paul offer.

Blair did not return my telephone calls, so I wrote him on August 14, informing him of my representation of Hextall and suggesting that we talk about a new contract. No response. I wrote again on August 22. His secretary told me he was out of town. On September 5, I wrote again. This time the letter had a sharper tone—I demanded a meeting. Blair responded but suggested that no meeting could be arranged until September 17. He also mentioned that the club's legal counsel, Ralph Strangis, would be present. I was puzzled by the delay in the meeting date, as well as by the inclusion of the club's legal counsel. I still did not know that the contract had been dated September 16. Hextall was the only person with all the information.

On September 17, I appeared at the meeting with Blair and Strangis. I went to law school with Strangis and know him to be an excellent lawyer. I was finally informed that the contract had been dated September 16 to avoid any obligation for legal fees due to me. Further, it was the club's position that since the parties had agreed on the terms of the contract and had intended it to be binding, the contract was binding and legal in spite of the fact that it hadn't been signed by Blair. Strangis then provided me with written legal authority that he claimed supported his position. As far as he was concerned, they had a deal. I was stunned and embarrassed.

After the meeting, Hextall and I met to discuss the matter. We never discussed the postdating of the contract. I told him that, in my opinion, there was no legally binding contract. After much agonizing, Hextall agreed that the St. Paul offer was too good to pass up and we should grab it quickly before it was too late.

Meanwhile, Blair cleverly announced to the media that Hextall and the club had agreed to terms on a new four-year contract. He didn't know about the St. Paul meeting, but his timing couldn't have been better. The folks in St. Paul were pretty stunned when they read Blair's remarks in the newspapers on Sunday, September 23. However, after a lengthy explanation, a telephone call to Hextall's former agent, and assurances by us that there was no valid contract, the St. Paul contract was signed. The final "whopping" contract was an amazing four-year, guaranteed contract in the amount of $600,000 ($150,000 a year), including a $40,000 signing bonus to be paid immediately.

The following day, when I went to the St. Paul club's offices late in the day to pick up the $40,000 signing bonus check, the St. Paul club's representative provided me with a copy of a letter from Mr. Strangis threatening the St. Paul club with litigation in the event it interfered with what the North Stars alleged was an existing long-term contract between the North Stars and Dennis Hextall. As a result of the letter (an extremely clever move on the part of Mr. Blair and Mr. Strangis), the St. Paul club refused to deliver the signing-bonus check, and claimed that the agreement was null and void on the technical grounds that Glen Sonmor, the club's general manager, did not have the authority to initial the one-paragraph change in the contract after team president Fred Grothe left.

This was a hopeless mess. On the one hand, the North Stars claimed to have a legally binding contract with Hextall for the next four years for $337,000, which Hextall denied; and on the other hand, Hextall claimed that he had a legally binding contract with the Saints for four years in the amount of $600,000, starting one year later, which the Saints denied. Moreover, the Saints refused to give Hextall the $40,000 signing bonus, which Hextall wanted to supplement his $38,000 salary under the last year of the North Stars' contract. The St. Paul signing was a well-kept secret that amazingly has never been made public until now. St. Paul's refusal to honor the contract later turned out to be a wonderful stroke of luck for Dennis.

It appeared that the question of the legality of the Hextall/North Stars contract would have to be settled in the courts. I recommended to Hextall that he honor the final year of his North Star contract. He had a good case, and if he won perhaps the Saints' offer would still be available. If not, perhaps there would be an offer from another club in the other league. Hextall followed my advice.

During the 1973–74 season, Hextall had his best season in professional hockey. He scored 20 goals with 59 assists for a total of 79 points, and was selected to play in the NHL All Star Game. It was an amazing feat considering his confused contract status.

The first crack in the contract dispute came in December 1973, during the middle of the season. We reached agreement on two important points. First, since the beginning of the season in October, the North Stars had been paying Hextall at the rate of $78,000 per year, the amount called for under the new contract the North Stars claimed to be binding on the parties. Hextall had refused to cash any of those checks because of my concern that acceptance of the money would imply acceptance of the contract. At this point, we agreed that Hextall could cash all of the back checks, and future payments, without any adverse legal consequences. It was also agreed that if Hextall went elsewhere after the season was completed, he would pay back the amounts advanced in excess of $38,000. Secondly, we negotiated an agreement providing that the legality of the contract would be submitted to binding arbitration. If the arbitrator found that the agreement was binding, Hextall would be bound to play for the North Stars under the terms of the contract he had signed. If the arbitrator found the agreement was not binding, Hextall would also be obligated to play for the North Stars, but under a contract identical in terms to the one offered by the St. Paul club (four years for $600,000). The North Stars did not know the contract had actually been signed. This was a substantial concession on the part of the North Stars, and a major breakthrough for us. Unfortunately, we were unable to agree on the arbitrator.

The big break came in March, just before the season ended. The North Stars' president, Walter Bush, summoned Hextall to a meeting. Bush was Blair's boss. At the lunch meeting, Bush urged Hextall to play his very best in the remaining few games of the season, and not to stir up any controversy regarding the contract dispute. Bush informed Hextall that major changes in the organization would take place as soon as the season was completed, and that the club was willing to work out a new contract with Hextall. The message was clear but unstated—Wren Blair would soon be removed as the North Stars' general manager. On April 24, 1974, Blair was unceremoniously fired and replaced by the club's head coach, Jack Gordon.

Good fortune had indeed smiled upon Hextall and me. After Blair's departure, negotiations commenced. Blair never would have done this.

The North Stars had done poorly during the previous season, and the club wanted to show the public that it was doing everything possible to retain its top player, Dennis Hextall. In May, despite the legal cloud that had scared them into backing out of their contract, the Saints offered a new six-year, guaranteed contract for $795,000, an average of $132,500 a year. The Saints also agreed to pay all of Hextall's legal fees incurred in connection with any lawsuit with the North Stars.

At the same time, the Vancouver Blazers of the WHA got into the bidding. Now we had a ménage à trois. Vancouver lured Dennis by offering a contract not only to Dennis Hextall but also to his two brothers, Bryan and Rick. The club expressed its intention of using them on the same line so they could play together. Although brother Bryan was not as good a player as Dennis, he was good enough to be playing with Atlanta of the National Hockey League. Their younger brother, Rick, had been playing in an amateur league for the Oakville Seals Manitoba Senior A Hockey League while he worked for the Manitoba Highway Department plowing snow. Rick had good skills, but his questionable attitude and work habits kept him out of professional hockey. Vancouver had come up with a gimmick that was extremely appealing to Dennis and that could at the same time be an excellent gate attraction. Dennis and his brother Brian met with Joe Crozier, the club's coach and general manager, and Jim Pattison, the club's major principal, in Vancouver.

When Joe Crozier, the Vancouver GM, started talking to me about guaranteed contracts for all three players with boxcar figures, I immediately hopped onto an airplane to Vancouver to explore the matter further. I met with Crozier and several of the club's principals. After extensive negotiations, Vancouver offered Dennis a six-year, guaranteed contract at $170,000 a year; Brian a four-year, guaranteed contract at $90,000 a year; and Rick a two-year contract at $40,000 a year. None of the players would be traded and Vancouver would pay Dennis's legal fees in the event of a lawsuit with the North Stars. The offer was almost too good to be true.

Dennis was very excited about the prospect of playing on the same line with his brothers, not only because it would be a big pay day for him with great security, but also because he could help his brothers' careers. It was agreed that Crozier would meet with me in Minneapolis on June 8 to attempt to iron out the details. Meanwhile, St. Paul's contract offer of six years at $132,500 a year was still on the table for Dennis only.

In late May the North Stars offered a four-year contract at $560,000, or an average of $140,000 a year, with a deadline for acceptance of June 14, while making it clear they did not intend to abandon their legal position in the event the offer wasn't accepted.

Although Vancouver's offer was the most attractive, Crozier didn't show up for the meeting of June 8. I suspected he was encountering problems with his principals, who were having second thoughts about such a risky and complicated offer. We were facing a North Stars deadline, a fading Vancouver, and an unreliable St. Paul. The timing was right to promptly conclude a deal with the North Stars.

The North Stars' "final" offer was extremely generous—a raise from $38,000 to $140,000 a year. Not bad. I decided to focus all of my energy on concluding the contract. Hextall was now 31 years old. A fifth year on the North Star contract for Hextall would be fantastic. A fifth year would assure him of playing in the NHL through age 35, several years past the normal retirement age of an NHL hockey player. I arranged a final meeting with Walter Bush and Jack Gordon. At the meeting, I was able to negotiate a fifth year to the contract for a final total of $690,000 guaranteed. Dennis and I had come a long way from the three-year, $205,000 offer that had appealed to him and his agent a year earlier.

My fee agreement with Hextall provided that my fees would be 25 percent of the amount in excess of the $205,000, three-year contract he had been prepared to accept. Since the total package was $690,000, under the agreement the fee would have been $121,250. However, I charged Hextall only on the basis of the first three years of the contract, so my fee was $56,250. Hextall's former agent also prepared his income tax returns, and when he discovered the fee, he pointed out how excessive it was. Hextall replied that he was delighted to pay every penny—it was one of the best investments he had ever made.

The Minnesota Fighting Saints folded in 1977 after only seven seasons of professional hockey. Four teams from the WHA (Hartford, Winnipeg, Vancouver, and Quebec) survived to join the NHL in 1978.

In 1978, high player salaries led to the sale of the North Stars by the Bush group to the Gund brothers. Bush remained with the club until 1984. Bush later became president of the Amateur Hockey Association of the U.S., a member of the International Ice Hockey Federation Counsel, and was inducted into the U.S. Hockey Hall of Fame. Blair became general manager of the Pittsburgh Penguins, and a few years later he was (for a short time) general manager of the Los Angeles Kings. Blair has for many years been out of professional hockey. He lives in Canada. Rick Hextall never played professional hockey. Dennis Hextall was traded to the Detroit Red Wings in 1976 and played his last season (1979–80) for the Washington Capitals, retiring at age 37. Today he is a manufacturer's representative selling design components for automotives and the military, and a vice-president of MAYBEE Associates, Inc., in Brighton, Michigan. He is married, has four children, and lives in Farmington Hills, Michigan, a suburb of Detroit. Although I haven't seen Hextall in a number of years, we remain friends.

My friend Glen Sonmor later became associated with the Minnesota North Stars in several capacities, including a stint as head coach. He still lives in the Twin Cities area, scouting for the Philadelphia Flyers.

Hextall's former agent is a successful businessman who lives in the Twin Cities area, and we have recently become friends.

Wren Blair and I never became friends.

According to the Minneapolis *Star Tribune*, mishandling of the Hextall matter "was one of the main factors in [Blair's] dismissal."

Sweet revenge.

4
NEAL BROTEN'S OWN BERLIN CRISIS

IT WAS SEPTEMBER 1991, AND I WAS ON AN airplane about to touch down in Berlin, a city without a wall. I was there to visit my client, a 31-year-old hockey player named Neal Broten.

John F. Kennedy had stared down the architects of the Iron Curtain by proclaiming, "All free men are citizens of Berlin." In the same spirit, Neal Broten was staring down his stubborn hockey bosses by exercising his prerogative as a free agent to come to Berlin, temporarily leaving behind an 11-year pro career with the Minnesota North Stars for a position on a team in the top German league.

Neal Broten is a Minnesota hockey legend. He learned the game skating on the frozen ponds and lakes of Roseau, Minnesota (population 2,500), 30 miles from the Canadian border. Hockey is to Minnesota what football is to Texas and what basketball is to Indiana. The Minnesota Twins are the only major league baseball team compelled to announce high school hockey results at spring training games in Florida. Broten led little Roseau High School to the state tournament three times in the mid-70s. He was the best hockey player in the state, and in 1979 starred for the University of Minnesota's NCAA champs. A year later, he was part of the U.S. Olympic "Miracle on Ice" in Lake Placid. In 1980–81, Broten was the first winner of the Hobey Baker Award, the Heisman Trophy of college hockey. He signed his first professional contract in March 1981, and joined the North Stars in their march to the Stanley Cup finals. He never played a day in the minors.

In 1985–86, Broten totaled more points (105, with 29 goals and 76 assists) than any American in the history of the National Hockey League. He is the Stars' all-time leader in points, assists, and games. In 1992, he was one of the six players fans voted to the North Stars All-Time "Dream Team," receiving more votes than any other player in the franchise's 25-year history.

After his 1989–90 season, Broten went into the option year of his contract with the North Stars. He had the choice of playing out the option at the agreed-upon salary of $350,000 and then becoming a free agent, or of attempting to negotiate a new contract starting with that season at a higher salary. He elected to play out the option.

We knew that as a 31-year-old free agent Broten could be signed by any club. The signing club would not be penalized by being required to pay the North Stars compensation in the form of players, draft choices, or cash for the loss of the player; however, there was one major hitch: The North Stars retained the right to match any other offer. This "right of first refusal" deters other clubs from signing free agents: Owners don't want to drive up prices on one another only to find their efforts are for naught because the other club matches the offer and retains the player.

In 1980, the average player salary in the National Hockey League was $108,000, while in the National Football League it was $78,000, in the NBA it was $184,000, and in major league baseball it was $190,000. However, by 1990, the average salary of a pro football player rose from $78,000 to $360,000, a pro baseball player from $190,000 to $557,000, and a pro basketball player from $184,000 to close to $1 million. The average hockey salary only rose from $108,000 to $220,000.

Hockey salaries started to change for the better in the summer of 1990 when Ron Caron, general manager of the St. Louis Blues, broke from the pack and signed the club's own free agent, right winger Brett Hull, to a four-year, $7-million contract. Caron then signed free agent Washington defenseman Scott Stevens for over $5 million for four years. Washington didn't match the offer, and the Blues had to give up five first-round picks over the next four years as compensation to the Capitals for losing Stevens. These signings shook the foundation of the NHL salary structure. Owners attempted to brush the signings off as the foolhardy work of a misguided GM. I chose to believe the two moves would trigger a wild escalation of pro hockey salaries.

That same summer, Norm Green, an egocentric multi-millionaire Canadian real estate mogul, became the principal owner of the North Stars. He hired Bobby Clarke as his general manager. Clarke, a 41-year-old Canadian, was perhaps the greatest player who ever played for the Philadelphia Flyers. He was a three-time MVP, won two Stanley Cups, and in 1987 was elected to the Hockey Hall of Fame. Like all former athletes, his largest payday was a mere pittance compared to today's salaries.

Immediately after his retirement from the Flyers, Clarke was named the club's general manager, a job he held for six years, until he was fired in August 1990. Green hired him almost immediately.

Clarke found it difficult to leave Philadelphia. He told me, "When I walk down the street in Philadelphia, everybody knows me. Here, no one recognizes me." He was just another guy wearing a suit.

In the aftershock of the Brett Hull and Scott Stevens contracts, it was difficult to predict where the salaries were headed. Were these two contracts unique, or was this an indication of things to come? This was a point of discussion when I first met with Clarke to talk about Broten. I argued that the Hull and Stevens deals were a harbinger. He disagreed. It was the first of many disagreements between us.

When I faced off with Clarke a week before the 1990–91 season, I discovered that he relied on the power play to prevail in negotiations. Power plays win hockey games but not contract negotiations. Clarke offered a one-year contract with a one-year option at $375,000. I suspect he would probably have gone, at most, to $400,000, a raise of about $50,000. A year earlier this probably would have been a good offer, and I probably would have grabbed it. But now I was betting on a dramatic rise in future salaries. Besides, when Broten and I had talked about contract goals during the summer, we had agreed that since this contract would likely be his last, our emphasis should be on the length more than the amount per year. At age 31 and with a bum shoulder, Broten had set his sights on a contract that would cover him through age 34 or possibly age 35. Naturally, for the same reasons, Clarke wanted the short contract. We were miles apart. I decided it was pointless to make a counteroffer. The timing wasn't right. We decided Broten would play out the option. It seemed like a good gamble.

Clarke was not pleasant to work with. When there was a conflict, he was quick to anger and became nasty. Everything was personal, and I was the enemy. He threatened to trade Broten and chastised me when we differed on Broten's value. He hasn't learned that one can disagree without being disagreeable, a basic tenet I try to follow. When passion not reason prevails, negotiations often become protracted and bitter. In sports, players can become less effective during these kinds of negotiations, and after an agreement is finally reached the club sometimes doesn't end up with the good will that brings out the best in a player's performance. Clarke may be an outstanding judge of hockey talent, but he doesn't have the temperament for handling contract negotiations.

Broten is a modest, unassuming guy. He has an even temperament, is eager to please, and reluctant to make waves. He is only 5'9" and 175 lbs., small by NHL standards, but he is a great skater and stick-handler, valuable on the power play as well as in killing penalties. His greatest strength is as a play maker. Neal was not a hard-liner when it came to money, but like most athletes he wanted to be paid fairly in relation to other players of similar ability. He had two concerns about playing out the option at $350,000 and becoming a free agent. First, there was some risk that he could be slowing down because of his age. If so, maybe after the season he wouldn't be offered as much as the $400,000 he could get now. Second, and more importantly, Broten had dislocated his left shoulder a couple of years earlier and during that offseason had had surgery to correct the problem. His shoulder socket was looser now and the shoulder sometimes popped out when he got hit.

Things went well in the first half of Broten's option year. At the mid-point, he was the North Stars' leading scorer and ranked 22nd in the league scoring race. His shoulder was holding up well. Also, there was talk about the formation of two new leagues—the North American Hockey League and the Continental Hockey League. Our decision was looking good. In December, I opened negotiations with a proposal asking for $3 million over three years, plus an option year. Clarke never responded. He considered my offer outrageous.

Meanwhile, the North Stars weren't drawing many fans and the new owner decided to embark on an aggressive season ticket sales campaign for the '91–'92 season. To run the effort, the team hired Pat Forciea, a hotshot political consultant in his mid-30s who was fresh from engineering the stunning upset of a longtime U.S. Senator from Minnesota. Forciea asked Broten to help with the promotion. Never one to turn down a request, Broten said okay. Little did he know that the promotion involved a sales pitch signed by him urging 62,000 of his "closest friends" to buy season tickets next year: "So join us and become a part of the hottest game on ice. Together we can fill up the Met in the 1991–92 season. . . . I'm looking forward to seeing you at the Met Center soon." As a season ticket holder, Broten got a sincere-sounding letter from himself. The letter gave me my first inkling that Green was not a man of high integrity. So I wasn't surprised when he uprooted the 26-year-old franchise and moved it to Dallas after the 1992–93 season.

Broten never saw or consented to the letter. He felt he had been used and was embarrassed about making a sales pitch to people who enjoyed watching him play when it was quite possible he wouldn't even be there next season. My letter to Norman Green protesting the use of Broten's name went unanswered, like my December contract proposal to Clarke. Their silence would not earn them high marks in a Dale Carnegie course. The negotiations were off on the wrong foot.

The second half of the season was a nightmare. In January, Broten's left shoulder popped out three times. He was concerned that the injury would have a devastating effect on his value when his contract expired so he didn't tell club officials. Instead of going to the team trainer or doctor, he maneuvered his shoulder back into its normal position. This was incredibly painful. Once his wife, Sally, observed him turn blue in the face on the bench during the process. He feared he would need surgery to tighten up the shoulder joint. Neal was having second thoughts about the gamble. He was injured and depressed and his point production was dropping badly. The coach switched him to a defensive line.

At times like this, the athlete's normal instinct is to grab the last contract offer on the table, good or bad. He envisions a poorer contract, or worse yet none at all, if he waits. This is when the club goes for the kill. A prior offer is either lowered or pulled off the table. The club takes a "wait and see" attitude. It's a lot like a bank loan—when you desperately need it, the bank doesn't want to risk it; when you don't need it, you qualify easily.

As an agent, you can't panic. You mustn't make a deal from a position of weakness. This is the time to stay cool, stay the course, and offer encouragement to your client. Take a look at the rest of the cards. Play out the hand.

Neal and I made arrangements for him to be seen by an outside physician, Dr. Harvey O'Phelan, a semi-retired orthopedist who years earlier was the North Stars' team physician and who had done the surgery on Broten's shoulder. When Dr. O'Phalen examined Neal in late January 1991, he concluded that surgery was unnecessary and that the shoulder would improve if Broten did exercises to strengthen the muscles surrounding the shoulder socket. Broten mentioned to the team trainer there was weakness in the shoulder and that he would like to do exercises to strengthen the surrounding muscles. The exercises worked. The shoulder improved. But Broten's production continued to drop and he scored only two goals during the second half of the season. In terms of the contract, his timing couldn't have been worse.

Then came the playoffs. The North Stars had been sloppy and lethargic throughout the regular season, but they were sprinkled with stardust in postseason play. Minnesota shocked the hockey world by upsetting Chicago, St. Louis, and Edmonton in the first three rounds. They wound up in the Stanley Cup finals against the Pittsburgh Penguins. Neal played a big part in the turnaround. He had nine goals and 13 assists in the playoffs and might have won the Conn Smythe Trophy for playoff MVP if Minnesota had won the cup. Pittsburgh won it in six games, but Neal's performance reestablished him as a top player and gave me the necessary ammunition with which to battle for a good contract. We had survived the option year.

Clarke didn't call. The silence wasn't interrupted until mid-July when I got a call from St. Louis Blues' general manager Ron Caron. He said the Blues were looking for a center, would very much like Broten, and invited me to make a one-time "take it or leave it" proposal.

I was ecstatic. This was the same Ron Caron who had shocked the NHL hierarchy in the summer of 1990 by engineering the signing of free agent Stevens. Caron was on a spending spree and was said to be courting Boston's 31-year-old free agent Dave Christian and New Jersey right winger Brendan Shanahan. Caron had signed Chicago's Michel Goulet to a four-year, $2.9-million pact but the Blackhawks had matched the offer.

When Clarke learned of Caron's offer to Broten, he told the Blues' GM, "Lay off. We'll match any offer. You're wasting your time."

I thought Broten and Goulet were players of comparable ability, so I proposed a four-year, $3-million deal. Caron seemed amenable to both the length and the amount of the contract, but indicated that he was going on a fishing trip and would get back to me in a couple of days. I anxiously awaited the verdict, but was counting the money when Caron called two days later and said, "The club has decided to go in a different direction." It turned out that the Blues had successfully signed Christian away from Boston when the Bruins chose not to match the offer. St. Louis also signed Shanahan at a big risk because compensation would have to be determined by an arbitrator. There was no money left for Broten.

The most crucial element in almost every negotiation of any kind is the existence of a viable alternative. Leverage, not fairness, determines the outcome of negotiations. Consequently, the player's representative must utilize all his creativity and imagination to dig up an alternative if at all possible. In the Broten case, the St. Louis Blues alternative had come and gone. There were no other NHL bidders on the horizon. It was late July, and Clarke had yet to respond to my proposal of the previous December, some seven months earlier. An alternative was important. Training camp would open in early September, without Broten if he didn't have a contract.

European hockey was the only alternative I could come up with. It was a long shot, as the two foreign players allowed on each club were usually signed by mid-May. They reported to training camp in early August. A few agents specialize in placing players in Europe, and I had only one contact—Craig Sarner. Sarner was a former hockey player at the University of Minnesota. He played for the U.S. Olympic Team in 1979 and then turned professional, playing much of the time in Europe. In 1991 he was coach of the Berlin club. In late July I contacted him and asked about his club's interest in Broten. He was very excited about the prospect of acquiring Neal. I explained to him that I would have to have an "escape" clause in the contract permitting Broten, at his option, to return before the NHL regular season started on October 3. This condition was a must for maximum leverage. Under NHL rules if Broten played in Europe after the first NHL regular season game, he would not be allowed to play in the NHL that season. European clubs rarely consent to such a clause because it's disruptive to the team and difficult to find a good replacement at that time.

The club initially said no, but a couple of days later had a change of heart and said it would be willing to explore a one-year contract with an escape clause. We got lucky. Apparently one of the foreign players under contract had refused to report until after his wife's expected delivery of their first child in October. We both agreed that the range would be $150,000 to $200,000 for the season, or $20,000 to $25,000 a month. I warned Sarner that I intended to use this contract offer in negotiations with Bobby Clarke, and that there was a chance a deal would be reached with the North Stars. This was clearly Broten's preference, but I also told him there was a good chance it wouldn't happen. Sarner was realistic. He understood. We were lucky. I had my alternative.

When I first talked with Neal on August 1 about the German proposal, his reaction was total rejection. It was a radical proposal, almost unheard-of for a player of his talent. Neal Broten playing hockey in Berlin would be like Kirby Puckett playing baseball in Tokyo.

On the same day, I met with Clarke. I told him Neal had an opportunity to play in Germany, but had to make a decision no later than August 7, the day their training camp opened. Clarke proposed a four-year, $2-million contract, with some of the payments deferred and a requirement on Broten's part to make a number of personal appearances for the club without charge for the next eight years. The four-year term was good, but the money was too low. We were about a million dollars apart. It appeared to me that we'd never be able to close the gap unless I used the Berlin alternative as leverage. But I didn't want to get caught bluffing. To be effective in negotiations, you need to be prepared to follow through with your proposals. If you take a stand and then have to back down you lose credibility, and your words then carry little weight with the other side. I had to persuade the reluctant Broten to be prepared to play in Berlin if negotiations with the North Stars club failed.

It wasn't easy. The decision to leave his team and his country was a difficult one, made more difficult by the fact that most of his friends and family told him to either accept the North Stars' offer or to hold out in Minneapolis. Neal was clearly going through an agonizing bout of indecision. On August 2, he reluctantly agreed to be willing to go to Berlin. But on the morning of August 4, he tracked me down to let me know that he was having serious second thoughts. Later that evening, he left a message at my home reversing himself yet again. He would go to Germany after all. The decision was final and reflected his confidence in my judgment, although he spent the next day grumbling to his wife, Sally, "There's no way I'm going to Berlin."

I pushed the "Berlin alternative" over the "home holdout" for several reasons. First, I didn't think we could reach our goal on a contract unless the club was pressured to sign Broten by the club's fans and supporters. His age was working against him, and he had a problem shoulder. In order to generate public pressure, we not only had to state clearly a persuasive case for our salary demands, but also had to establish that Broten would play elsewhere and the North Stars would lose him for the entire season if he wasn't treated fairly. If Broten merely sat at home, the North Stars could sign him at any time during the season. There would be no threat of his playing elsewhere, the situation wouldn't cause concern to North Star fans, and therefore it wouldn't get media attention. In the Berlin situation, however, if the September 25 deadline passed, Broten would be with that club the entire season.

Second, our leverage would be much greater if Broten was earning substantial money playing hockey and staying in good condition.

Third, if he was at home Broten would become bored and impatient, and he would be constantly getting flak about the holdout. Pressure from well-meaning family, friends, and teammates to sign would mount, and his desire to join his teammates at training camp would increase. Worse, North Stars' officials would be knocking on his door every day with scare tactics. We would be dead meat. On the other hand, if he was in Berlin, the distance alone would protect him from all of these outside pressures.

In any negotiation, you need to know your customer, to understand his tolerance for disputes, his patience for protracted negotiations, his attitudes about money, the size of his pride and ego, his temperament, his ability to handle this kind of pressure, who influences his decisions, and the amount of confidence he has in you. All of these factors differ from client to client.

Fourth, my hope in Broten's case was that if other NHL clubs saw that the North Stars had allowed him to go to Berlin, it might shake loose some good offers from clubs encouraged that the North Stars wouldn't match their offer.

With these thoughts in mind, I hammered out an agreement with Sarner providing Broten with $45,000 American dollars, tax-free, for the period from August 9 to September 30 if he chose to return home. If he played the entire season, he would be paid $180,000 tax-free. He would be one of the highest paid players in Europe, but these salaries were small compared to what the NHL now offered, and we'd already turned down $500,000 a year from the North Stars. The agreement would be signed by

Broten only if we couldn't reach agreement with the North Stars before the deadline of August 8.

While this was going on, the North Stars' Pat Forciea was plotting to discredit me and confuse Broten through a campaign of disinformation. He apparently was taking a page from the political books by preparing a bag full of "dirty tricks." The first dirty trick came when Clarke's $2-million offer was reported by North Stars' officials as $2.4 million. At the time, I assumed it was an innocent mistake and paid no attention to it. The public was led to believe that the North Stars' offer rejected by Broten was 20 percent better than it was. Neal was disturbed. Had I misunderstood the offer, or was I deceiving him? Either was not good. Even I began to wonder.

On August 7, I set up final meetings with the Brotens (1:00 P.M.) and Clarke (4:00 P.M.). When I met with Sally and Neal, I pointed out that the North Stars' offer on the table was four years at $500,000 a year, of which $100,000 would be deferred to years five through eight. I calculated the present value of this package at $1.9 million. I told them that in my opinion, the Berlin move would eventually result in a North Stars' contract for four years that would earn him an additional $350,000 to $500,000, plus the $45,000 tax-free ($70,000 equivalent) he would earn in Berlin for eight weeks' work.

I reasoned that Broten's value would increase because I anticipated that new player signings in the next eight weeks would be higher than Clarke had anticipated, and that the pressure from the public to re-sign Broten rather than lose him for a season in Berlin would be enormous and could not be ignored.

We talked about the obvious risk. If Neal suffered a significant injury while playing in Berlin, he would be damaged merchandise. He had to stay healthy through the several preseason games and the eight league games prior to the October 1 termination date. I pointed out that the fear of injury was much greater than the actual risk. The odds of an injury were small in comparison with the gain of $350,000 to $500,000 I projected if he didn't suffer an injury.

The agents that deserve the big fees are the ones who make forceful recommendations, almost making the decision for the client. Weak agents carefully and cautiously point out each of the alternatives to the client, then ask the client to pick the alternative. If the alternative selected by the client doesn't work out, the agent is off the hook.

The Brotens were not only clients, they were also good friends. In my heart, I knew I was much better qualified to make this decision than they were. To do otherwise would have been a cop out. I told them in no uncertain terms that I thought Neal should go to Berlin if Clarke didn't come up with a new offer later that day—an offer worth at least $2.5 million. The Brotens agreed.

The Berlin club was becoming extremely impatient, and understandably so. We had reached agreement on the terms but neither side had signed. At 3:30 P.M. on August 7 I got a call from a man in a Berlin restaurant. It was not my patient friend Sarner but his boss, the club's general manager. He was blunt: The offer was open for 60 minutes more. If I faxed to them a contract signed by Broten within 60 minutes, we had a deal. If not, the club's offer would not only be withdrawn, but the North Stars would be notified that the club's offer was withdrawn, leaving us at Clarke's mercy. Luckily, the meeting with Clarke had already been scheduled for 4:00 P.M. This gave Broten and me 30 minutes in which to make a deal with Clarke.

The Berlin ultimatum was an excellent negotiating tactic. It was made after we had had a reasonable period of time in which to consider their proposal, so we had no cause to be offended, yet it now forced our hand. We had to make a quick decision and no longer had sufficient time to use the Berlin offer to improve the North Stars' offer. It placed us in the difficult position of losing our leverage with the North Stars if we didn't quickly accept the Berlin offer. It is a clever tactic for preventing your counterpart from creating a bidding war.

Broten still didn't want to go to Berlin. Two million dollars is a lot of money, and he didn't want to lose it because of an injury in Berlin. He was also still upset about the disparity between the $2-million contract offer I had reported and the $2.4-million contract offer reported by the media. Berlin was demanding an answer. I was about to meet with Clarke. The pressure was mounting.

Although I rarely include my clients in meetings with GMs, I decided it would be best for Neal to join me to erase any doubts about the terms of the first offer. I also wanted him to hear firsthand any other last-minute proposals to eliminate possible misunderstandings.

I left the unsigned Berlin agreement with my secretary and told her that I would be calling her before the 4:30 deadline with a "yes" or "no."

Broten and I arrived at Clarke's office at 4:00 P.M., and I told Neal about the Berlin ultimatum. Clarke kept us waiting until 4:10. Twenty minutes remained. I had to be abrupt.

Neal spoke from his heart to Clarke about his feelings and his desire to be treated fairly. I explained to Clarke that we were running out of time on the Berlin option and urged him to make another offer if he was willing to do so. First, however, I asked Clarke to confirm that his previous offer was for four years at $2 million, which he did. My credibility with Broten was shored up. Clarke then sweetened the pot by adding $600,000 to the package, to be paid $100,000 a year starting nine years from then and ending 15 years from then. Clarke's total package was now $2.6 million, up from $2 million, but with the extended deferred payments had a present value of about $2.2 million up from $1,900,000. Still not chicken feed.

Our quick counterproposal for $3 million over four years with $250,000 a year deferred to years five through eight had a present value of about $2.8 million. Clarke considered the offer way too high. He was perturbed. "I'd like to sleep on it. I want to think about it until tomorrow morning." Not an unreasonable request, yet I knew he wasn't serious. The contract wasn't ripe for negotiation. The club didn't need Broten under contract on August 7—only in early October, when the season began. Moreover, I anticipated new, bigger contract signings in August and September that would increase the market value of unsigned players like Broten.

I had to inform Clarke that Broten would be signing a contract with Berlin immediately if the offer wasn't acceptable. Proposing ultimatums or setting unreasonable deadlines are usually poor negotiating techniques. The normal reaction of the recipient is to accept the challenge by rejecting the ultimatum. Anger is another typical response, and when emotions take over, you can't make a deal. However, in this situation I had no choice.

Clarke reacted predictably. He went ballistic. He told us Minnesotans would forget about Broten, he could stay in Berlin forever, and that although he previously thought Broten was a team man, it was now clear he was selfish and greedy. If there had been any doubt about Berlin in Broten's mind, Clarke's cutting words had just pushed him over the edge. We rejected the request and made no further proposals. He had called our bluff, but we weren't bluffing.

Broten and I hurriedly walked out of Clarke's office to an adjoining room. It was now 4:25 P.M., 11:25 P.M. in Berlin. I discussed the matter briefly with Broten and recommended that the Berlin contract be signed. We had only five minutes left. He went along with me, but made it clear that he would opt to return on October 1. I warned him to tell no one about his plan. I called my secretary and told her to sign Broten's name on the agreement and to immediately fax it to Sarner. Broten never did sign that contract. We ran out of time.

Minnesota's hockey legend was leaving the North Stars to play in Berlin. He was heading for Kurfurstendamm, the city's main drag, shortened to "Kudamm" by Americans. Berlin officials were organizing a special airport welcome, North Stars officials were angry, the Brotens were scared and disappointed. I was busy planning my next move—the handling of the media.

Neal and I met Sally at a private club near the Met Center, coincidentally the place where Broten had been presented with the Hobey Baker Award ten years earlier.

"Pack your bags. We're going to Germany," Neal said. Sally was disbelieving. This was no celebration. We were all disappointed and depressed. As we were commiserating, Broten left to return several of a flood of messages. He returned somewhat ashen and shaken, reporting that he had returned a call from Stanley S. Hubbard, Jr., who owned the ABC affiliate Twin Cities TV station and was one of the five wealthiest Minnesotans. Hubbard was an ardent hockey enthusiast and was a big supporter of the North Stars as well as being a local college and high school hockey fan. Hubbard told Broten he was making the biggest mistake of his life by going to Berlin. He assured Broten that the North Stars' offer was an excellent one and his advice was to accept it. He added that if Broten went to Berlin, the North Stars' offer might not be on the table later. I didn't doubt Hubbard's sincerity, but I wondered who had told him about the situation and provided him with Broten's unlisted number. Anyway, the call raised doubts in Broten's mind about the decision and about my judgment. Had this come from the North Stars' bag of dirty tricks?

While driving home that night, I heard Forciea being interviewed on a major radio station about Broten's defection. Forciea calmly assured listeners that Clarke and I were still negotiating and were close to a deal. No wonder many players' wives referred to him as the "Viper" and a local sports columnist called him the "Spin Doctor." I was finally beginning to catch on. This would not be business as usual. This war would be waged in the media. Public reaction would determine the winner.

Five minutes after I hit the garage, I had hired a long-time friend, David Mona, a top PR man with an excellent sports background, to help me fight the media battle. Mona suggested a press conference at my house as quickly as possible, quickly enough to make the 10:00 P.M. news. I made the arrangements. Mona emphasized the "key message" strategy. Neal and I must emphasize Neal's long-term contributions to the team and the community. Neal was clad in a sweatshirt with the word "GERMANY" emblazoned on the front. Unrehearsed, both Neal and Sally spoke about their disappointment, and Sally broke down in tears. Her reaction was sincere and spontaneous, but a Hollywood actress couldn't have done better. A tearful Sally was shown on every local TV station, sitting beside her glum husband. The morning papers featured the same picture. This was good. Broten was the fair-haired Minnesotan; Green and Clarke were the outsiders.

As the press conference was ending, a telephone call came from Broten's father in Roseau. Neal's dad had worked hard most of his life. He was a blue-collar city maintenance man, and he knew the value of a buck. Neal told me his father thought Neal was crazy to turn down $2 million dollars but he said, "You're a big boy now. You have to make your own decision."

In a *USA Today* article, Clarke was reported as saying, "The [contract] numbers won't be the same when he comes back. I hope he's making the decision on his own and not taking someone's advice."

The next morning, one of the club's assistant coaches, Andy Murray, called Broten several hours before his scheduled departure and warned Broten that once he played in a game in Europe, he would be ineligible to return to the NHL for the entire season. This was incorrect. I had told Broten he could play in as many games as he wanted in Europe, as long as he returned by the start of the NHL season in early October. Murray had coached in Europe for six or seven years in the '80s and should have known better. I suspected this was another North Star dirty trick. It worked. Broten was really shaken up. More doubt was created. He called me that morning about his conversation with Murray. I reassured him that my information was correct, but I sensed he still had doubt in his mind. I urged him to call the NHL Players Association for confirmation. He did, and he was satisfied that I was right.

At the airport, he was depressed about his departure for Berlin. No sooner had Sally and the two children arrived home from the airport than the phone was ringing. It was Neal. A shocked Sally's first thought was that he had never boarded the plane and was calling from the airport. Neal was calling from the European-bound airplane. "Oh my God, Sally," Neal said as he was sobbing. "I can't believe I'm going to Germany." Although Neal received a hero's welcome at the Berlin airport, complete with club officials, flowers, speeches, and plenty of media, he was miserable the first several days.

These were the worst days of his life. He was alone, separated from family and friends, a complete stranger in a strange land, and worried about losing a $2-million-dollar offer to an injury. Communication with his teammates and others was frustrating and difficult. The language barrier created misunderstandings, some of them amusing. A few days after his arrival, when media types were obtaining photographs of him, one noticed the standard words "Choice for me—Drug Free" imprinted on the shaft of a hockey stick Broten had brought from the U.S. The next day, Broten and a close-up of his stick were prominently pictured in the Berlin newspaper with a feature article critical of Broten for favoring "free drugs" for everyone. You can imagine this caused quite a stir. Broten's angry teammates boycotted the reporter, while coach Sarner tried to straighten out the mess. Sarner, Broten's friendly teammates, and the arrival of Sally helped Broten make a good adjustment after an unsettling first couple of weeks.

After the news broke of Broten's departure, the sports pundits had a field day. One radio sports talk-show host called me a "nut case." A Twin Cities sports columnist, poking fun at Broten and me, wrote in the St. Paul *Pioneer Press* his own definition of certain words.

"Why didn't he sign with the Stars? Perhaps Broten was suffering from "temporary insanity".

tem-po-rar-y in-san-i-ty: n. 1. Passing up a guaranteed contract worth millions. 2. Signing with a German hockey team. Of course, we can't rule out the possibility he got bad advice.

bad ad-vice: n. 1. An agent who advises you to sign with a German team."

Mona, my PR man, was busy encouraging people who agreed with Broten's position to speak out publicly through letters to the editor, calls to the North Stars, and call-ins to sports talk shows. Ten days later, two letters to the editor of the Minneapolis *Star Tribune* were printed in support of Broten and critical of the North Stars. This was no accident. Neal made himself available to the media by telephone from Berlin. We didn't want this story to have a one-day shelf life. Our strategy would fail if the public forgot about Broten.

A week after Neal's departure, the "end run" began. The club's strategy was simple: ignore Simon and divide and conquer by negotiating directly with the Brotens. Forciea contacted Sally, who was planning to visit Neal in Berlin in a week. They met for a drink and some talk. Forciea explained that he was there at the behest of Green, who was in Calgary, "sick" about the turn of events but his hands were tied. Later he said he could see where the offer was unfair. Clarke had to be given free rein on decisions like this. This is the "good guy, bad guy" act. It works like this. Clarke's a bad guy, he's too tough; but I'm a good guy, I'll help you get a fair contract. Trust me. Work with me. He indicated he would not be staying on with the club too much longer because he was frustrated with the way it was operated and he wanted to be involved in the 1992 State Democratic party summer convention. That convention came and went and Forciea remained a fixture in the North Stars' organization. He left the club in the spring of 1993 only because he did not want to move when the team was moved to Dallas.

He said: "I've been on the phone with Clarke the past two days. Clarke has a very large ego, definitely wants Neal back, but refuses to negotiate with Simon." In other words, get rid of Simon and you and I can cut a deal quickly. He also conceded that the club had received numerous calls in support of Broten, some threatening to cancel season tickets. He suggested he deliver a new proposal to Sally. Sally entertained the idea because she and Neal could see no harm in it. The North Stars were progressing on their "end run."

I was angry. I had to nip this tactic in the bud or Neal would be at the disadvantage of negotiating without an agent, and I would be out a client. I told Sally in no

My father, I. E. Simon, had a tremendous influence on me. He taught me to be deliberate, made me respect hard work, and steered me toward law school. My mother, Gertrude, supported my decision to initially try the practice of law rather than join the family business.

I have been a sports fan since my grandfather took me to my first baseball game when I was seven, and I love to play competitive sports. This photo of the tennis team at the University of Minnesota was taken in 1956. I am at the front left.

Here I am in 1960, a freshly minted lawyer, with then Minnesota Attorney General (later U.S. Vice-President) Walter Mondale.

After leaving the University of Minnesota, I maintained close ties with the alumni association and became a supporter of the athletics at the University, a connection that helped me get my start in contract sports. Here I am chatting with Dave Winfield (another Minnesota alumnus) and Bob Hope before our participation in half-time ceremonies at a 1980 Gophers' homecoming game.

One of my early court cases that steered me toward sports representation came after the infamous 1972 "Basketbrawl" in Minneapolis. I represented Minnesota player Corky Taylor in a bid to reverse his season-long suspension. Here we are after completing the hearing in front of the Big Ten athletic directors. (AP Photo)

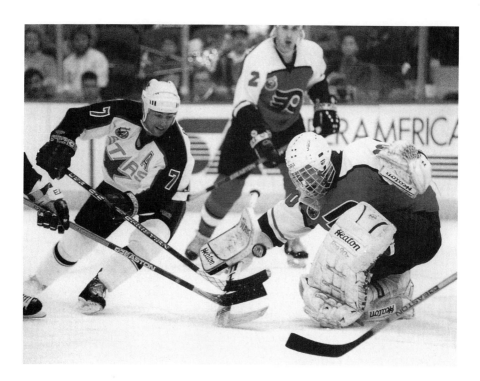

Neal Broten of the Minnesota North Stars played on the famous 1980 U.S. Olympic hockey team. A local favorite, in 1992 he received the most votes of any player selected for the All Time North Stars team. (© 1993 STAR TRIBUNE/Minneapolis–St. Paul)

Looking glum, Neal Broten prepares to follow my advice and board a plane to Berlin to play in the top German hockey league. It was painful for him to leave his friends and family, but six weeks later the strategy paid off to the tune of $1 million, and fans welcomed him home with a thunderous standing ovation. (© 1991 STAR TRIBUNE/ Minneapolis–St. Paul)

Mutt and Jeff—Kevin McHale and I on our way back from Europe in 1980.We had made the trip to Italy after contract negotiations with the Boston Celtics had broken down. McHale was the first unsigned rookie to miss a Celtic rookie camp. (AP Photo)

A statue of Boston Celtics' formidable president, Red Auerbach, graces Boston's Faneuil Hall. When I visited it recently, I finally felt I had Red's undivided attention.

Keith Fahnhorst of the San Francisco 49ers was a cornerstone client. He had faith in me early on and enjoyed an illustrious 14-year career in the NFL, including two Super Bowl championships in the 1980s.

uncertain terms that by permitting Forciea to talk to her instead of to me, she was playing right into their hands, because club officials knew they could make a much better deal if I was out of the picture. Sally must tell Forciea that I was the only person they could talk with about the contract. She agreed and told me she would insist that all dealings be with me hereafter, but nothing changed, and that made my job more difficult. I knew, however, that Sally would soon be returning to Berlin and geography would limit the club's contacts with the Brotens.

Forciea's new proposal provided the two Broten children, Brooke and Lara (then ages six and eight respectively), $10,000 a year for each of the four years to go toward their college education. In short, the package was sweetened by $80,000. Big deal. It was a token increase. Sally rejected the offer. We hadn't sent Broten to Berlin to pick up $80,000.

During September, Forciea's dirty tricks continued. Several times radio and TV stations received word that the North Stars and Broten were close to a deal. This was totally untrue. One day in early September Jim Kaat, a client of mine and the Twins' TV color analyst, called my office, asking my secretary if I was back from Berlin yet. When she informed Kaat that I had not gone to Berlin, he was baffled. He said, "I was listening to the radio a couple of days ago, and some guy from the North Stars—I think his name was Pat Forciea—was on the air. Some guy called in, complaining that they would never go to another North Stars' game because of the Neal Broten situation. Forciea tried to pacify the caller and said, 'Ron Simon is on his way to Berlin right now to talk to Neal and bring him back to Minnesota.'"

Rob Leer, a sports reporter at a major Twin Cities' TV station, told Sally that an unidentified person sounding like Forciea left a message on his VoiceMail indicating that Broten and the North Stars were close to a deal.

In mid-September in the late evening, I received a call from Sid Hartman, Minneapolis *Star Tribune* sports columnist. He said that one of the North Stars' representatives had told him that the club was close to a deal with Broten, and he wanted confirmation for his column to be published the next morning. I told him the information was total nonsense and that we weren't any closer to a deal than we had been on August 7 when Broten left for Berlin. Hartman had to scramble to strike the misinformation from his column before it was printed.

I suspect that all this disinformation came from Forciea or other club executives to calm the fans, hoping to relieve or reduce the tremendous pressure on the club to sign Broten, and perhaps to minimize the negative impact on the season ticket sale campaign.

Clarke continued to ignore our requests that he deal with me. He called Sally a few days before she was going to return to Berlin, telling her that Broten's defection to Berlin was "blackmail." Thus, even if he was now willing to pay Broten more money, he couldn't do it because he would be giving in to blackmail, and the other players could then pull the same stunt, expecting the same result.

After Sally returned to Berlin, I decided to give it one last shot with Clarke. It was generally known that Broten had an option to return before the NHL season started. (We had made sure that this information was leaked.) When I met with Clarke in mid-September, I told him that I was leaving for Berlin on September 21 to visit with Neal and to make some major decisions. Neither of us budged. Clarke continued to call our tactics blackmail and said while he was the Philadelphia GM, the biggest mistake he ever made was to give in to the demands of goalie Ron Hextall, who refused to report unless his contract was "renegotiated." He said, "When I gave in to him, it ruined the franchise. I'm not going to repeat that mistake."

I suggested that Broten could be paid additional money under a separate personal service contract providing for his token appearances on behalf of the club after his retirement. I mentioned that Texas pitcher Nolan Ryan and Washington defenseman Rod Langway had such contracts. He didn't get it. It passed over his head.

The pay under the seldom-used personal service contract is usually in reality mostly additional compensation for the athlete's performance under his other contract. However, unlike the other contract, the terms of the personal service contract remain confidential because there is no requirement that this contract be filed with the league or with the Players Association. The player ends up with the aggregate deferred compensation he is seeking, and his obligation is only to provide token postcareer services to the club. The club, on the other hand, has fulfilled its obligation to the player while avoiding establishing a harmful precedent for teammates of similar ability because the terms of the personal service contract are confidential, and the club can also justify the additional pay for postcareer services. Like Ryan and Langway, Broten was a perfect candidate for this arrangement. He was a top player, had been with the club for many years, was nearing retirement, and was popular in the community. It was a win/win situation that went by the boards.

One advantage of face-to-face negotiations is that you can size the other guy up. Sometimes body language or facial expressions will tip you off. I could see clearly that Clarke was under pressure to sign Broten. Finally, he mistakenly mentioned that failure to sign Broten "could cost some people their jobs." After this slip of the tongue, I had renewed confidence. My strategy was working.

The breakthrough came the day before my departure. Clarke came up with a big offer. Green and Forciea had assessed the loss from a public relations standpoint—the impact on the club's image and its effect on ticket sales—and they had overruled Clarke and Head Coach Bob Gainey. Their previous four-year offer of $400,000 a year plus $100,000 a year over the next ten years (a $2.6-million package worth approximately $2.2 million at present value) was substantially increased to $350,000 a year for the first four years and $200,000 a year over the next ten years—a package of $3.4 million up from $2.6 million. The present value of the package had increased from about $2.2 million to about $2.65 million.

The offer also included valuable non-monetary concessions not usually included in hockey contracts, like the club's waiver of its usual right to buy out Broten's contract for much less money. In other words, unlike most hockey contracts, Broten's contract was fully, not partly guaranteed for four years. Moreover, the payments due under the contract from the North Stars were guaranteed personally by Green, making it one of the few or perhaps the only contract in the NHL personally guaranteed by the owner. I felt an unbelievable sense of relief. I had not had a decent night's sleep from the time Neal had left for Berlin. My judgment had been vindicated. The pressure was off. I knew that the money was right and that a deal could be made.

When I telephoned the Brotens with the news, they were relieved. Broten had until September 25 to make a decision, but it was a foregone conclusion. I went to Berlin anyway to discuss the offer with the Brotens, and also to attempt to improve the unresolved non-monetary terms of the contract prior to the September 25 deadline. Although the items open for negotiation were important, make no mistake—it was a done deal. Neal was going home. However, it is important to remember that the only effective time to negotiate the final points—even the fine print—is while you are still in a position of leverage. Once the pressure is off, you'll have a difficult time resolving any sticky points in your favor. The best place to negotiate effectively was from Berlin.

I went to Berlin and watched Neal's team defeat Düsseldorf. After the game, the Brotens and I met to discuss the contract situation. We quickly agreed that the Berlin contract would be terminated on September 25, but that the club would not be informed of our decision until the 25th and negotiations would continue with the North Stars on the remaining non-monetary issues.

Late in the evening on September 24, Green telephoned Neal, and in his absence, talked to Sally. He assured Sally that the "loose ends" would be worked out satisfactorily if they would come home. The Brotens returned on October 1, and the negotiations on the remaining loose ends were successfully concluded on October 5, the day of the Home Opener with the Chicago Blackhawks.

After the deal was made, Green was quoted in USA Today as saying, "I'm sorry he [Broten] went to Germany because the strategy had zero value. He got the same deal he would have received had he stayed."

I say, "NOT!"

If the strategy had "zero value," as Green indicated, why did the club up the ante that August day when Clarke was informed that Broten was going to Berlin, and why did the club finally come up with the big bucks and the guarantees the day before I left for Berlin? Why did Green make one last desperate call to Sally late the evening before the September 25 deadline to persuade them to return and assuring them that the "loose ends" would be worked out?

Mona, the PR expert, agreed. "During the time Neal was in Berlin, there was seldom more than a two- or three-day period in which Neal's progress was not in the local media. It's hard to imagine that the public's interest in getting Broten signed would have been nearly as high had he remained in the Twin Cities with no other option than to sit out the season or to accept their offer."

Larry Wigge, the *Sporting News* columnist who writes the "NHL Report," summarized the situation:

"Neal Broten is $1 million richer now that he has returned from Berlin to sign a new, four-year contract with Minnesota. The veteran center's threat to play in Germany enabled him to reap a $350,000-a-year deal, plus $2 million in deferred payments for ten years after the contract expires."

When Broten returned to Minnesota, the ever PR-conscious North Stars ran a clever ad in the newspapers: "You'll love the 'Brots' we brought back from Germany! Auf Wiedersehen, Germany. Native son Neal Broten is back in Minnesota, and unlike defensemen all over the league, we couldn't be happier. So Neal, Sally, Brooke, and Larissa—the entire Minnesota North Stars organization welcomes you home."

It was a good gesture. However acrimonious the negotiations, once they have been completed, it is important to put them behind you. Allow the wounds to heal. Don't burn your bridges. You have to work with these people again. Today's enemy may be tomorrow's ally.

Less than a year later, I was flattered when Gainey, then also the general manager, and his assistant, Les Jackson, approached me to find out if I would be interested in representing the club in certain sensitive player contract negotiations. I declined, but only because of the conflict of interest it would have created with the hockey players I represented, not because of any bad feelings from my previous experience.

I do believe some bad feelings lingered between Broten and Clarke, however. Predictably, Clarke left the North Stars and returned to Philadelphia as club vice-president in the spring of 1992. A year later he relinquished what he called his "largely ceremonial job" and accepted the position of general manager with the new South

Florida franchise.

After a one-year roller coaster ride, we ended up with a contract that fell within the range of our goals, provided some important guarantees, and Broten picked up $45,000 tax-free in Berlin to boot—not bad preseason pay when compared with the $2,000 his teammates were paid for training camp.

Broten did not dress for the North Stars' Home Opener against the Blackhawks on October 5, 1991, because he'd missed the entire training camp. I was there, and I watched and listened to the traditional introduction of each of the North Stars players. In a break with tradition, Broten also was introduced. The thunderous standing ovation that greeted his introduction sent chills up and down my spine. Only then was I finally satisfied that we had done the right thing.

5
KEVIN MCHALE
IS CALLED FOR
TRAVELING

He is best known for his Herman Munster physique and his unstoppable moves on a basketball court, but like most kids from northern Minnesota's Iron Range, Kevin McHale grew up on skates. The McHale family lived in Hibbing—famous for taconite mines, hockey players, and Bob Dylan. The U.S. Hockey Hall of Fame is located in Eveleth, a few miles from Hibbing, and McHale spent the better part of his youth on the outdoor ponds of the Iron Range. While he was in high school, McHale grew from 5'9" to 6'9". It was obvious to everyone that it was time to come indoors to the nice toasty gymnasium. Nobody's interested in a tall hockey player, but a 6'9" kid who can tie his shoelaces without bending over gets the attention of all basketball coaches.

In 1976, McHale led Hibbing High School to the finals of the State Tournament and was recognized as the top high school player in Minnesota. He was courted by scores of colleges, but most of those letters from big-time schools in the East and West were never opened. Always loyal to his roots, McHale knew he was going to the University of Minnesota in Minneapolis.

At Minnesota, McHale became the second-leading scorer and rebounder in school history. During his career with the Gophers he grew to 6'10" and developed his inside game. (Today McHale is recognized as one of the greatest post-up players in the history of basketball.) He was also a terrific shot-blocker and team leader. In 1980, following his senior season, McHale played in the usual postseason college All Star games, including the Coaches All American Game in Indianapolis, the Pizza Hut Game in Las Vegas, and the Aloha Classic in Hawaii, where he was named MVP.

McHale selected his agent in much the same way as he had selected the university he attended. Boxes of letters and telephone messages from agents were ignored. His coach, Jim Dutcher, met with Kevin to discuss the selection, and after the three of us met, Dutcher recommended me. I had never represented a basketball player. McHale's instinct was to "go local," and to go with someone whose livelihood was not dependent on representing him. McHale's father, Paul, toiled in the taconite mines for over 40 years, and he raised sons who understood loyalty and the value of a hard-earned dollar.

I liked McHale. He was down-to-earth, casually dressed, fun-loving, and personable. He didn't take himself seriously and certainly wasn't overly impressed with his status as a basketball star. People had been telling him how great he was for more than four years, but he did not think of himself as special. He was the only tall person in his family and he realized that if the height had gone to his brother, then his brother would be the one getting all the attention.

We made quite a pair walking down the street together. McHale is 6'10" and I am 5'8". Mutt and Jeff.

Mindful of my lack of experience with pro basketball players, I decided that it was in Kevin's best interests for me to hire the very best pro basketball consultant I could find. Many people make the mistake of refusing to admit to themselves what they don't know. They believe that such an admission is a sign of ignorance which will tarnish their image. They attempt to undertake a task or provide an answer when they don't have the necessary knowledge, information, or experience. We see evidence of this every day. Think about when you encounter a person on the street and ask for directions. People will give you the directions, even when they really don't know or aren't sure themselves how to get where you're going. I wasn't going to take Kevin McHale for a ride and get lost because I was embarrassed to look at a map. If Kevin was less impressed with me, or had less confidence as a result and decided to make a change, so be it. It was more important to me that his contract negotiations be handled with the greatest skill and competence.

My man was Larry Fleisher, a New York lawyer who graduated from Yale Law School, who was then the full-time boss of the National Basketball Association Players Union. In addition to holding this position, Fleisher negotiated the contracts for a number of the top players in the NBA. I doubted very much that he would be willing to associate with me as a "behind the scenes" consultant on an hourly rate fee basis. Prepared to be shot down, I called him on the phone and gave him my story. Although he was businesslike and curt (typical New Yorker, I thought), he agreed to serve as my consultant. He later charged me a very fair fee of $3,000 for his advice.

In 1980 none of the NBA players' salaries or contract terms were available to agents or players, and thus as in football in 1974, the only people who had information on players' contracts were the few player agents who had actually negotiated those contracts. Fortunately, Fleisher was not only one of the elite among this group, but as head of the union had access to the terms and conditions of every player's contract. He was the perfect consultant.

McHale was one of only five college players invited to attend the NBA draft, and this indicated he was certain to be one of the first players selected. I accompanied McHale to the draft, which was held in New York City on June 10, 1980. Kevin and I arrived the afternoon before, and I proceeded to make inquiries about when Kevin would be selected. The consensus was that Joe Barry Carroll (a big center from Purdue), Darrell Griffith (the high-scoring guard from Louisville), and McHale were the top three players. Boston, Utah, and Golden State had the first three picks, and it was expected that Carroll would go to Boston, Griffith to Utah, and McHale to Golden State.

McHale dreamed of playing for the fabled Boston Celtics, the club with the greatest tradition and prestige in the NBA and perhaps the best-known sports team in the world. The Celtics are to basketball what the New York Yankees are to baseball and what Vince Lombardi's Green Bay Packers were to football in the '60s. Kevin's wish to play for the Green appeared hopeless because Boston was picking first and Carroll was everybody's number one.

While McHale slept and dreamed of leprechauns and parquet floorboards, Red Auerbach and Bill Fitch in Boston were conspiring to pull off the greatest heist in the history of the NBA—a deal that would benefit McHale and the Celtics for more than a decade. Hours before the 1980 draft, Boston traded its number-one pick to the Warriors for young center Robert Parish, plus Golden State's number-three pick. The Warriors wanted Carroll, the Celtics wanted McHale, and Parish turned into a "throw in" for Boston.

We knew Golden State would choose Carroll. Utah was still in the way, and McHale and I were concerned that the Jazz might select him with the second pick. At about 1:00 A.M., I made contact with Utah Jazz general manager Frank Layden. He told me that Utah would use its second pick on the first round to select Darrell Griffith and would not select Kevin McHale, even if he was available and Griffith was not. McHale was relieved.

The draft was held the following day at the Imperial Ballroom at the Sheraton

Center in Manhattan. NBA Commissioner Larry O'Brien announced that Golden State's first selection was Joe Barry Carroll. It seemed like only a few seconds passed when the commissioner returned to the microphone to announce the selection by the Utah Jazz of 6'4", 190-lb. Darrell Griffith from Louisville. So far the draft was running according to form. Boston used its full allotment of time before making a selection, and McHale and I were squirming in our seats. Finally, there was smoke from Auerbach's cigar. Commissioner O'Brien returned to the podium and announced: "Boston selects 6'10", 235-lb. Kevin McHale from Minnesota."

"That's me!" McHale shouted, genuinely excited.

The Celtics ended up with two-thirds of a front line (McHale, Parish, and Larry Bird) that many people say was the best in the history of basketball. The Warriors got Joe Barry Carroll, a chronic underachiever nicknamed "J.B.C."—"Just Barely Cares."

After the celebration and the interviews, McHale and I were prepared to return to Minneapolis but were told by Boston officials that Auerbach, the Celtics' president, general manager, and legendary former coach, would like us to fly to Boston immediately to attend a press conference and to meet Auerbach and head coach Bill Fitch.

Auerbach is the godfather of the NBA. He's been with the league since its inception and won eight consecutive championships as head coach of the Celtics. He is probably the most successful head coach and general manager in the history of sports and he's never been embarrassed to tell you. Red's arrogance has infuriated people through the years, but he's always had the teams to back up his boasts. Who else could get away with lighting a victory cigar at the end of games?

Fitch was a friend whom I knew quite well from his days as head basketball coach at the University of Minnesota in the late '60s. This would be our first meeting since Fitch left Minnesota ten years earlier.

At 3:20 P.M., McHale and I walked into the Blades and Boards Club at the Boston Garden and, before a large gathering of news media and other salty insiders, took our seats next to Fitch and Auerbach. McHale said, "Boston. I can't think of a better place for a white Irish Catholic guy to play basketball."

McHale was happy to be drafted by his dream team, but I could see it was going to be difficult getting him signed. Fleischer had warned me that Auerbach could be the toughest negotiator in the NBA. Red was as old as the NBA and I was an NBA novice. This looked like a mismatch.

Kevin's girlfriend, Lynn (now Mrs. McHale), presented one of my first obstacles. Lynn's father was a Hibbing businessman who sold air filters to the mining companies and also dabbled in real estate. Lynn's family lived across town from Kevin's, on the "right" side of the tracks. Lynn was attending the College of St. Thomas in St. Paul and had one year remaining before she obtained a degree. She didn't want to be separated from Kevin, so she decided to transfer to a college in the Boston area for her final year. Boston University or Boston College were the likely choices, and I offered my help in accomplishing the transfer.

When it appeared that the transfer requests for these two schools would be rejected, Lynn suggested that perhaps admission could be obtained with the help of Mr. Auerbach or others in the Boston organization. I was strongly opposed to this arrangement for several reasons. First, I didn't want to be indebted to Mr. Auerbach during a period when he and I were engaging in sensitive negotiations involving hundreds of thousands of dollars. Second, looking ahead, I didn't want to be in the position where Lynn would be moving into a dormitory at a college or university in Boston in late August, a complete stranger to the community awaiting the arrival of her unsigned boyfriend. How seriously would Boston view a "holdout" in Minneapolis or a threat to play in Europe when Kevin's girlfriend was alone in Boston? We would be playing right into Boston's hands. Kevin agreed with me. He told Lynn that he hired me to represent him in connection with his basketball contract, and not to arrange for her smooth transfer to a college in the Boston area. Lynn stayed in Minnesota that school year.

Although McHale, Carroll, and Griffith were clearly the top three players in the draft, McHale's situation following the draft was quite different from many of the high first-round picks. Carroll, Griffith, and other top first-round draft choices Mike Gminski (number seven, New Jersey), Mike O'Koren (number six, New Jersey), Kelvin Ransey (number four, Chicago), and others were expected to provide immediate help to their clubs, all of them much weaker than the Celtics. Boston had finished with the best record in the NBA the previous year, all of its players were returning, and the Celtics probably had a stronger front line than any club in the league. This didn't allow much room for McHale, and we knew that if negotiations stalled, McHale had only two practical alternatives: He could hold out until the contract was satisfactory or he could play basketball in Europe.

In Europe, only two foreigners were allowed on the roster of each team. Routinely, the two foreigners were the team's best players. The European clubs' highest priority was a white, big man—a forward or preferably a center. McHale, a forward who could also play center, answered every European team's problems. Back then, the European alternative was for NBA players in the twilight of their careers or young basketball players who weren't quite good enough to play in the NBA. Players could earn significant income, but not nearly as much as they'd be paid in the NBA.

In 1980, there had never been a player selected as high as Kevin McHale who opted to play in Europe his first year. The quality of basketball in Europe was not nearly as good as in the NBA, and playing in Europe was not as prestigious. American players often had difficulty adjusting because of the different culture and language barriers, and many were lonesome and became homesick because they were away from their family and friends. Nevertheless, it was an alternative. The players played fewer games, the pay was significant, and there were substantial tax benefits (some of which were not legal). Several lower NBA first-rounders had played in Europe in the past, including Bill Bradley and Tom McMillen. Bradley and McMillen, however, were pursuing overseas studies as Rhodes scholars. Basketball was secondary. Eventually, both players went on to the NBA and then the U.S. Congress.

I began to formulate reasonable goals for McHale's contract. Rick Robey had been the third pick in the first round two years earlier, and Indiana had agreed to pay him an average of $220,000 a year for five years. Bill Cartwright, the New York Knicks center, had been the third person picked in the first round the previous year, and he had reached an agreement providing for average compensation of about $250,000 a year for four years. These long-term contracts of the first-rounders were all guaranteed, meaning that if the club terminated the player because of injury or inability to play well, he received full pay nevertheless. To complete my evaluation it would of course have been helpful to know the contract terms of the top 1980 draft choices. As it turned out, however, these figures never became available to me before McHale signed.

In those years, most high first-round draft picks ended up with five-year, guaranteed contracts. I was convinced that often these long-term contracts were not in the players' best interests but were of substantial benefit to the agents, whose fees were based on a percentage of total compensation under the contract. The club also often benefited because rookies who developed into good players ended up being paid far less than their value the last several years of their contract. More often than not, I strongly believe that the more highly skilled players, especially in the early stages of their career, are much better off with a shorter contract. This is so primarily because of the history of escalating salaries from year to year (the past 15 years in particular) in football, basketball, and baseball. Often, after several years, rising salaries and improved player performance combine to render a previous contract obsolete.

After I completed my evaluation, I concluded that if McHale wanted security, a reasonable goal would be a five-year, guaranteed contract for an average of $250,000 a year. Fleisher concurred, but in the back of my mind was some lingering doubt about the wisdom of such a long contract. In July, Auerbach and I had several telephone conversations. I made an initial proposal about 20 percent higher than my final goal, and attempted to justify it on the basis of the Cartwright and Robey contracts and the expected increases due to inflation. Auerbach angrily rejected the proposal on the grounds that the other NBA clubs were stupidly managed and he had no intention of being bound by their folly. He made a token offer that I couldn't even consider seriously. We were going nowhere.

In August, Fitch began to call me. He claimed that Auerbach was very angry with McHale and me, and that he was intervening as a mediator to restore calm. On more than one occasion, he lowered his voice to a whisper, warning me that he could talk no longer because the unsuspecting Auerbach was approaching. I was amused by this novel approach by my old friend, but it would strain credibility to believe that Fitch and Auerbach were not working in tandem. It was also highly unusual for a head coach to become involved in the contract negotiations. I had never run across it before. This was typically the job of the general manager. It appeared that Fitch had become Red's front man because of our previous friendship in Minnesota.

In August, Auerbach finally offered a five-year package, guaranteed at $175,000 a year. Red refused to provide me with any basis for his offer, although it was clearly an offer substantially lower than the third person picked in the first round in the two previous years. Auerbach merely reiterated that the other clubs were stupid to pay Robey and Cartwright that much money, and if the offer wasn't acceptable, McHale could sit out the year. He also advanced the theory that playing for the Boston Celtics was such a great privilege and pleasure that the player should accept less than the going rate. I was concerned that Red might soon be asking Kevin to pay the Celtics for the privilege of playing for them.

I began to look for a possible alternative, and remembered a letter buried deep in my files. The letter was from an American, Dan Peterson, who was the successful head coach of the basketball team in Milan, Italy. Milan was perennially one of the top two or three basketball powers in Europe. The club had lost one of its two foreigners, a center, and badly needed to replace him. Peterson had inquired about McHale's interest in playing pro ball in Italy.

The Celtics were playing hardball. It was time to hook up with the overseas operator. Peterson had not yet found a center. He remained interested in McHale, but indicated a decision would have to be made not later than mid-September. In the meantime, he intended to continue his search for a replacement.

On August 19, in an effort to sign McHale before the Celtics' rookie camp, Auerbach made what he described as his "final offer." He renewed his previous offer of a five-year, guaranteed contract for $675,000 (average $175,000 a year) and added a $50,000 signing bonus. I rejected it, and McHale did not attend the rookie camp.

A word about "final offers." I have seen people—including some quite experienced and highly regarded negotiators—panic when the opposition utters the feared words, "This is the final offer." This reaction too often is followed by an unconditional surrender. I've found that sometimes a final offer is not a final offer. The difficulty in any negotiation lies in discerning when it is and when it isn't.

No unsigned rookie had ever dared to miss Celtic rookie camp, and Fitch told me that if McHale missed the camp, his chance to play in his first year would be greatly diminished. I indicated McHale would not show without a signed contract. On August 26, Fitch left a message that Boston was withdrawing its offer if I didn't return his telephone call that day. I didn't return the call, and Boston didn't withdraw the offer.

By the end of August 1980, none of the first seven draft picks on the first round had signed. Auerbach was putting pressure upon me to come to Boston with McHale to conclude the contract negotiations during the first two weeks in September. He was threatening to have McHale sit out the entire season if he and I did not promptly conclude the contract negotiations in Boston. He was claiming that because McHale had missed the rookie camp, it was imperative that he be present at the beginning of training camp or he would have little value to the team the first year, and it would be pointless for Boston to sign him. I struggled to stall the Boston trip until some of the other top first-round picks had signed. Finally, I came up with the perfect excuse for avoiding the trip.

Auerbach and I are both Jewish. The Jewish High Holidays, the two most important holidays and the holiest days of the year (one or two days of observance of the Jewish New Year and nine days thereafter one day of observance for the Day of Atonement), fell in that year during the first two weeks of September. Most Jews observe the high holidays by attending services at the temple or synagogue and by spending time with their families rather than working. Because of our common background, Auerbach would certainly "buy" this excuse.

I immediately called Auerbach.

"Red," I said, "Kevin and I would like to come to Boston in the next few days to meet with you, but as you know and can appreciate, this is just not possible now because of the upcoming Jewish holidays."

"No shit?" said Auerbach. "I didn't know McHale was Jewish."

I was running out of options. The possibility of playing in Europe had to be pursued quickly because most of the European teams had filled their rosters with their two foreigners for the upcoming season. Training camps were about to open (the Celtics' camp was to open on September 13), and on September 10 the top eight draft choices remained unsigned. Milan had agreed to hold a spot open for McHale until September 15.

On September 10, I finalized plans for McHale and me to meet with Coach

Peterson and club officials in Milan. The meetings were set for September 13, the same day practice began for Boston. Fleisher and McHale approved of the strategy, and I notified Fitch of our impending departure.

McHale was disappointed. He had wanted so badly to play with Boston. Yet he understood the situation, agreed with my approach, and promised me that if the Celtics' offer did not improve and we received the kind of offer we anticipated from Milan, he would play in Italy for one year. This was not an easy concession for him to make at the time. Ten years later, Danny Ferry and Brian Shaw started a trend of good young players opting for Italy, but in 1980 nobody was doing it, especially no top-three pick. When McHale and I went to Italy fully prepared to sign a contract, we did not think of ourselves as pioneers. We simply did not believe we were receiving fair treatment at home.

McHale's promise to play in Italy was important because I did not want to be in a position where I was bluffing. If you point the gun at somebody, make sure it's loaded. If not, no one will ever take you seriously again.

Not giving up on Boston entirely, I scribbled down Bill Fitch's unlisted Boston telephone number and arranged for a return flight from Milan to Minneapolis that stopped in Boston—just in case. In either event, I decided it was imperative to reach an agreement with one of these two clubs before we left Italy, regardless of how much time it took us. I was unwilling to place McHale in a position where he did not have an agreement with either club after Milan's September 15 deadline. McHale would then have been at the mercy of the only bidder, Red Auerbach.

Never underestimate the human and emotional elements in high-stakes negotiations. Clients are subjected to heavy pressures from within. I saw this kind of pressure when McHale called his family in Hibbing several days before our scheduled departure, and he was informed that his passport was nowhere to be found. He was told he must have lost or misplaced it. McHale and I were in a state of near-panic because it would take about two weeks to get a new passport. The trip would have to be cancelled and by that time, the Milan deadline would have passed. McHale returned to Hibbing a day before his departure. He looked throughout the house without success and repeatedly questioned his mother, who finally confessed that she had hidden his passport because she didn't want him to play in Italy.

This was tough on Kevin. He is neither greedy nor materialistic. He and I both believed Boston was being unfair. This first experience with the business part of sports was a bitter one for which he was unprepared, and it took a toll on him and on his family. He didn't feel any better when he read Fitch's reaction to our Italian tour. The coach said, "Let him eat spaghetti."

Peterson and his contingent greeted us at the Milan airport and took us to a basketball game between Milan and another Italian club. McHale evaluated the play as about on a par with the Big Ten teams, but a far cry from the NBA. Spectators stared at McHale and during the game he was hounded by the Italian news media.

The following afternoon while McHale worked out at a nearby basketball court, I met with Dan Peterson and a club official to discuss a contract proposal at their offices. Milan offered a one-year contract that included a $20,000 signing bonus, an "unofficial" contract for $40,000, plus payment of the Italian tax on the "official" contract. (American players commonly don't pay U.S. taxes. This is illegal, which is why the Italians offer "official" and "unofficial" contracts.) We valued the total package to be in excess of $120,000. We had hoped to improve the offer to about $140,000. Given the tax breaks, legal and illegal, it was similar to Boston's offer. When I spoke with McHale, it was clear that he was not happy about playing in Italy but, as he had previously promised, he was willing to play one year there if the deal could be sweetened a little bit. We were very close to a deal. There was no question in my mind that the Italians would grant us the additional concessions.

One of the reasons for playing in Italy for less money for one year was to place Kevin in a superior bargaining position with the Celtics after the first season. If the NBA arbitrator ruled the Italian league "amateur," Boston would have to sign Kevin to a contract before the next NBA draft or completely lose the rights to him and Kevin could be drafted again the following year. If not, Boston would retain his rights.

At this point, all of the current top draft picks still remained unsigned. I wasn't going to get any help from them, so I abandoned my goal of a five-year, guaranteed contract averaging $250,000 a year with Boston. It wasn't going to happen. The alternative was a three-year contract. If I could get the shorter term, I would be quite satisfied with average income of less than $250,000 a year. Naturally there was less security and more risk, but if McHale was the player Auerbach projected him to be, he could make a fortune on a new contract after three years.

It was a good compromise and offered Boston an opportunity to save face. I always consider how my counterpart will look in the eyes of his principal if he recommends acceptance of my proposal. Concern for my opponent is not altruistic. Rather, I have found that the probability of reaching an agreement in a difficult negotiation is substantially increased if my counterpart ends up with an agreement that doesn't make him look bad. Appearance can be more important than reality.

I decided it was time to dig out Fitch's unlisted telephone number for one more shot at the Celtics. I told Fitch that it looked as if Kevin would be signing with Milan. I casually dropped the concept of a three-year contract as a possibility, a "trial balloon."

Fitch told me he was going to go over Auerbach's head and talk directly with the club's owner, Harry Mangurian. I presumed that Auerbach's pride and ego would not allow him to be directly involved in bettering the "final offer." Auerbach had taken his stand and if the owner wanted to overrule him, so be it. For selfish reasons, Fitch naturally wanted McHale signed by the Celtics because the addition of McHale would likely improve the team's record. Fitch assured me that I could call him the following day at noon Milan time, the appointed time for the final meeting with the Italians, even though it would be 5:00 A.M. in Boston. Fitch indicated that he would be awake doing his daily exercise of hanging from his heels in his inversion boots.

Shortly before noon the next day, Peterson and the Italian contingent contacted us from the lobby to announce their arrival. I called Fitch. Presumably hanging upside down as we spoke, Fitch told me that he had talked directly with Harry Mangurian and that Mangurian was awaiting my call. He thought Mangurian would go along with my request for a three-year contract "if the numbers were right." This turned out to be the deal maker. I called Mangurian and we negotiated for ten minutes while McHale looked on anxiously. Finally, McHale nodded as we concluded a three-year pact at an average of $220,000 per year.

When the dust settled five years later, McHale's earnings far outstripped those of the other top seven picks. After McHale's three-year contract expired in 1983, he signed a new four-year contract in which he averaged approximately $1 million a year, including the 1983–84 and 1984–85 seasons. Most of the other high draft picks in the first round were earning $200,000 to $325,000 a year in the same two seasons still under their initial contracts.

McHale was extremely relieved, but now we had to break the news to the Italians waiting in the lobby. They were disappointed but remarkably understanding. Auerbach and Fitch welcomed us warmly as we arrived in Boston. The contract was signed at about five in the afternoon, and at Auerbach's insistence, the exhausted McHale was immediately whisked off to practice, which was already in session.

Dave Cowens, the aging star Celtics forward, retired one month into the season, providing McHale with an opportunity for playing time. Fitch used McHale as the "sixth man," a proud role in the Celtics' storied history. Frank Ramsey and John Havlicek served as "sixth men," in the days when Auerbach invented the role.

McHale went on to have an outstanding first year as a reserve who played in every game for Boston. He averaged ten points, was a great shot blocker, and rebounded well. The Celtics met the Philadelphia 76ers and Julius Erving in the conference finals, and McHale played a key role in the Celtics' come-from-behind victory. McHale left tickets for me for the seventh and deciding game of that series, and my brother Howie and I witnessed a pulsating 91–90 Boston victory. After the game, McHale arranged to have us join him in the winner's locker room. We celebrated with Kevin, Larry Bird, Robert Parish, Tiny Archibald, and yes, Bill Fitch and Red Auerbach. I shall never forget the sight of Julius Erving walking into the Celtic locker room and shaking the hands of the Celtics. Even in defeat, Erving was the personification of class and dignity. Boston went on to easily beat Houston for the NBA championship. McHale was a Celtic and he was a world champ. It sure beat spaghetti.

I felt a real closeness with McHale. We had been through a lot and it had worked out well. A year later, my wife and I returned to Boston to visit with Kevin and Lynn, who was living with Kevin at the time. Kevin and Lynn were engaged to be married, but apparently Lynn's parents were kept unaware of the living arrangement because they would not have approved.

Kevin arranged for us to join Auerbach for a bite to eat in his office at the Boston Garden before the game. Auerbach traditionally shared cocktails and his favorite deli food with friends before Boston home games. Red was polite but understandably not overjoyed at serving as my host. During the conversation, I explained to Red that my wife had always wanted to motor through New England to see the famous foliage. We had heard from many people about how breathtaking the drive through New England was. It was almost impossible to get reservations at the quaint inns that dotted the New England landscape. Auerbach didn't seem enthusiastic. Rather, he suggested we would have a much better time going to Cape Cod, where he owned a hotel. When I asked him why we should skip the foliage, he said, "If you've seen one tree, you've seen 'em all."

Thanks, Red.

At the conclusion of the 1981–82 NBA season, I was wrapping up a major medical malpractice case, which I had initially accepted about four years earlier. I was winding down this part of my practice as my involvement with professional athletes was growing, but this trial attracted a lot of attention. It was held just ten miles from Hibbing, Kevin's hometown. I represented a lady in her mid-20s who was in a semivegetative state in a Duluth, Minnesota, nursing home as a result of severe permanent brain damage she had suffered. The lawsuit was against a Virginia, Minnesota, doctor. When the lengthy legal process had run its course, the jury returned a verdict in our favor in the amount of $1.45 million, at that time the largest medical malpractice verdict ever returned in the State of Minnesota. In my honor, my law firm held a reception at the office after work several days later. This verdict was the highlight of my career, and I allowed myself to bask in the glory of this success. I had been through the humbling experience of informing clients that cases had been lost. This was sweet victory.

My euphoria was short-lived. Several days after the jury returned its verdict, I received a call from Kevin. The Celtics had just been eliminated from the playoffs, and I congratulated Kevin on an outstanding season. Kevin had heard about my successful jury verdict in his hometown area and he congratulated me. I was surprised that he knew about the trial, especially since he'd just been involved in the playoffs.

Then he dropped the bomb. He told me he wanted to change agents immediately. He said he was happy with the way I had handled the contract negotiations, but he needed someone else to take over. He said his decision was final and irrevocable. I was shocked. He had never voiced any dissatisfaction and there were no signs of any problems in our personal relationship. My wife and I had visited with him and Lynn less than two months earlier, and all had appeared well. He refused to go into details regarding the reason for the change, or to talk with me in person about the decision, even though he was returning soon to Minnesota. He asked that the files be transferred immediately to John Sandquist, an unknown agent from Seattle.

Kevin later stated that his reason for making the change was because I was too busy. Apparently he believed my big malpractice case had taken up a great deal of time. He said I had too many irons in the fire and he needed more personal attention, which he didn't think I would be able to provide him, especially with negotiations for a second contract coming up in a year. I knew this couldn't be the real reason, because I had never neglected McHale's affairs.

I was despondent. I had trouble sleeping and didn't feel like eating. I make a living based on trust and judgments, and I'd totally misread my relationship with one of my most important clients. I was deeply hurt that what I thought was a close friend would not at least meet with me before he took the drastic step of changing agents.

I thought back to all we had been through together, the struggle with Auerbach and the trip to Italy. During his first season, I visited Kevin in Boston. I handled all of his business and financial affairs, received his paychecks, and doled out a monthly allowance to him based on a previously agreed-upon budget. I came to Boston to assist him in the closing of his condo purchase. Whenever I came to Boston, Kevin was always a great host. Whenever possible, he personally picked me up at the airport. Wherever he went, he took me along even if I wasn't invited. In the summer of 1981, my wife, my two children, and I motored to Hibbing to visit Kevin and Lynn. We had dinner at his parent's home and also met Lynn's parents at their home. Schatzi and I spent time with Kevin and Lynn in Boston in March 1982. When Kevin took us to the airport, his parting comment was an invitation to me and my son Stephen (then 12 years old) to come to Boston for the NBA playoffs. I really appreciated that gesture.

Kevin did not need to be concerned about me, let alone about my 12-year-old son, during the playoffs, but this was typical, he was friendly, thoughtful, and generous.

All of the above deals only with my personal feelings and relationship with McHale. There was also the professional aspect to consider. This was a career crisis. I felt embarrassed and humiliated. How could I explain to others that I no longer represented the hometown hero? I was gravely concerned about the snowballing effect my discharge by McHale would have on my career as a sports attorney. McHale was extremely popular and visible in the Twin Cities area, and my competitors were certain to point out (and did as I subsequently discovered) that easygoing McHale had sacked me after only two years. I feared that this firing could be a fatal blow to my sports practice.

I talked to a couple of people close to McHale who seemed to believe that he was discouraged when he paid his taxes in April 1982. It was the first time he had had to pay any substantial income taxes, and apparently he had been shocked by the size of the bill. At this time tax shelters were the investment of choice for high-income earners, including professional athletes and entertainers. During locker-room talk, players often bragged about how little they paid in taxes, implying that any player who paid the regular taxes was stupid and ill-advised. I generally disapprove of tax-shelter investments because the risk of loss of the entire investment is too high, and the income is often deferred to a later period when the player's earnings are actually higher, resulting in higher taxes. I suspected that McHale was receiving comments from family or friends to the effect that his taxes were too high because he was receiving poor advice from me.

My first step in damage control was to talk to my client Kent Hrbek, a 21-year-old baseball prospect who was playing his first full season with the Minnesota Twins. Still shaking from the McHale bombshell, I telephoned Hrbek and asked him if I could drive out to his house to see him about an important matter.

When I arrived at Hrbek's place, I proceeded to embark on a long dissertation about my investment philosophy and the evils of tax shelters. I asked him if he was comfortable with the investment ideas I had just outlined, and he said he was. Kent was courteous but obviously bored and puzzled. I asked him if he would promise me that if he was ever unhappy with the way I was handling any of his matters that he would immediately tell me of his dissatisfaction. He promised he would do so, but continued to be puzzled. I finally explained the McHale situation. I didn't want him to hear it elsewhere first. His response was, "So what?"

Several months later when I was in New York City, I dropped by to see Larry Fleisher. By then the pain had only slightly diminished, and I felt the need to cry on an understanding shoulder. Fleisher was unsympathetic. He said it was common among pro basketball players to switch agents, but he was surprised that McHale had. He said several had switched from him to other agents. Conversely, he had represented a number who had changed agents. It came with the territory.

In May 1993, Kevin McHale, age 35, retired from basketball. He played for the Boston Celtics during his entire 13-year career. During this period, Boston won the NBA Championship three times: 1981, '84, and '86; and lost to the L.A. Lakers in the finals in 1985 and '87. McHale was a seven-time NBA All Star and will likely be inducted into the Basketball Hall of Fame.

After McHale left me, I was never able to attract a top professional basketball player as a client; however, none of my then-existing athlete clients left me as I had feared. For several years, my competitors effectively used the McHale firing to their advantage, and no doubt I lost certain players who ordinarily would have associated with me as clients.

Some permanent scars remain from the incident, but I bear no resentment or ill-will toward McHale. I believe he was influenced by outsiders, and he appears to be the same likable guy that I knew in the early '80s. Eleven years later, I still have not fully recovered from the shock of McHale's phone call. The wound was deep, the pain was great, and the healing period was long.

6
THE FAHNHORST BROTHERS GO FROM ST. CLOUD TO THE SUPER BOWL

KEITH AND JIM FAHNHORST GREW UP IN ST. Cloud, a small Minnesota town about 50 miles from the Minneapolis–St. Paul area. When Keith was six years old, a year before Jim was born, their father, a truck driver, became disabled due to a back injury. Their mother was a maid at a hotel in St. Cloud. Keith and Jim and two other siblings learned to survive on their mother's modest income and the small disability payments their father was receiving. The boys learned that money was hard to come by. Nobody was spoiled in the Fahnhorst household.

KEITH FAHNHORST

Keith was the first to make a splash in sports. As a high school senior he was a 6'6", 185-lb. tight end. He was very lean for a college prospect, but the University of Minnesota offered him a scholarship and Keith and his family were delighted. The coaches at the university must have seen something that eluded other recruiters. Keith's physical development during his college years was remarkable. His hours in the weight room and the dining hall enabled him to add 60 lbs. of muscle to his large frame. At 245 lbs. he could compete in the Big Ten, and in his senior year in 1973 he was named an All Conference offensive tackle. Pro scouts rated Fahnhorst one of the top 50 draft-eligible prospects in the country.

He was swamped with letters and telephone calls from agents, including me. Although I had represented several professional hockey players, I had never negotiated a contract for a football player, but Keith selected me anyway. He was taking a big risk with me, and I have always been grateful to him for the confidence and trust he placed in me. The first client in any sport is by far the most difficult to get. Keith is affable, mild-mannered, down to earth, and soft-spoken—he reminded me of a St. Bernard—and we hit it off right from the start.

In 1974, the NFL draft was held in January. (It's now held in April.) Keith was selected by San Francisco in the second round, 35th overall. In the first round, the 49ers drafted Wilbur Jackson, a running back who was the first black to play for Alabama under Coach Bear Bryant, and Bill Sandifer, a defensive tackle from UCLA.

Today the terms of each football player's contract for the previous years and the current year are made available to any agent through the Players Association. Unfortunately, in 1974, the terms of all player contracts were confidential. If you had not represented other top picks in the current year's draft or similar selections in drafts of the recent past, you just didn't have the information and without any comparisons it was difficult to determine your player's worth. Experience, which I didn't have, was critical.

I considered my situation and decided to approach Keith's contract negotiations differently from other football agents. I reasoned that if I followed the pack, it would be impossible to distinguish me from the competition. Lee Iacocca, chairman of the board of Chrysler Corporation, expressed my feelings best in a June 1990 commencement address at Michigan State University when he said: "Uniformity is an advantage, but it's also an anchor on creativity, a stifling sameness." I decided I was not going to follow the conventional wisdom. I was going to bring a fresh perspective to the table. This was easy to say but hard to do. And it was risky.

The competing World Football League was in its embryonic stage, planning to play its first season in 1974. A couple of years earlier, I had observed firsthand the positive effect the new World Hockey Association had on NHL player salaries. I saw no reason why the World Football League would not have the same effect on the NFL player salaries.

Maximum leverage in contract negotiations is obtained when a person has a reasonable alternative. My plan was to wait until the WFL had established its credibility, until I had a respectable offer from a team in the WFL, and until most of the other top draft choices had signed. I would then have more information about the market value of the players and the maximum leverage with which to negotiate. It was also my impression that I would have a decent chance to pick up some unusual concessions if the signing club didn't have to worry about setting a precedent that would effect the demands of other unsigned players.

In the real world, any butcher, baker, or candlestick maker can check out a number of prospective employers. He can then pick the job he likes best. This is not the case in professional sports. Pro football, basketball, baseball, and hockey each hold an annual draft of individuals eligible to play their sport professionally for the first time. Each club selects a player from this group in a predetermined order on each round. The drafted player can sign a contract with only the team in that league that drafted him. In the past, the legality of the draft has been successfully challenged twice in the courts when no collective bargaining agreement was in effect. In 1970, the courts held the NBA basketball draft to be in violation of anti-trust laws. In 1978, the NFL football draft was ruled invalid for the same reason. However, in each instance the draft still exists because the unions have allowed it to continue as part of a broader collective bargaining agreement with the owners. Nevertheless, in my opinion, a draftee coming out of school could prevail in a court challenge of the draft on the grounds that he should not be bound by a previous agreement of a union in which he was not a member when he was drafted. In reality, it is unlikely that any rookie would test the draft in court, because his legal fees would be prohibitive, and he would not be able to recoup the enormous loss of salary he would suffer during the years it would take for the litigation to run its course. Even if the player recovered substantial damages, he probably would still have lost his skills during the interminable litigation process. Contrary to popular belief, most athletes want to play. A damage award is not a substitute. Baseball is exempt from anti-trust laws by virtue of a 1922 Supreme Court decision.

In those days in football, the jock played with the club that drafted him or he didn't play at all. Yes, there was always Canada, but the pay was usually much lower, the level of play inferior, and the taxes much higher. Under NFL rules one could always sit the year out and then enter the next draft, but the player lost a year's earnings and his skills got rusty, reducing his appeal in the next draft. To my knowledge, only two draftees in the history of the draft—Tom Tupa, a punter from Ohio State, and Kelly Stouffer, a quarterback from Colorado State—sat out a season. Tupa was drafted by another club in the succeeding draft, and Stouffer signed a day or two before the succeeding draft when the St. Louis (now Phoenix) Cardinals who drafted him traded his rights to the Seattle Seahawks.

The upstart new leagues—the World Football League from 1974–76 and the U.S. Football League from 1982–84—provided an alternative for a time, but the high risk of failure of the leagues deterred most of the rookies from chancing them.

In the future, fewer football players will be victimized by the draft because under a new agreement between the clubs and players, the number of draft rounds has been reduced from 12 to seven. This change will provide players who previously would have been drafted in rounds eight through 12 the freedom to sign with any interested NFL club. However, their contracts may not be more favorable as a result of the competition than if they had been drafted, because of restrictions on rookie salaries.

When Fahnhorst was drafted by San Francisco, the 49ers' incumbent tight end was Ted Kwalick, an All Pro who was recognized as the best tight end in the game. The 49ers coach, Dick Nolan, had indicated that although Fahnhorst was a tight end, at some time in the future he could be converted to an offensive tackle because of his size and strength.

A few days after the '74 draft, Lynn "Pappy" Waldorf, a San Francisco 49ers' scout, camped on my doorstep in Minneapolis in an effort to quickly conclude the signing of Fahnhorst. Waldorf, a soft-spoken, portly gentleman in his 70s, was one of those coaching greats whom I had read about when I was growing up in the '40s. I was quite impressed that he had flown to Minneapolis to work with me to conclude the signing. Waldorf suggested that Fahnhorst was the type of guy who, because of his size, strength, and position, could play 14 years in the NFL—a rather bold prediction, especially since the average career has never exceeded four years. Pappy Waldorf turned out to be exactly right.

Negotiating for the 49ers, Waldorf recited the usual litany of what the previous year's second-round draft choice (Willie Harper, a linebacker from Nebraska) had been paid. Harper's three-year contract was for approximately $90,000, or an average of $30,000 a year. Waldorf suggested an even better contract would be available to Keith if the matter could be concluded quickly. I politely declined Mr. Waldorf's offer. A quick signing was not part of my game plan.

A month later, San Francisco general manager Jack White offered a three-year package of $120,000, including a signing bonus of $30,000, or an average of $40,000 per year, one-third higher than Harper's $90,000 contract. I rejected White's proposal.

While most agents were signing their players to NFL contracts in February and early March at figures higher than previous years, I was waiting and hoping that the new league would take hold. It was a risky proposition. If the new league didn't get off the ground, the 49ers could reduce their previous offer. I was attracted by the upside, however. If the new league became more credible, the competition could create big bucks for us.

The 49ers held their annual three-day rookie orientation camp from February 22–24 without Keith. In those days, such an absence was rare. The club told me that it wasn't done, and Keith got a little scared when he learned that all of the other 49er rookies attended the camp.

From my point of view, I wanted to avoid any risk of injury to Keith, and I also wanted to send the club a signal that we meant business. Meanwhile, I was desperately trying to elicit an offer for my client from the World Football League. Fahnhorst had been drafted by New England in the WFL's first draft, but he was a fifth-round pick and their best offer was a three-year package for $84,000, far less than the 49ers' initial $120,000 offer. The WFL Portland club acquired Fahnhorst's rights, but later, because of financial constraints, were not able to make an offer.

I didn't have a competing bid. Meanwhile, Fahnhorst was under tremendous pressure from family and friends to sign. They reminded him that his agent had no previous experience in representing professional football players, that he had antagonized the club by not appearing at the rookie camp, that all of the other top draft choices (all with experienced agents) had already been signed, that the 49ers didn't really need him because they had Ted Kwalick, and that perhaps he would be offered no contract at all if he continued to buck the system. Fahnhorst was in desperate need of money and certainly could have used the signing bonus the 49ers had offered.

Fahnhorst is a man of even temperament and great loyalty. I knew the situation was tearing him up on the inside, but I also knew that he had faith in me. It was difficult for him to bite his tongue, but his silence permitted me to attain a favorable result. Had he expressed his desire to sign quickly, it would have created pressure on me and I would have been inclined to conclude the contract negotiations quickly for substantially less to please the client and avoid any risk of losing him. This is one way impatient clients hurt their own cause unknowingly.

Our first break came near the end of March. The new league stunned the sports world by announcing the signings of three high-profile members of the world champion Miami Dolphins—running backs Larry Csonka and Jim Kiick, and wide receiver Paul Warfield. These signings by the Toronto Norsemen gave the new league instant credibility.

Following these signings, our offer from San Francisco increased significantly. Keith called to find out if the time was right yet. I told him it was not. He was disappointed, but accepting. I continued to wait, in the hope that I would be able to obtain a better offer from the WFL. In late March, Portland indicated that although it was not able to make an offer, it would allow me to work with any other club in the WFL. I tried, but none was interested.

By late March all of the 49er draft picks except Fahnhorst had been signed. I decided to manufacture my own offer. I called my friend Steve Arnold for a favor. In

1972 I had befriended Arnold when he visited me to discuss a WHA contract for Cesare Maniago. Some of Arnold's friends were the founders and promoters of the World Hockey Association, and now the World Football League, and he was able to acquire the WFL's Houston franchise for little or no money. He told me that his club had no interest in Keith, but that as a favor to me he would provide a bogus letter from the Houston club offering Fahnhorst a three-year $150,000 contract with a guarantee for the first two years.

Unscrupulous as this was, I had my "offer" from the other league. In late March, I mentioned the Houston offer to White and proposed a three-year, $175,000 contract, guaranteed. White said he would come closer to $150,000 but under no circumstances would Keith be given a guarantee of salary payments for any year. This just wasn't done in the NFL.

An NFL contract is not a contract. Most people are under the impression that the large football contracts they read about in the newspapers are guaranteed. Wrong. Although the player is bound to play only for the team under contract during the term, for the agreed-upon salary, the club is not bound to keep the player during that term. Under the form contract, the club can release the player at any time before, during, or after the football season, and the club would no longer have any obligation to pay the player except for modest severance pay to certain veteran players.

The situation is a little better in other major sports. In baseball and basketball, almost all multi-year contracts are guaranteed, and in baseball once the season starts almost all of the one-year contracts are thereafter guaranteed. In hockey, the contracts are also guaranteed, but the club has the right during a limited period each summer to buy out the player's contract. The club is obligated to pay either one-third or two-thirds of the remaining compensation due, depending on the age and years of service of the player. But the player is then free to sign with any club. However, in basketball and hockey the contracts of unproven players often provide for a much lower salary while the player is in the minor leagues.

In mid-April, driving home through the rain late at night with my family, I heard a car radio report that 49ers superstar tight end Ted Kwalick had signed a contract to play for Hawaii in the WFL. I was so excited that I pulled over to the side of the road and let out a scream of joy. In the back seat, my children woke up and asked what Dad was doing. I knew what I was doing. It finally was time to make a deal. The contract was ripe for negotiation.

When I arrived home that night, I called Fahnhorst to tell him that now was the time. The 49ers' only possible replacement for Kwalick was Dick Witcher, a marginal player who was really a wide receiver and not a tight end. The 49ers could not afford to lose Fahnhorst, Bay Area fans were in an uproar over the loss of Kwalick and from a public relations standpoint, the immediate signing of Fahnhorst would help quell the fans' unrest. Keith, my wife, and I flew to San Francisco the next day, Easter Sunday.

Good timing is crucial to the success of any negotiation. If the contract is not ripe for negotiation, you can stand on your head or pound on the table, but you won't get it done right. In this instance, the three signings that gave the new league credibility as an alternative for Keith, the letter from Arnold that appeared to offer an alternative, and now the 49ers' loss of an All Pro with no backup at Keith's position combined to create the ideal conditions for concluding a successful negotiation. I had waited patiently, and at some risk. But now I was hopeful I could reap the rewards.

We got the royal treatment in San Francisco. Team representatives met us at the airport and transported us to the swanky Fairmont Hotel on Knob Hill, where we stayed at the 49ers' expense. Fahnhorst was overwhelmed by the lavish accommodations and said, "I thought the Holiday Inn in St. Cloud was something!"

The next morning, a limousine driver picked Keith and me up at the hotel and delivered us to the 49ers' office in Redwood City where, after some cordial negotiations with GM Jack White, an agreement was reached covering three years for $205,000, including a guarantee for the first two years and a signing bonus of $70,000. (During the meeting, I had showed White the bogus letter from Houston of the WFL, which included a guarantee for the first two years of the contract.) Circumstances had combined to produce a super contract. The pact was believed to be better than the contract of almost any first-rounder in that year's draft. The two-year guarantee was a rare concession, one of only a handful given to any NFL player during that period. As it was then, it is now—less than one-half of 1 percent of NFL players have guaranteed contracts.

Fahnhorst was so ecstatic about the deal that he had a difficult time containing his enthusiasm before we actually signed the contracts. I pulled him aside before we were to enter the general manager's office and told him it was important for him and me to maintain poker faces. I knew that some day we would be negotiating contracts with the same organization, and perhaps the same people. I did not want them to know our emotional reaction to the outcome. If my counterpart perceived that we were overjoyed by the result, he could conclude he had been too generous. He would be prepared on our next encounter to make certain that it didn't happen again. On the other hand, it would have been inappropriate for us to appear sullen. Keith would then appear to be an ingrate or one with an attitude problem. Some sage described my sentiments best: "When you win, say little; when you lose, say less."

The bogus Arnold letter was very helpful in obtaining the contract and the guarantee, but now that I've had a lot more experience I believe that such tactics, although tempting, are not honorable and can be harmful over the long haul. If discovered, this kind of deceit destroys one's credibility. If your counterpart does not respect you and believe you, it makes it almost impossible for you to be persuasive. After this episode with Keith Fahnhorst, I made it a point never to mislead my counterpart during the negotiation process.

As the years passed, my wife and I became very friendly with Keith and his wife, Susan. During the off-season, the Fahnhorsts would sometimes come to our house for dinner. The mammoth 278-lb. Keith held his own at our dinner table, but I was surprised he didn't eat more than he did. One night after dinner, my wife asked Susan why a huge man like Keith seemed to eat like a normal person. Susan laughed and whispered that it was Keith's practice to have a large dinner at home before going out for dinner. He didn't want to embarrass himself.

In addition to negotiating Fahnhorst's contracts, I handled miscellaneous legal matters, provided tax planning, and managed his business affairs, including budgeting his expenses, helping with investment decisions, and approving major expenditures. I did everything "from soup to nuts."

Susan Fahnhorst is generally a conservative spender, but has a soft spot for fur coats and jewelry. Keith and I devised a plan early in his career, providing that when Sue requested his permission to purchase a luxury item, he would approve it on condition that it was acceptable to me. When Keith and Sue asked for my approval, most of the time it would be withheld on the grounds that the budgeted funds were not sufficient to handle the purchase. This way, Keith always came out as the good guy. However, on one occasion following the end of the football season, Sue spotted a beautiful diamond ring in Sacramento, California, which she badly wanted to buy. Keith (who was with her at the time) as usual did not want to incur the expense, but he also did not want to alienate his wife. He followed the "game plan" and indicated he had no objection if I also approved. On the spot, Sue attempted to reach me at my home. Unfortunately I was not home, but in my absence my wife (a friend of Sue's) suggested as a compromise that Sue purchase the ring on condition that the jeweler provide her with a letter indicating that she would have 30 days in which to return it and receive a refund on the purchase price. She was a well-trained lawyer's wife.

Sue purchased the ring and the jeweler gave her the letter. A few days later, Keith and Sue returned to their offseason family home in Minneapolis, at which time Keith and I met for our usual season-ending meeting. The first order of business on my agenda was the ring. I suggested to Keith that the ring be returned immediately to the jeweler, and asked him if there would be any problem. He paused for a moment and said, "No, but the finger would have to be attached." So much for the right of return.

Unfortunately, sometimes neither the player nor his agent recognize the importance of good advice regarding the player's financial affairs. Tragically, the list of highly paid athletes who have gone "busted" because of financial mismanagement reads like a "Who's Who" in sports. Among the most notable from the recent past are baseballers Rollie Fingers, Steve Carlton, Jack Clark, Bill Madlock, and George Foster; cagers Hal Greer and Kareem Abdul Jabbar, and gridders Johnny Unitas and Billy Sims.

Early in his career, Fahnhorst discovered that his game-day performance would be enhanced if he took amphetamines. The pills were illegal but had the effect of making the player more aggressive, giving him more stamina and endurance and sharpening his ability to concentrate. Dave Casper, the All Pro Oakland Raiders tight end, once told Fahnhorst that he used to find amphetamines in his left shoe prior to games. He was never certain who put them there, and didn't want to know, but suspected it was one of the trainers. When Keith was with San Francisco, one of the 49ers' offensive line coaches often used to say to his players, "Go into the cookie jar if it will help."

One Saturday night before the 49ers played in Minnesota, my wife and I invited Keith and his teammates Wilbur Jackson, Delvin Williams, and Jim Obradovich to dinner. We naively asked if it was true that some players took "uppers." They feigned ignorance and changed the subject, but Keith later told me that on the ride back to the hotel, Delvin Williams rolled down his sock and displayed his stash of uppers. One pill usually meant that the player would not sleep the night following a game. The pills are commonly used in the NFL today.

One of Keith's few bad times with the 49ers came in 1985 when he retired (briefly) in the middle of the season due to a series of disputes with head coach Bill Walsh. The feud started when Walsh overruled Keith's selection as team captain for the season opener. Walsh kept firing. After an October loss to the Chicago Bears, he took an indirect dig at Fahnhorst's age (33)—"With some players on the downside of their careers, only time will tell." Finally, in the November 3 game against Philadelphia, Fahnhorst was stopped as he headed onto the field for the 49ers' first offensive series. Keith was told that Walsh had decided to replace him with guard Guy McIntyre. Nice touch. The next day Fahnhorst did not show up for practice and expressed his intention to retire.

Walsh was unpopular with many of the players because they felt he grabbed too much of the credit. Walsh used these feelings to his advantage. Antipathy for the head coach served to unite the players. Walsh knew what he was doing.

On the day of Keith's walkout, Walsh went to Fahnhorst's home to talk with

Keith and Susan. A day after the meeting, coach Walsh sent Susan a plant and a card that read, "You have a magnificent husband. I have taken him for granted, but this plant marks the day that I begin to acknowledge his greatness." Keith came back. He retired after the 1987 season due to a back injury.

As predicted by Pappy Waldorf, Fahnhorst played 14 years in the NFL, all with the 49ers. The highlights were many, including playing in and winning two Super Bowl championships in the '80s (January 1982 and 1985), being selected offensive captain by his teammates for many games and several years, being selected as First Team All Pro and Pro Bowler in 1984, being the highest paid offensive lineman in the NFL in 1986, the club's elected player representative during the labor strife that led to the players' strike in 1982, and starter of 92 straight games at offensive tackle for the 49ers.

He also continued his education in the offseasons and got his degree from the University of Minnesota in 1977. Today he lives in Minneapolis with Susan and their three daughters, and is a stockbroker for a regional brokerage house.

JIM FAHNHORST

Jim Fahnhorst is seven years Keith's junior. He also was an outstanding athlete and followed Keith's big footprints to the University of Minnesota, where he was an inside linebacker. He was 6'4" and 235 lbs., and in 1981 (his senior year) he led the conference in tackles and was named to the All Big Ten team.

On April 29, 1982, Jim received a telephone call from Bud Grant informing him that he had been selected in the fourth round of the NFL draft by the Minnesota Vikings. A lifelong Minnesotan and a die-hard Viking fan, it was Jim's dream to play professional football for the hometown team. He was pumped.

My reaction was a little different. As Jim's agent, I knew that his being drafted by the Vikings could be a major problem. During the reign of general manager Mike Lynn, the Vikings were notorious for paying draft picks far less than other clubs in the NFL. Lynn's philosophy was different from that of all of the other general managers. His view was that the unproven rookies were being overpaid by other clubs, and that rookies were not entitled to that kind of pay until they became established players. When I returned to Minneapolis, I explained the realities to Jim. Although his enthusiasm was diminished somewhat, he had hopes for a quick resolution.

The Vikings' training camp was scheduled to open on July 29. Meanwhile, there was some vague talk about the formation of a new league—the United States Football

League. The USFL had not signed any players and its plan was not to start training camp until January 1983.

During the summer, I met several times with Mr. Lynn to talk about a contract for Jim. The best offer I was able to elicit was a $20,000 signing bonus, a 1982 salary of $33,000, and a 1983 salary of $38,000, for a total two-year contract of $91,000. Of course, there was no guarantee that Jim would make the club and be paid the 1982 or 1983 salaries. The club would have the right to terminate him at any time. The offer was consistent with Vikings' offers to other draft choices and fourth-rounders from previous years. It was far below what the average fourth-round pick had received on a two-year contract in 1981, which was about $130,000, as well as far below what was being paid to all of the other fourth-round picks in the 1982 draft.

The problem was further aggravated by the fact that Fahnhorst's closest friend and teammate, offensive guard Ken Dalliafor, drafted in the fifth round by the Pittsburgh Steelers, had signed a two-year contract for an aggregate amount of $168,000, a far cry from Fahnhorst's $91,000.

I was desperate to find an alternative. The Canadian Football League was out for a number of reasons. My only other option was to contact the USFL. I was referred to John Ralston, former Stanford and San Francisco 49ers head coach who was temporarily the spokesman for the West Coast teams in the USFL. I knew Ralston from his days as assistant GM of the 49ers when he and I had worked together on one of Keith Fahnhorst's contracts. When I finally found Ralston in mid-July, he told me representatives of the new league were meeting to conduct league business, including working on a uniform player contract and assigning Jim Fahnhorst and a few other available players to teams. He said the USFL was more interested in the 1983 crop of college seniors than competing with the NFL for 1982 draftees like Fahnhorst. The new league did not plan to start training camp until January 30, 1983, with regular-season games running from March through July to avoid conflict with the NFL.

At the end of July, as the Vikings' camp opened, Ralston informed me that Fahnhorst had been assigned to Los Angeles. Unfortunately, Los Angeles did not yet have a coach or general manager, and the league had not drawn up a uniform player contract. Meanwhile, back in the Twin Cities, Lynn was publicly predicting that Fahnhorst would be in a Vikings uniform. Setting aside logic for the moment, Jim and I steadfastly refused to accept the Vikings' offer. We hoped Minnesota would sweeten the pot to get Fahnhorst into camp, although this was not likely because he was not expected to help the team that year and he was not a top draft choice. The USFL was still a long shot.

By the end of July, Jim was ready to accept the Vikings' two-year offer if the signing bonus was increased from $20,000 to $30,000. Minnesota refused to budge. Shortly after the Vikings' camp opened on July 29, Darrin Nelson, the Vikings' first-round draft choice, ended his holdout and signed a contract, leaving none of the 336 draftees from the 1982 NFL draft unsigned except Jim Fahnhorst and Tim Wrightman, a wide receiver drafted in the third round by the Chicago Bears.

It was an awful time for Jim. His friends and family were critical of his rejection of the Vikings, and his best friend (drafted later than Jim) had signed a contract to play for almost twice what he had been offered. It got so bad that after mid-July, Jim and his girlfriend (now wife), Kim, seldom went out and Jim refused to attend his five-year high school reunion in St. Cloud. He continued to work out daily at the university weight room. A week after the opening of training camp, Jim encountered Sid Hartman, the long-time and nationally respected sports columnist for the Minneapolis *Star Tribune*.

A word about Hartman: He's got more clout than any Twin Cities columnist. While in his 20s, he was a part-owner of the Minneapolis Lakers, now the Los Angeles Lakers. Sid knows everybody. He's got contacts in sports throughout the country and his sources provide him with scoops and interviews not available to anyone else. The morning after Roger Maris hit his 61st home run to break Babe Ruth's record for one year, Hartman phoned Maris's hotel room for an interview. The receptionist told Hartman that 58 other people had already attempted to contact Maris, and he had refused to talk to every one of them. Hartman persisted, asking to talk with the manager of the hotel. The receptionist became impatient and connected with Maris, who told her to put Sid's call through. Sid got the interview with Maris when no one else could. The day after Al Kaline, the all-time great Detroit outfielder, got his 3,000th hit, he talked with only two people—President Gerald Ford and Sid Hartman. You can run, but you cannot hide from Sid. He once stepped into a locker room shower to interview Joe Namath.

In the Gopher weight room, Sid approached Jim. "Jimmy, what are you doing?" he asked. "You're making the biggest mistake of your life. Simon's a great lawyer, but he's making a big mistake this time. You have to get to camp immediately or you're not going to make the team!"

Sid was close with owner Max Winter and head coach Bud Grant. Jim was scared, but he stuck with me. I had a good track record with his brother, and we both knew the Vikings' offer was not good enough.

With the pressure mounting. I did something that I had never done before. I decided that Jim could only endure this disappointment and retain his confidence in me if he saw the Vikings' intransigence firsthand. Generally this is a bad tactic because football players don't have the experience or training to be good "poker" players. A player present in a negotiating session can unconsciously send messages that are too revealing or inconsistent with your position. Making matters worse, players can be intimidated by their bosses and succumb to scare tactics because of the "imbalance of power."

Despite these reservations, I invited Jim to join me in a meeting with Mike Lynn. The strategy worked. Jim wanted only $10,000 added to his signing bonus, but Lynn wouldn't budge. The meeting angered and frustrated Jim. His resolve strengthened, and his confidence in my judgment was fortified.

A week after training camp had opened, I encountered several friends who inquired about the Fahnhorst holdout. They admired my tenacity but inquired about my alternatives. They were concerned that Fahnhorst's holdout would jeopardize his career. I responded by sharing with them a story that best reflected my attitude toward the Fahnhorst predicament:

A powerful Arab king was very attached to his favorite horse. The horse had sustained an injury due to the neglect of the long-time horse trainer. The penalty for such malfeasance was always death.

The horse trainer was brought before the king and his court, and he was asked if he had any final words to say before he was executed.

The trainer fell to his knees, begged the king's forgiveness, and promised the king that if he was confined to jail for one year rather than executed, he would teach the king's horse to fly.

The king was angered by such an outrageous promise, but because of his love for his horse, and the visions he conjured up about his flying horse, he granted the request.

Two guards, agitated by his promise, grabbed the trainer, and took him away. One angrily asked him, "Trainer, have you gone mad? Are you crazy? Nobody can teach a horse to fly. You will surely be put to the worst kind of death after a year."

The trainer responded with a smile, "In a year, I may be dead. In a year, the king may be dead. And in a year, who knows? Maybe I can teach that goddamn horse to fly!"

A few days later, while poring over the fine print of the sports pages, I saw a tiny squib indicating that Tim Wrightman had signed a contract with the Chicago Blitz of the USFL. It was one of the first contracts signed by any club in the new league, and it contradicted Ralston's version of the league's game plan.

I decided to track down George Allen, new head coach and general manager of the Blitz. Chicago, of course, didn't even have Fahnhorst's rights, but I figured I had nothing to lose by talking with Allen, the legendary professional football coach for both the Los Angeles Rams and the Washington Redskins. Allen compiled an unbelievable record (116 wins, 47 losses, 5 ties) in 12 years as an NFL head coach and never had a losing season in the pros. He loved defensive players and had a reputation as a generous spender. When Allen was fired in Washington after the 1977 season by owner Edward Bennett Williams, the owner said, "I gave him an unlimited budget—and he exceeded it."

I located Allen and asked about his interest in Jim Fahnhorst. He told me he would get back to me. Later that day, he called me back to tell me of his strong interest. George Allen believed a winning football team was built with defense, and he had a very high regard for Big Ten football and the midwestern work ethic. He assured me that he would do whatever was necessary to obtain Jim's rights from the Los Angeles club. We began negotiations. Meanwhile, Lynn continued to predict publicly that Fahnhorst would be in camp soon. My negotiations with the Blitz were complicated because the new league still did not have a form player contract. All of the existing sports leagues have lengthy uniform contracts covering most of the terms, with only the length of the contract, the compensation, and other special provisions to be added.

While negotiating with the Chicago Blitz, I not only wanted a generous contract, but I also wanted Jim in a position where he had the option of returning to the NFL with the Vikings or any other club after two years. At the time of our talks, a provision in the NFL Collective Bargaining Agreement provided that if a drafted player played elsewhere his first two years, he could thereafter sign with any other club in the NFL, although the club that initially drafted him would have the right to match the contract offer. Therefore, although Chicago wanted a contract for more than two years, I insisted on only a two-year contract. Chicago agreed and made an offer much larger than the Vikings' proposal.

Sensing a problem, Lynn sweetened the Vikings' proposal by offering a $20,000 interest-free loan to be forgiven later if Jim signed a second contract with the Vikings. Lynn also urged me to allow Jim to meet with head coach Bud Grant after Grant and the team returned from its second preseason game in Atlanta. Lynn was finally courting Jim, but I was moving closer to a deal with Chicago.

Jim met with Grant. Grant was an All American end at the University of Minnesota in 1949. He was also an outstanding baseball and basketball player, one of the few athletes in the history of the University of Minnesota who lettered in three major sports. He went on to play professional football with the Philadelphia Eagles and then the Winnipeg Bluebombers in the Canadian Football League. He also played professional basketball for the Minneapolis Lakers. At 28, he became the youngest coach ever in the Canadian Football League. He returned to Minnesota to become head coach of the Minnesota Vikings in 1967. Under his leadership, the Vikings went to four Super Bowls from 1969 through 1976. Fahnhorst, like so many other people in the Minnesota community, was in awe of Grant.

When Jim met face to face with the legendary coach, it was clear that Grant was not going to offer additional money. Grant listed all of the benefits of the NFL: prestige, competition, great coaching, and large crowds. He mentioned that this was a great opportunity to play for Minnesota because the incumbent linebacker, Jeff Siemon, had just been traded to San Diego. And of course Grant emphasized the joy of playing for the home team, and the opportunities for local employment following Jim's career with the Vikings. Grant did not hesitate to state that the new league was inferior in every one of these respects and was not likely to survive. He warned Jim that he might not get paid even if he had a contract with the USFL. Grant's final message was, "We need you in camp right away."

Fahnhorst was very impressed with Grant. He listened intently, but he remained unpersuaded.

Jim was not moved because I had "poisoned the well" earlier that day with a story about a young pro football player named Bud Grant who jumped to the CFL after his rookie season with the Philadelphia Eagles. Grant had a terrific first season in the NFL, but got into a contract hassle the next year and played out his career in Canada. He urged Fahnhorst not to do exactly what he had done 30 years earlier. And he didn't even mention his own experience during his heartfelt discussion with Jim.

The following morning we decided to make a deal with the Chicago Blitz. I met with Blitz GM Bruce Allen in my office. The son of George Allen, Bruce is a pleasant, savvy young man who was still in his 20s when we first met. He came equipped with a wad of snuff in his cheek and a paper cup in which to spit. The Vikings found out about our meeting, and Mike Lynn made several calls to my office while I was meeting with Allen. We were in the process of drafting our own lengthy agreement (the USFL still didn't have a boilerplate contract) and each time Lynn called, he was rebuffed by my secretary. As we were about to close the deal, I extended to Lynn the courtesy of advising him that we were accepting the Chicago offer. Lynn insisted that he be permitted to come to my office to talk with Jim, his fiancée Kim, and me to dissuade us from making this big mistake. But he still had no intention of sweetening the pot. Fahnhorst told me to tell Lynn it was too late.

I felt a strong moral obligation to conclude the contract with Bruce Allen, George Allen, and the Chicago Blitz. They had rescued Jim from the depths of despair, and I didn't intend to turn my back on them now. We signed a two-year deal worth $155,000 (as opposed to the Vikings' $91,000). Jim would also get $5,000 a year to report and pass the physical each year. Best of all, the contract was guaranteed. He would receive the money even if he wasn't good enough to make the club, or if he suffered an injury that prevented him from playing. The Vikings guaranteed nothing. The Blitz also agreed to pay for his housing during the season. Perhaps most important, the Blitz contract also expired prior to the start of the 1984 NFL season, giving Fahnhorst the opportunity to play in the NFL two years later.

Fahnhorst was a starting middle linebacker who played well for Chicago in 1983 and again in 1984, when the team moved to Arizona under Allen. Jim won't forget when coach Allen held practices at night because of Phoenix's extreme heat during the summer days. At one practice, there was a continuous downpour accompanied by much lightning. Allen refused to cancel practice. When a power outage plunged them into total darkness, Allen still would not yield. He ordered the players to pull their cars to the perimeter of the practice field, and car batteries weakened while the headlights gave Allen enough light for practice.

Allen didn't like talking with reporters. He was a physical fitness nut who headed the President's Council on Physical Fitness. At age 66, he ran three or four miles a day during the heat of the day and would talk only to reporters who ran with him. Interviews were rare. Players loved this.

In March of 1984, when Fahnhorst's contract was set to expire, I began negotiations with Bruce and George Allen. The Vikings still had Jim's rights and he wanted to play in the NFL. After the May 1, 1984, draft, all NFL clubs would be able to negotiate with us, but the Vikings would have the right to match any offers.

In mid-April, I notified every NFL team of Fahnhorst's availability and the 49ers, for whom Jim's brother Keith played, quickly made their interest known. GM John McVay and I began to spar, each attempting to elicit the first proposal from the other. I steadfastly refused, and McVay finally came forth with a substantial offer—one larger than I would have demanded if I made the first proposal.

Whenever possible, don't make the first offer. Once in a while, the other offer is so much larger than anticipated that you can safely raise your settlement goals. On at least two occasions in the past, my counterpart's first offer was larger than the amount I had set as a goal. If the other side is also unwilling to make the first offer, I propose a simultaneous exchange of offers.

The negotiations presented several problems. The Vikings still had exclusive rights to Jim until draft day on May 1. Meanwhile, the 49ers needed to know if Jim Fahnhorst would be with their club before the draft was held. Their priority was finding a middle linebacker. If Jim was not interested, they would use a high pick to select an inside linebacker. If Jim was going to be with the club, they would use the pick for an outside linebacker. Meanwhile, I was anxious to conclude the contract negotiations because Fahnhorst was still playing football for the Arizona Wranglers, whose season did not end until July. If he suffered an injury before the contract was signed, any offers would be withdrawn. Negotiations were concluded—unofficially of course—with the 49ers on April 30 one day before the draft.

Fahnhorst's new four-year contract included a deferred signing bonus in the amount of $535,000, with base salaries of $200,000, $225,000, $260,000, and $325,000 for 1984, 1985, 1986, and 1987 respectively, the grand total coming to $1,545,000 for four years.

The agreement also provided that if Fahnhorst was hurt while concluding the 1984 USFL season, he would be entitled to the signing bonus of $535,000, even if he was unable to play professional football. After we officially reached agreement with the 49ers, they were concerned that Minnesota would match the offer. McVay contacted Mike Lynn and offered to trade him a draft choice in exchange for the rights to Jim Fahnhorst to eliminate this possibility. Lynn refused to deal with McVay, however, because he was angry with the 49ers for offering such a hefty sum to Fahnhorst.

Lynn had publicly announced that he would match the offer if he could reach agreement on a trade with another club. To close that loophole, McVay and I merely agreed to add a clause providing that Fahnhorst could not be traded to any club other than San Francisco, San Diego, or the Los Angeles Rams. The clause effectively destroyed Lynn's ability to trade Fahnhorst, while at the same time providing Fahnhorst with trade protection that probably no other football player in the National Football League had.

The Vikings did not meet the San Francisco offer, and thus were not entitled to receive any compensation for the loss of Fahnhorst. When Lynn announced his decision, he described the contract as "mind-boggling."

In an article in Sid Hartman's column in the Minneapolis *Star Tribune* of Sunday, June 24, 1984, Lynn stated: "The total package breaks down to an average salary per year of $386,250. This is an offer to a player who didn't make the USFL All Star Team. The contract offer to Jim Fahnhorst would make him the second highest paid player on the 49ers' team, behind only quarterback Joe Montana. Fahnhorst's contract would also make him the fifth highest paid linebacker in the NFL. . . . Do you think we are going to make a player who is going to have a difficult time making our squad our second highest paid player?"

Jim was one of the few people who ever had to play two football seasons continuously without a break. Starting in January 1984, he played a full season for the Arizona Wranglers, including playoffs, then went right to the 49ers. On December 2, 1984, the 49ers were playing against Atlanta in Jim's 37th game of the year (the NFL regular season is 16 games). Jim was hurting so much that he had to have a shot in the leg, the foot, and the rib to numb his pain. During the game, he suffered a serious knee injury involving the medial collateral ligament. The injury was due to slow reactions caused by fatigue. He was out for the balance of the season, missing the last five games. The 49ers went on to win the Super Bowl.

Jim Fahnhorst was a reserve inside linebacker for the 49ers from 1984–90. During his tenure with the team, they won three Super Bowls. McVay still says that the 49ers were happy with the Fahnhorst deal, because Jim played well for the club for a number of years and was also a great guy to have on the team because of his attitude. The only problem was that players and their agents during contract negotiations with the club were constantly comparing their contracts to Fahnhorst's.

George Allen died on the final day of 1990. He was 72. Without Allen, Jim never would have had the unique pleasure of playing with the San Francisco 49ers during a period when they were the most dominant team in football. Without Allen, Jim would not be the wealthy young man he is today. Without Allen, I never could have taught that horse to fly.

7

The Irresistible Force vs. the Immovable Object:
NEGOTIATING WITH THE MINNESOTA VIKINGS

I N 1 9 6 1, T H E N A T I O N A L F O O T B A L L L E A G U E awarded Minnesota an expansion franchise. Five principal owners plopped down an aggregate $600,000 for a team that is now worth approximately $125 million. A return of over 200 times on the money over 32 years is not a bad investment. No need to break out the crying towel for the owners.

Joe Six Pack watching from his living room or the upper deck of the Metrodome might see pro football only as a game. But it is also a big business. Yet, unlike most other businesses, the success of a sports franchise is not necessarily measured by the bottom line of the financial statement.

Paul Beeston, president of the World Champion Toronto Blue Jays, told me after the club's World Series triumph that he and his associates "judge the success of the franchise based solely on the win/loss record. Good financial results will often follow." His counterpart, Chicago Cubs general manager Larry Himes, feels differently. "Eight teams in baseball made money last season," he said recently. "The Cubs were one of them. Should we apologize for that? I don't think so. We're in the business of business."

The same paradox exists in the National Football League. During the 1980s the Vikings made a profit every year but had a mediocre .500 record and never got to the Super Bowl. During this same period, the San Francisco 49ers were losing millions but won three Super Bowls. Which franchise was more successful? Ask Joe Six Pack. Then ask your accountant.

The ten seasons starting in 1968 and running through 1977 constitute the glory days of the Vikings' franchise. There were nine playoff appearances, six conference championship games, a win/loss record of 104–35–1 (.746), and four trips to the Super Bowl under head coach Bud Grant.

Jim Finks, now the New Orleans Saints' general manager, ran the Vikings from 1964 until early 1974. He left the team when owners refused to sell him 3 percent of the club's non-voting stock. Finks's position was assumed by then-Vikings' President Max Winter, a founder, who sought a yes-man assistant. Lynn, a 38-year-old neophyte from Memphis, applied for the job. At the time he applied to be GM of the Vikings, he'd been heading a Memphis group seeking an NFL expansion franchise. He had run NFL preseason games in Memphis. That was it.

When the new WFL located a franchise in Memphis in 1974, it killed Memphis's chances of getting an NFL team, and Lynn was in debt to the tune of $50,000 and out of a job. He wrote to Max Winter, seeking an interview for a job with the Vikings. It was probably one of several dozen desperation letters mailed by Lynn. Winter wrote back in July, indicating he was too busy to talk with Lynn. He said the only position open in the organization was the GM's job and noted that it would require a man who has been in the NFL for a great deal of time.

Four weeks later, Winter called Lynn and asked him if he would be interested in a job with the organization. Lynn responded: "I'll be up there on the next plane." Lynn was hired as Winter's assistant, and Winter wasted no time throwing Lynn into the fire. Lynn was assigned the task of negotiating 27 player contracts for the upcoming season.

"I really don't know what Lynn can do," Winter told the Minneapolis *Star Tribune*. "I asked him if he would be interested in a job that didn't provide any future security unless he proved he could produce. Once we hire a general manager, Lynn might be out of a job." Nice endorsement.

A month later, Finks started getting calls from Viking players, asking him about Lynn. Who was this new guy negotiating their contracts? When a top NFL official queried Winter about the newcomer, Winter responded, "The new man is named Mike Lynch, and he's hired on a trial basis." To this day, some of the old-guard owners and NFL officials mockingly refer to Lynn as Mike "Lynch."

In his younger days, Lynn had been a poor-to-average student. He had so many incompletes his senior year in high school he had to go to summer school to get his diploma. However, he was street smart and had a master's degree from the school of hard knocks. His New Jersey high school recently recognized him as the Outstanding

Student of the Past 25 Years.

Michael E. Lynn III lasted 17 years with the Vikings. During his stewardship, Minnesota was the only NFL club that showed a profit every year (in '82 the Vikings were the only NFL team that made money). He came in a pauper and left a multi-millionaire. He manipulated for himself a lucrative long-term employment contract and a slice of the luxury box rental that netted him over a million dollars a year. He was able to purchase some Vikings stock, which he sold in 1992 for a reported $7.3 million. In comparison, Finks's request to purchase a measly 3 percent of the stock would have been the bargain of the century.

Lynn was a clever, shrewd, and tough negotiator, but his style created acrimony. Early on, he decided he would be a more effective negotiator if he could create a certain mystique about him. He believed this would be intimidating to the players. To do this, he remained invisible and aloof, encountering players only during the negotiation process. He also developed a strategy of not returning agents' telephone calls the first 10 or 15 times. When he finally chose to return their calls, he warned the agents how difficult he was to reach, and he would urge that the negotiations be concluded then when the agent had the opportunity. In face-to-face encounters, he would lean back in his office chair, clad in a very expensive suit, pausing between puffs on a cigarette. He always had a smirk on his tanned face. He was slick and slippery. Most of the players disliked him intensely. Mick Tingelhoff, the Vikings' perennial All Pro center, ended one negotiating session by driving his fist through the wall of Lynn's office. All Pro defensive end Carl Eller ended another meeting by hoisting a 300-lb. desk and dumping its contents onto Lynn's lap. Happy Valley, it wasn't.

My first of two unusual sorties with Lynn occurred one year after his baptism. I was representing an obscure middle linebacker named Ollie Bakken from the University of Minnesota who was drafted on the 12th and final round by the Vikings in 1975. This one should have been a no brainer. Not many 12th-round picks make it in the NFL. Usually the terms of a rookie's contract are based primarily upon what the other players drafted in the same round that year are being paid. Simple common sense: A late-round draft choice had no bargaining power. The contracts usually included a small signing bonus, maybe $2,000 to $5,000, and a modest salary with some performance bonuses. We didn't even bother to meet. Negotiations were handled by telephone.

Rookie contracts awarded by the clubs were already artificially low by virtue of their monopoly. The ambitious Lynn, intent on picking up some quick brownie points with Winter, went the other clubs one better. He offered the Viking players drafted in each round significantly less than other clubs had offered their counterparts. Now there were two rookie pay scales: Minnesota's, and all of the other clubs'. Lucky us.

The 1974 and 1975 Viking draftees and their agents screamed and hollered, but all of them eventually fell in line, all except Ollie Bakken and me. We refused to submit to what we felt was an unfair contract. The numbers in dispute weren't that large, but it was a matter of principle. I was able to land Bakken a job in the Canadian Football League. The pay was almost as good, and although the taxes were higher, Bakken did have a much better chance of making it in the weaker league. In pro football, if the player doesn't make the team, he usually doesn't get paid. Bakken went on to have a successful career in Canada.

Seven years later, Lynn and I went at it again over a rookie contract. This time, I was representing University of Minnesota linebacker Jim Fahnhorst, another home-grown talent who was drafted on the fourth round by the Vikings in 1982. Lynn was still paying much less than the market, and I was still insisting on market. Different player, same result. Fahnhorst ended up playing with George Allen's Chicago Blitz in the newly formed United States Football League. Lynn and I were 0 for 2. When the Twin Cities sports media gave Lynn heat about losing the local prospect, he responded, "I've successfully signed all drafted players each year except two over the past nine years. Both were represented by Ron Simon." I considered it a compliment.

In the late '70s, Lynn developed a clever approach to veteran contracts. He had the vision to foresee rapidly rising salaries in the future. He would lock the better players into long four- or five-year contracts. While most of the lodge brothers were not offering veterans a signing bonus to re-sign, Lynn was happy to oblige. He dangled the up-front money as bait for the long-term contracts. The signing bonus was especially attractive to most of the players because they were often short of cash. The bonus was also, in effect, a partial guarantee, because if the player was later cut or couldn't play because of injuries, he at least had the signing bonus. In addition, the salaries under the contract sometimes looked generous at the time of the signing. There were several "catches" however. There always were with Lynn.

First, Lynn's signing bonuses were paid out over eons, and because the interest rates in the late '70s and early '80s were at an all-time high (the prime rate was over 20 percent in 1981), the present value was sometimes little more than half the amount of the bonus. Thus, the amount of the signing bonus was illusory. I referred to Lynn's signing bonuses as "funny money."

Second, during this period inflation was rampant, and each year football salaries were escalating by leaps and bounds. The average salary of the NFL player rose from $78,000 in 1980 to $360,000 in 1990, over 400 percent, an average of over 40 percent per year. Consequently, an annual salary of $100,000 that had looked generous in 1981 when the contract was signed could look puny only three years later. (The average player's salary in 1981 was $82,400; in 1984 it was $177,400.) Then the players were stuck for another two or three years under the old contract with way below market pay.

Third, a four- or five-year contract was sometimes mistakenly considered by players to provide security, when in fact, the player could be dropped at any time with little or no severance pay.

Fourth, during the term of the contract, average players often developed into outstanding performers, but they couldn't cash in because they were still tied up.

I called these contracts "Mike Lynn Specials." One could understand that the players were no match for Lynn when it came to business matters, but how about the players' agents? Where were they when the players needed some sound advice? Lynn had figured that out, too. Sometimes, he would offer the player the new proposal a year before his old contract expired. The offer looked so attractive, sometimes the player wouldn't even consult with an agent. He figured he could save the agent fees. No matter; Lynn knew that even if an agent was involved, he would likely go along for the ride.

One doesn't have to be a Harvard math major to figure out that the 5 percent fee on a five-year contract is more than double the fee on a two-year contract. The work is the same either way, and since the players often switch agents, the representative doesn't have to worry about losing the client after a couple of years. He has the proverbial "bird in the hand." This abuse finally became so widespread that in the mid-80s the NFL Players Association had to step in. In an unusual action, it enacted a maximum fee schedule for agents, which provided that the agents could receive a fee only on the first three years of any contract negotiated by them. Some agents still ignore this prohibition, but predictably the number of four- and five-year contracts has dropped off dramatically.

In most cases, I knew a one-year contract was actually preferable. Lynn knew I knew, and he recently admitted I was right.

RASHAD

In 1982, I was the lawyer for Ahmad Rashad, the Minnesota Vikings' wide receiver. Rashad was one of the top receivers in the game. He was a Pro Bowler from 1978 to 1981, who became the all-time leading Minnesota Viking in receptions with 400 catches before he retired. He was the "big play" guy who made a circus catch in the end zone on a "Hail Mary" pass as time ran out in the final regular-season game against the

Cleveland Browns in 1980. The victory propelled the team into the playoffs. He was very popular with the fans and as a team leader he had the ear of the players. He had brains and personality as well as athletic prowess. Unfortunately, he couldn't hang onto a buck. Regardless of how much his income was, he never seemed to have much left. He owned a home in suburban Minneapolis—a bachelor pad with a swimming pool and a tennis court on which he and I had some heated battles. He also had a Ferrari and a Rolls Royce to boot. He still owns the home and visits periodically.

In the summer of 1982, Rashad asked me if I would help him renegotiate a contract he had signed with the Vikings. (I was not involved in negotiating that contract.) Rashad had been hooked on a Mike Lynn Special. In 1979, Rashad, then 29, had signed a five-year contract covering the 1979 through 1983 seasons. By 1982, the fourth year of Rashad's contract, his yearly compensation of $136,000 ($75,000 salary, $15,000 debt forgiveness, plus about $46,000—the yearly prorated share of the present value of the signing bonus) paled in comparison to the pay of the other top receivers of the day.

Ahmad was unhappy and wanted Lynn to sweeten the pot for the upcoming 1982 season. He was not concerned about the 1983 season, because he was plotting a second career in television and had decided that the 1982 season would be his last. He was at the top and he wanted to walk away while he was still able to.

"Renegotiation" is a dirty word in the sports dictionary. It's one of the few things that owners and fans agree on. I respect the sanctity of a contract. If the club has to pay the player more money if he plays better, then shouldn't the player accept less money if he plays worse? A deal is a deal. On principle I am opposed to the renegotiating of a contract. Sounds simple. It isn't.

In 1978, I was representing Paul Hofer, then a backup running back for the San Francisco 49ers. Hofer was a 1976 11th-round draft choice who beat the odds by surviving the club's last cut. During his first two years he played sparingly, and each year he was "on the bubble" before he survived the final cut. I negotiated a three-year contract for Hofer covering the 1978 through 1980 seasons at modest salaries that reflected his backup status. During the second half of the 1978 season, Hofer got his break when starter O. J. Simpson went down with an injury. Hofer moved into a starting role and wound up a team MVP. Unfortunately, he still had two more years left on a contract that made him one of the lowest paid players on the team. Before the start of the next season, I asked the 49ers to add a couple of paltry bonuses to the contract for the 1979 and 1980 seasons, but I naively reassured them, in writing no less, "It has always been our policy not to request renegotiation unless the circumstances are extremely unusual." They happily agreed.

In 1979, Hofer became the regular running back with the over-the-hill Juice as his backup. Under new coach Bill Walsh, Hofer was averaging five yards a carry and led the team in both rushing and receiving. There was no longer any correlation between his salary and his value. Every regular on the team was making more than he was. O.J.'s salary was much larger, and he was Hofer's backup. The "Juice" was constantly on Hofer to get his contract renegotiated. Hofer complained to me. I did nothing. I was opposed to renegotiation.

In late November, coach Walsh cornered Hofer after a practice and suggested that Hofer's 1979 contract could be renegotiated by adding some easily attainable bonuses, and that perhaps the 1980 contract could be scrapped for a better one. Needless to say, Hofer was upset with me. I don't blame him. The initiative to improve his contract had come from the club, not me. If he'd waited for me to make a move, it never would have happened. The 49ers voluntarily renegotiated the 1979 and 1980 seasons, almost doubling Hofer's money for 1980. I looked bad. What do you think Hofer thought of me? The 49ers were willing to renegotiate and I wasn't. I learned a valuable lesson. No more Mr. Nice Guy.

It would be nice if all clubs had a conscience like those 49ers of 1979. But that's not the way the world works. It certainly was not part of Mike Lynn's world. Lynn was adamant about refusing to renegotiate any contract. He made it clear time and again that there was a club rule against it, and there were no exceptions.

He had been tested several times in the past, and had fended off demands from some of the great Viking players of the '70s. I was one of the agents representing the Vikings' All Pro guard Ed White, who was badly underpaid by the third year of a four-year contract that he had negotiated himself. After a two-year squabble, which included a training camp holdout by White, Lynn traded him to San Diego rather than change his contract. Lynn feared that if he ever renegotiated one contract, the floodgates would be open. After he left the Vikings, Lynn admitted to me that it was perhaps the biggest mistake of his 17-year regime. "I should have figured out a way to work it out somehow," he said.

I was reluctant to get involved in Rashad's renegotiation. The Ed White incident was a painful reminder of Lynn's stubbornness. I was concerned that the plan was destined for failure, but the Hofer experience had changed my outlook.

Contract renegotiation is usually requested when a player is unhappy with his salary under his contract. Often, the player offers threats, veiled or otherwise, that he will not play unless his pay is increased. Under the typical renegotiation, the player's compensation for the remaining years of his contract is increased, and the club receives no additional benefit. Clubs usually reject these demands, fearing that acceptance will invite the player's teammates to make similar demands. Clubs often agree to contract extensions, however. Under a contract extension, in football, the time is extended one or more years, the player receives a salary raise for the additional years, and usually a signing bonus, but the salaries for the initial years are untouched. The theory is the club benefits by keeping a good player in its organization for a longer period at reasonable salaries. An extension is permissible; a renegotiation is frowned upon. In reality, sometimes there is a very fine line between a renegotiation and an extension, and a creative general manager can make one look like the other.

Rashad and I made our plea to Lynn and, surprisingly, he went for it, tossing an extra $55,000 into the kitty for the 1982 season. We were really pleased. Ever mindful of the disastrous precedent a "renegotiation" would set, Lynn cleverly disguised the transaction to conceal its true nature. Rashad was to be paid $25,000 for the club's option on his services for yet another year, the 1984 season, at the same salary of $75,000. Rashad and I knew (and Lynn of course had to know) that Rashad would then be 34 years old and would not be playing football for the Minnesota Vikings, especially not at a salary of $75,000. In reality, Lynn got nothing in return for his $25,000, and knew it.

It was also agreed that $10,000 in loans to Rashad from the club would be forgiven, and to boot, Ahmad would receive from Viking Enterprises (a company to soon be purchased by the Minnesota Vikings) $20,000 for agreeing to serve as honorary chairman of a celebrity golf and tennis tournament run by the Vikings to raise money for charity each summer. Rashad had already served as the honorary chairman in 1981 without pay, and we all knew he intended to do so again in 1982. Some of the terms were only evidenced by handwritten notes, and you can bet that none of the papers were ever filed with the league and the Players Association as required by NFL rules.

Lynn camouflaged the transaction well, leaving no paper trail. In the unlikely event that word got out, Lynn would have characterized the change as an extension. After all, Rashad had granted the club an option on his services for 1984. Make no mistake, it was a renegotiation. If it walks like a duck, quacks like a duck, and looks like a duck, I say it's a duck.

After the 1982 season, Rashad hung it up "in one piece" and moved on to a successful career as a television sports analyst with NBC Sports. He later married Phylicia Ayres-Allen, a star of the "Cosby Show." He expanded into acting and other fields of entertainment. Today, Rashad is one of TV's most popular characters. His versatility is impressive. In addition to football, he has covered the 1988 and 1992 Summer Olympics. He also has hosted "NBA Inside Stuff," "NBC Live," has written a book, and is host of "Caesar's Challenge," a daytime game show on NBC.

STUDWELL

In 1982, Rashad introduced me to Vikings' linebacker Scott Studwell at a lunch meeting. In the next two years, I ran into Studwell once or twice and we merely exchanged greetings. In the middle of the 1984 football season, Scott called me and asked me to represent him. This is most unusual. A top pro athlete usually selects a representative from among those who have made a direct pitch to him. Ordinarily, an agent isn't considered for the job if he hasn't hustled the player. These people have been recruited all their life. If an agent doesn't call, the assumption is the agent isn't interested. Often, the winner is the best salesperson, not the best representative.

Studwell had played at Illinois, where he broke all of Dick Butkus's records for tackles made in a season. He was certain he'd be picked in the NFL draft in the first five rounds. A disappointed Studwell was still waiting by the telephone when the Vikings grabbed him on the ninth round of the 1977 draft. By 1979, he was the starting middle linebacker. He loved playing football so much that he once told me he would gladly play for nothing if the other guys didn't get paid. I never mentioned this to Lynn. Studwell even enjoyed training camp. He told the Minneapolis *Star Tribune*, "Where else can you go and put aside the rest of your responsibilities and just concentrate on football for four or five weeks, and act like a kid again?" He was a little disappointed when the Vikings moved from Metropolitan Stadium to the Metrodome in 1982. He's one of those macho guys who disdained the sideline hand warmers during those frigid Decembers.

Studwell was such a nut on conditioning that the day after each season ended he began his daily workouts, pumping iron and doing various types of aerobics in preparation for the next season. One time I asked him how many days he works out each week in the offseason. He said, "I work out every day, seven days a week."

Studwell was a throwback to the old-time days of Bobby Layne and Norm Van Brocklin. Play hard, party hard. Unfortunately, the nightlife took its toll. His best friend, teammate Tommy Kramer, ended up in a treatment center in California several times. Studwell was one of a number of teammates recommended for the Hazelden Treatment Center in Minnesota. Scott resisted at first but ultimately agreed to take the cure. There was one hitch. Scott had his ten-year high school class reunion in Evansville, Indiana, coming up. The bash was scheduled during the four-week in-patient treatment period. Studwell contacted Lynn and said, "Mike, I'll go to Hazelden but only for two weeks. I've got an important class reunion I want to attend." Scott apparently figured if he was dry for two weeks, he'd really be ready to get wasted with his old Hoosier buddies. Nice try.

Studwell says the treatment was a turning point in his life. During this period, he met his wife, Jennie, who was extremely supportive during this difficult time, and they now have two children. He is a model citizen and family man.

Like Rashad, Studwell was the victim of a Mike Lynn Special, a five-year pact covering the 1981 through 1985 seasons. Under the agreement, Studwell got a $275,000 signing bonus, and salaries of $75,000, $85,000, $95,000, $100,000, and $110,000 for the five seasons for a grand total of five years for $735,000. Looked like a hell of a deal. It wasn't. It turned out to be a disaster. When the deal was signed, the prime rate in this country hit an all-time high of 20.5 percent. The $275,000 signing bonus was strictly "funny money." It was payable over seven years: $15,000 in 1981; $20,000 in 1982; $25,000 in 1983; $30,000 in 1984 and 1985; $50,000 in 1986 and 1987; and $55,000 in 1988. If anyone had bothered to put a pencil to it, they would have discovered that its present value based on the prevailing interest rate was about $130,000.

By 1984 Studwell had led the team in tackles in four of the previous five years and was closing in on the Vikings' all-time record for tackles made in a career. He had played eight years and his career earnings totaled $715,000, less than $100,000 a year. He was 30 years old and on the downside of his career. He came to me frustrated and upset about his contract, which still had one year to run at a salary of $110,000. Even under NFL rules, the new minimum salary for a nine-year veteran like Studwell could not be less than $130,000. Benchwarmers around the NFL were doing better. He and his previous agent had tried to renegotiate the contract prior to the 1984 season with no luck. Lynn stonewalled them, after promising Studwell that he would "make it right." That effort died during a somewhat heated, unplanned meeting between Lynn and Studwell in a Washington, D.C., airport.

The Hofer renegotiation and the Rashad renegotiation—OOPS! extension—were fresh in my mind. I had an advantage no one else had. I knew about the Rashad deal.

Studwell wanted the contract changed to provide for more money in 1985. Would I try to renegotiate the contract with Lynn? Of course not. Renegotiation was out of the question with Lynn. Everyone knew that. Instead I would do a Rashad-type "extension." I contacted Lynn to measure his reaction and found him amenable to talk. As I expected, Lynn insisted upon playing word games. Semantics don't bother me. I knew from the Rashad experience that it was important for Lynn to characterize the transaction as an extension. I was happy to oblige, as long as Studwell received substantially more money in 1985. Sometimes you can get what you want just by calling it by a different name. Lynn and I never mentioned the words "holdout" or "renegotiation." It wasn't necessary. The "H" word dangled over Lynn's head like the sword of Damocles.

The day before training camp started we reached an agreement that included a $400,000 signing bonus, payable $100,000 following the 1985 and 1986 seasons, and $200,000 after the 1987 season. This bonus gave us the most bang for the buck because it had the same effect as a partial guarantee of the 1985–87 seasons. Two more years would be added to the contract—the 1986 and 1987 seasons—at salaries of $200,000 a year. Studwell would now be paid $210,000 instead of $110,000 in 1985, $300,000 in 1986, and $400,000 in 1987, or $910,000 over three years. Lynn was so worried about the impact the bonus would have on other players' demands that he asked us to throw in another season, 1988, at $300,000. He wanted to create the appearance that the signing bonus was paid for over as long a term as possible. None of us expected Studwell to play that year at age 34, so it didn't matter to us. By the time he had finished doctoring up the contract, he had tossed in the last year of the old contract, so it looked as if Studwell was getting a $400,000 signing bonus for four years rather than two. Now, when Studwell's teammates in the prime of their career demanded a big signing bonus "like the one Studwell got," Lynn could respond: "Give me four years at Studwell's salaries and I'll give you a big signing bonus." Lynn earned his large pay checks.

Studwell played the 1985, 1986, and 1987 seasons as expected. The 1987 season ended when the club lost a heartbreaker to Washington 14–7 in the NFC championship game. In a rare display of emotion, Studwell sat in the locker room after the game, crying his eyes out for about 10 minutes. The Super Bowl had apparently eluded him for the final time. His wife, Jennie, admitted feeling a little resentment because the stoical Studwell hadn't shown this kind of emotion at the births of their two daughters.

For the first time, Studwell was selected for the Pro Bowl in 1987. He surprised himself and everyone else by not only returning in 1988 but by playing well enough to be voted to the Pro Bowl again. Eight other Vikings, including tight end Steve Jordan, joined Studwell for the 1988 Pro Bowl in Hawaii.

STUDWELL AND JORDAN

Like Studwell, Jordan was a client whose contract expired after the 1988 season. Both players were now free agents. Big deal. In football, free agency was a misnomer as the player wasn't "free" to go to another club.

In baseball and basketball, landmark decisions or collective bargaining agreement changes led to true free agency. Movement of players and multi-million-dollar contracts are not uncommon. Not so in football, because under the system then in effect, the old club could always match the new club's offer, but more importantly, even if the offer wasn't matched, the new club had to give up two first-round draft choices to the old club as compensation for a good player. This isn't compensation. This is cruel and inhuman punishment outlawed under the Constitution. That's why the likes of Walter Payton didn't get so much as a phone call from another club when he became a "free" agent. Wilbur Marshall, a Chicago Bears' free agent signed by Washington, is the only significant player in all of these years who has moved from one club to another under free agency.

In December, 1992, the owners and football players reached an agreement on a settlement of lawsuits that the players had won in the trial courts. The settlement included a new Collective Bargaining Agreement and a $110-million payment to players who sustained damages as a result of regulations that restricted the movement of free agents. Now players will be able to become unrestricted free agents after playing four or five years in the league. Undoubtedly, many players' salaries will soar initially, but increased salaries for veterans are long overdue. In 1992, the average NFL football player's salary was $500,000, while the average NBA basketball player's salary was $1.2 million, and the average Major League baseball player's salary was $1.0 million. However, in a year or two I believe the salary increases will be less than anticipated by the players because there are just too many strings attached. The owners have outfoxed the players again. Some leaders of the football Players Association concede privately that the agreement is not a good one for the players, but they claim the Association had to settle because it no longer had sufficient funds to continue the expensive legal battle. We still haven't heard the last word on the settlement. I am co-counsel for a number of NFL players who are dissatisfied with their share of the damage settlement. The players are asking for the right to have their day in court individually.

In 1988 we were still operating under the plantation system. I went through the motions of contacting all NFL clubs and nobody wanted an All Pro linebacker or tight end.

Steve Jordan is not your typical pro football player. In high school in Phoenix, he was an A student who earned academic scholarships to five top schools. He picked Brown University, one of the Ivy League's most prestigious institutions. Brown has never been accused of being a football factory, but it was a place where a mediocre 6'3", 195-lb. tight end could make the team. When Jordan's grades slipped at Brown, his parents (both teachers) told him he'd be through with football if the grades didn't improve. Smart people. Perhaps they knew that out of the 100,000 graduating high school football players annually, only 400 go on to make an NFL roster. He cracked the books and, by his junior year, Jordan was an "All Ivy League" tight end.

During his senior year as a civil engineering major, Jordan had lined up an excellent job with a major New England construction company upon his graduation. While all of the other pro prospects were being invited to the usual postseason All Star Bowl games, Jordan was contemplating his career as a civil engineer. Surprisingly, the Vikings drafted Jordan in the seventh round in 1982. Jordan put the slide rule in mothballs and headed for Minnesota, where he made the club as the third tight end. Rashad dubbed him "Ivy."

In the next two seasons, Joe Senser, Bob Bruer, Dave Casper, and Don Hasselbeck all had cracks at the position ahead of Jordan, but a combination of injuries, luck, and talent put Jordan in the starting role by 1985 and he's still going strong today.

Jordan and Studwell were established Pro Bowlers and free agents when I went to work to cut deals for them in 1989.

The first step in the negotiation process is to assess your player's value, and then to set your goals for the terms of a new contract. The major factors considered include age, experience, ability, recent and career performance, health and injury history, and team record. Other important considerations are the salaries of comparable players at the same position on other teams, and the compensation of teammates who are negotiating new contracts at the same time. Often, however, subtle factors that don't show up in the performance statistics or payroll records play the most important role in determining the success of the negotiations.

After I completed my evaluations, I decided to shoot for a two- or three-year contract for Jordan averaging about $750,000 a year. For Studwell, the goal was one or two years averaging about $600,000 a year.

The Jordan goal was ambitious, but I believed it was achievable for three reasons. First, Jordan was one of the top three tight ends in football, rated slightly below Mickey Shuler of the New York Jets and Mark Bavaro of the New York Giants. They were being paid in the range of $700,000 to $800,000 per year. Of course, they were on big-city New York payrolls, a distinction not overlooked by Lynn. Second, the club didn't have anyone to fill Jordan's shoes. Finally, the most subtle factor. I knew Jordan was the perfect person to sit out until our demands were met. He was a man of very strong convictions and infinite patience. He and I were convinced that my contract goal was fair. Jordan had saved his money and he was a civil engineer prepared to start a new career, which would provide him decent pay, if necessary. Sometimes the most crucial factors in a successful negotiation have nothing to do with the player's ability on the field.

Studwell didn't have the same leverage. He would be 35 before the 1989 season started, was now removed in obvious passing situations, and his 1988 performance had been rated only 18th overall on the team. Yet he contributed in so many other intangible ways. He called the defensive signals and was a team leader. He was like a coach on the field. He was also a Pro Bowler who had a very good 1988 season. But his age would work against him. The coaches believed that he could be replaced with very little loss to the team. Ray Berry was waiting in the wings.

A goal must be carefully and realistically set, but more importantly, once established, there should be no backing off unless the circumstances change. I don't favor rigidity—there are many different ways to cast a transaction—but a goal is meaningless if it is abandoned the minute the going gets tough. Unfortunately, far too often the target is dropped during the final stages of negotiations as the pressure mounts and the deadline for a final decision approaches. Admittedly, the stress is uncomfortable, but if the goal was rationally reached, stick with it. Don't give in under pressure.

Vikings training camp opened July 30. When Lynn and I talked on the telephone at the beginning of June, he assured me that "all of the guesswork has been taken out of contract negotiations" because of his new system. He didn't elaborate. It sounded as if I'd been replaced by some robot.

Lynn's chutzpah never ceased to amaze me. When we met in his office in early June 1989 to talk about the new contracts for Studwell and Jordan, he couldn't wait to expand on his newest toy. I was barely seated in the chair when he said, "Ron, the Vikings now have an infallible computer system which rates each of the players and then extrapolates the amount of compensation to which they should be entitled. The system is managed by a full-time employee, a Ph.D. in Computer Science, Mike Ayers."

I thought he was kidding. I was smiling, amused by his sense of humor. I could always count on good old Mike for some jokes and funny stories. But this time he wasn't joking. He said, "There are 39 factors included in the rating system, the most important of which is the game-day performance. The 39 factors are not weighted equally." He went on to explain that the computer ends up with a rating number for each player, and the extrapolation is made to determine the amount of compensation he should receive. He said the system eliminated the need to negotiate contracts. He then began to tick off some of the 39 factors:

1) Coaching staff grade
2) Number of games started
3) Percentage of playing time
4) Special teams participation

5) Outside honors
6) Independent evaluation
7) Club rating
8) Player rank on team
9) Percentile rank in league among players at same position
10) Compensation to be earned by player based on average of six players ranked closest to the player in the league at that position
11) Club's recommendation regarding compensation

When he had finished his spiel, I asked, "Mike, tell me what the computer says is fair compensation for Studwell and Jordan."

Lynn said, "For Studwell, the proposed contract is a signing bonus of $50,000 and a base salary of $350,000 for a one-year contract."

"For Jordan," he said, "the contract will be for three years, with a signing bonus of $225,000, and base salary as follows: 1989—$380,000, of which $100,000 would be deferred for five years; 1990—$475,000, of which $150,000 would be deferred for five years; 1991—$580,000, of which $200,000 would be deferred for five years." The average salary came out to about $475,000 to $500,000 a year, depending upon how one evaluated the deferred payments.

I struggled to contain my laughter. I didn't want to insult Mike.

In the months that followed, I chose to ignore the computer system, and strangely enough, Lynn never mentioned it either. To this day I wonder why so much time, effort, and money were supposedly put into the system and why Lynn dropped it. Every time I think about the system spitting out the numbers on a contract, it draws a chuckle. Lynn still believes that player salaries in the future will be determined by similar computer systems. I doubt it.

About ten days before the start of training camp, Lynn and I met to talk about Studwell's new contract. He offered a $200,000 signing bonus plus a $200,000 salary for 1989 only. I countered with a $300,000 signing bonus, a $300,000 salary, and a $50,000 bonus if Studwell played a majority of the defensive plays. Lynn didn't respond.

Studwell had never missed a day of training camp in 12 years and didn't want to start now. He also didn't want to give his backup, Ray Berry, the opportunity to win the middle linebacker spot by default. Nevertheless, training camp opened without Studwell because the matter was still unresolved. Studwell was becoming extremely tense, nervous, and irritable. His wife, Jennie, grabbed the two infant girls and escaped to their cabin in western Wisconsin. Jennie recalled, "It was impossible to live with him. He was a bear."

Lynn knew Studwell's temperament and mentality. Too well. After training camp opened, Lynn pulled the "end run." He twice called Studwell directly. Each time he warned Scott that he was making a big mistake by missing training camp. "Scott," he would say, "at your age, you need to be in training camp from the start, and you don't need to give Ray Berry the opportunity to win over your starting job." The strategy was effective and Studwell became more anxious.

Studwell was cursed by his own "instant gratification" syndrome. Some of us elect to get unpleasant matters behind us by making a quick decision. When Studwell buys a suit, he usually grabs the first or second one off the rack. Many Americans have this mentality. Good negotiators from other countries are aware of this trait and take advantage of it by merely outwaiting the Americans until they get what they want.

Contract negotiations are particularly stressful for the athlete. Most of the time, however, the quick fix provides only temporary relief. Later when it becomes clear that the decision was a mistake, the pain is greater and lasts longer.

After several days of missed training camp, Studwell could bear the frustration no longer. He was ready to explode. He bolted into Lynn's office without me and demanded to know why the matter had not been resolved. Lynn held his ground. After the meeting, Lynn confided to a close friend that Studwell was so eager to get to training camp that there was no need to improve the offer. He merely had to wait Studwell out.

This is one of several reasons why I am almost always opposed to any of my players discussing contract matters directly with the general manager. It's a mismatch. The player tips his hand. He does not have the experience nor is he trained to be a good poker player.

When Studwell and I talked later, he insisted that we accept Lynn's one-year offer at $525,000, $75,000 short of my goal. Lynn, fully aware that he had the upper hand, also insisted upon and obtained an option on Studwell's services for 1990 for $500,000. The second year at $500,000 did not concern us much because Scott assured me that he would not be playing football in 1990 at age 36. If so, he said he would almost certainly be a reserve anyway and the $500,000 would be ample. Studwell signed the contract at 1:00 P.M. and was in training camp in Mankato, Minnesota, 100 miles away, by 2:30 P.M. after missing six days. He got his instant gratification, but it was expensive. I believe it cost him $50,000 to $75,000.

In negotiations, more goals aren't met due primarily to the client's impatience than any other single factor, including the opposition's intransigence.

Jordan was different. I met with Lynn on July 29, one day before the opening of training camp. He offered a signing bonus of $300,000 (some of which would be deferred) and a three-year contract of $500,000 a year, also partially deferred. We were miles apart. Lynn believed that the highest salary should be paid to the most highly rated player, the second highest salary to the second most highly rated, and so on. After the 1988 season, Jordan was rated the eighth most valuable player, behind Wade Wilson, Keith Millard, Gary Zimmerman, Joey Browner, Anthony Carter, Chris Doleman, and one other player. We had no quarrel with the evaluation, but every player ahead of Jordan had a different set of circumstances. Lynn was concerned that his payroll integrity would be destroyed if Jordan ended up the highest paid player on the team, and he worried about the demands that the players rated higher than Jordan would make next year.

When Lynn finally announced that this was "the best offer that will be made," it was crunch time.

A number of top football players in the past have sat out the entire season after rejecting a final offer, among them John Riggins (1980, Washington); Al Harris and Todd Bell (1985, Chicago); Mike Merriweather (1988, Pittsburgh) and Robert Jackson (1988, Cincinnati); Gary Anderson (1989, San Diego); Bobby Hebert (1990, New Orleans). In each of these cases, at some point in time the player and his agent had rejected the club's "best offer." These were all lose/lose situations, a disaster for the player and for his team. The player loses a year's pay and his skills erode; the club loses a valuable member of the team. We were staring a potential lost season in the face, or perhaps worse, the end of a career. The decision is a difficult one and has to be based on the negotiator's touch and feel. Is this the best offer? Is my goal still reasonable?

Jordan and I caucused. Nothing in the circumstances had changed since my initial evaluation. I recommended we stick to our guns. Jordan agreed. With trepidation I called Lynn's bluff. We rejected the "best offer that would ever be made."

In August, the discussions continued. I met with Lynn several times, during which we exchanged proposals. We tried a one-year contract, a two-year contract, and then a three-year contract, with and without signing bonuses, all without success. Nevertheless, the gap was narrowing.

During one mid-August meeting at Lynn's office, in the middle of negotiations that were going nowhere, I peered out the window and saw my clients Steve Jordan and Carl Hilton, the backup tight end, holding their own mini-workout with wide receiver Anthony Carter on a grassy field nearby. All three were training camp truants. Perhaps as an act of defiance, I decided to join them. There I was, dressed in full lawyer garb, scooping up passes from Carter and pumping the ball into Jordan's arms. The players had the decency to control their laughter, and the workout ended up reducing the tension for all of us. It was also quite a thrill for me. After all, how many guys get to throw the football around with some of the best players in the world?

When Lynn and I met on September 5, the tension had intensified. Training camp had come and gone without Jordan. The Vikings would be playing their first game in five days. It was agreed that if Jordan wasn't at practice the next day, he could not play in the first regular-season game on Sunday. Jordan would then lose one-sixteenth of his salary, and the positions would really harden. Who would be responsible for the lost paycheck? We were heading for a "lose/lose" situation. In 18 years, I had never had a client miss a regular-season game because of a contract dispute. My own personal record was on the line. Lynn upped the three-year offer to $666,666 per year; my counterproposal was $800,000.

I went home later that evening, discouraged and tired. I told my wife it looked bad. Had I miscalculated?

While watching the late evening news, the sports anchor reported that Keith Millard had signed a new contract averaging $850,000 a year, that Jesse Solomon (the only other player without a contract) had agreed to terms, and that Steve Jordan was the only unsigned player. I immediately turned to my wife, and in a complete reversal said confidently, "This baby is now ripe for negotiation and tomorrow we will make a deal."

All the conditions for breaking an impasse had been met. First, regardless of Jordan's contract, Millard would be the highest paid player on the team, eliminating Lynn's objection based on lack of payroll integrity. Second, Jordan was the only unsigned player, so his salary would no longer have an effect on any unsigned players and the much-maligned Lynn would be a hero if all his players were signed before the regular season commenced. (This is one of the reasons why I usually prefer my players to be the last on the team to sign.) Third, Lynn seemed to be shooting for the Super Bowl. He needed Jordan now. Tomorrow was the deadline for Jordan. If he didn't sign tomorrow, he couldn't play in the first game. If he couldn't play in the first game, there was trouble for everyone.

I was so excited about the change in circumstances and the prospects for reaching an agreement, that I awoke early and telephoned Lynn's assistant, Jeff Diamond.

"Jeff," I said, "there is no question in my mind that Mike and I can make a deal on Jordan right now." I asked for Lynn's unlisted home telephone number. When I called at 7:00 A.M., I was told he was already at the office. I reached Lynn, met with him a couple of hours later at his office and, as I suspected, when I reduced my demand to an average of $750,000 a year for three years, he met it. He also gave me a "throw-in" bonus. He called it his "Super Bonus": a $100,000 bonus if Jordan was elected to the Pro Bowl in each of the three years during the term of the contract. The size of the bonus, of course, was eye-catching—a typical Lynn trick—but Lynn knew the odds of earning it were quite remote. With a stroke of the pen, the $350,000 signing bonus and the $650,000 salary average per year made Jordan the highest paid tight end in the NFL.

Mike Lynn, former cheapskate and tightwad, was clearly changing his tune. For the first time, I saw that he was more interested in the Super Bowl than in super profit. The old Mike Lynn would never have capitulated.

I had attained a lofty goal in the Jordan negotiations and had fallen short in the Studwell negotiations. The reasons were unrelated to the players' skills on the field. Studwell was impatient and paid the price for instant gratification; Jordan was patient and had dug in his heels for the long haul. Studwell didn't want to miss a day of training camp; Jordan was willing to miss all of it, even though he believed he needed two weeks to get ready for the season. He began to enjoy the lifestyle away from training camp. He spent much more time with his family, worked out on his own, and played golf. "Hey, it wasn't so bad," Jordan told me. Jordan was prepared to give up football and to start a career as a civil engineer; Studwell loved football and would never give it up until he could no longer play effectively. Jordan relied on my advice; Studwell did not. Ironically, Scott and I did and still do have a close friendship, and he has always had confidence in my judgment. He conceded that at the time my advice was sound, but he didn't care that much about the money and playing football was his first love. He wanted the hassle over and done with.

A couple of months later, I ran into Lynn on a downtown street. We stopped to talk.

"Simon," he said, "I overpaid your man Jordan by quite a bit. I did it because at the time he was the only remaining holdout. I thought we had an excellent chance for a Super Bowl, and so I felt it was important to have all the players signed before the season started. If I didn't think we were a prime contender for the Super Bowl, I would have let him sit the whole season."

Exactly.

A couple of weeks later, my impressions were further corroborated when Lynn masterminded the infamous blockbuster trade for Dallas Cowboys' running back Herschel Walker. He was going one last time for the Super Bowl. Lynn admitted then that if the Vikings didn't make the Super Bowl with Walker, the trade was a bad one. They didn't, and before the end of the 1992 season Walker was released. *Pro Football Weekly* called it "the worst trade in the NFL in the past 25 years."

On November 24, 1991, Steve Jordan made his 401st reception for the Minnesota Vikings, and with that catch he became the all-time leading Minnesota Viking receiver for receptions, passing Ahmad Rashad. He was then selected to the Pro Bowl for the sixth consecutive season. Not bad for a guy who couldn't get a football scholarship. Meanwhile, the 36-year-old Scott Studwell, the Methuselah of football, again defied the odds. He had another good season as the starting linebacker—and decided to return for the 1990 season. Under the option year of his contract, he would be paid a salary of $500,000. He was satisfied.

During the offseason, I bumped into Lynn and casually mentioned to him that I would like to talk with him about a new contract for Studwell, who was entering his option year. Lynn told me in no uncertain terms there would be no new contract. Since this certainly was Studwell's last year, it made no economic sense for the Vikings to award him with a new contract this year. Fairness did not require it either, but I persisted because I had seen a new Mike Lynn, more concerned about keeping the players, rather than the stockholders, happy. In late July, about a week before training camp was to open, Lynn gave me an audience but only on one condition: that Studwell join me. I had no choice. These discussions essentially involved a "renegotiation" of the already existing 1990 contract and any crumbs Lynn would throw our way were found money. We had absolutely no leverage.

After Lynn and I sparred back and forth with offers and counteroffers in the presence of a silent Studwell, I came up with a proposal for a $220,000 signing bonus, a salary of $450,000, and another $50,000 if Scott made the team. Lynn rejected the offer. He suggested further compromise. I refused, quietly packed up my papers, put them in my briefcase, threw my coat over my left arm, and began to walk out. A reluctant Studwell trailed behind me at some distance, like an obedient but downhearted puppy dog. He was literally nauseated. He wanted to vomit. He was thrilled with Lynn's offer. He was sure I had blown it. I had sensed the change in Lynn, and I was gambling that the new kinder, gentler Lynn would go along with the proposal if I went the distance.

As I reached the door, Lynn called out: "Okay, Simon. Sit down. We've got a deal."

Studwell ended up with $720,000, not the $500,000 under the option year for 1990. However, this would be a renegotiation, so Lynn, ever vigilant, insisted on tacking on the 1991 season at $400,000. (Studwell would be 37 years old.) Lynn called it a two-year package, including a $220,000 signing bonus, $450,000 the first year plus $50,000 if he made the team, and $450,000 the second year, or a total of $1.17 million. The average salary per year was $535,000. Another Lynn "extension."

Lynn was no dummy. He knew he had just made a gift to Studwell of $220,000. I considered it an extremely generous gesture on Lynn's part. This was his way of compensating Studwell for being badly underpaid during a good part of his career. It was Lynn's way of recognizing Studwell's great contributions to the team and the organization, and his model behavior on and off the field. The transformation of Mike Lynn had been completed. The new Mike Lynn was more interested in fairness than in leverage, more interested in the present than the future. I also suspected that the new Mike Lynn was probably planning to leave soon, and one last time was pursuing his quest for that elusive Super Bowl.

A month later, Mike Lynn announced his resignation. At the end of the season, he would leave the Vikings to assume duties as president of the new World League of American Football. In July 1991, he was fired from the WLAF.

Scott Studwell ended up playing in more games than any linebacker in the history of the NFL other than Ted Hendricks. By prolonging his career two seasons, at age 35 and 36, he earned an additional $1,245,000—more money than he was paid his first ten seasons. Studwell is now on the management side in Player Personnel for the Minnesota Vikings. Some day, he'll be a general manager in the NFL.

On January 15, 1992, Jordan strolled into the Vikings' office to pick up his $100,000 "Super Bonus" for three consecutive years in the Pro Bowl. He's still a fixture at tight end for Minnesota and is still among the highest paid tight ends in the NFL.

Lynn did change in his last couple of years with the Vikings. He was more available, more open, and honest and more generous with the players. Unfortunately, too much damage had already been done and most disliked him to the end.

I didn't like the old Mike Lynn either, but I didn't have any problem with the new one. Neither did Studwell.

8

PAUL MOLITOR, MY FIRST $4-MILLION MAN

The police were called to my house on Christmas Day 1980. They had to break in to see if Paul Molitor was inside, dead or alive.

Molitor was in my house, sleeping off a wild night of cocaine abuse. I was in Florida on vacation with my family and had no idea what was going on back in the Twin Cities. I knew nothing of Molitor's drug habit and had no reason to suspect any substance abuse on the part of this fine young man who hailed from a large Catholic family in St. Paul.

In the winter of 1980–81, Molitor had everything any young man could want. He was handsome, single, wealthy, and famous. He'd already been an American League Rookie of the Year and an All Star, and there was so much ahead. He was a star infielder with the Milwaukee Brewers and the idol of thousands of fans in both Milwaukee and the Twin Cities. He was also my client, and I trusted him to look after my home and my dog when I took a December holiday in Florida with my family. Too bad Frosty couldn't talk. He would have had some stories for us.

On Christmas Eve, Paul invited some friends to my house for a cocaine party. After the revelers left, long after midnight, Paul was unable to sleep. High on cocaine, he stayed up all night. He unplugged all the telephones, then finally fell asleep somewhere between 6:00 and 7:00 A.M. While he was sleeping, his parents, six sisters, and brother were gathering for a family Christmas dinner at his parents' St. Paul home. When Paul didn't show by 11:30 A.M., his family became concerned. Later in the day, his girlfriend, Linda, was informed of Paul's absence and she called our house. There was no answer. Linda knew of Paul's cocaine use and became frightened. In the early afternoon she went to the house, rang the doorbell, and knocked furiously on the locked door. There was no response.

Because of Paul's fame, she didn't want to involve the police and risk discovery of Paul's habit. The repercussions could be far reaching: destruction of his reputation and career, not to mention possible prosecution. On the other hand, she feared for his safety. She was worried that he might be dead or dying. Finally, somewhere between three and four in the afternoon, a hysterical Linda summoned the police for help. The policeman broke into my house, and Linda accompanied him to my bedroom, where they found a just-awakened Paul. Fortunately, the police officer left immediately. Paul was ashamed and embarrassed. He later told me, "That was probably the low point of my life."

In the field of sports representation, your clients become a little like your own children. You learn and grow with them. You forgive and you go on. When I learned of Molitor's cocaine use, I couldn't help but remember the first time I saw his fresh face a couple of weeks before the major league baseball draft in June of 1977. My friend George Thomas, the assistant coach at the University of Minnesota, had called to tell me that his shortstop, Molitor, would be a first-round choice in the upcoming draft. This was unusual for a Minnesotan. Baseball players from the Upper Midwest are not good bets to become major leaguers because the poor weather conditions don't permit enough playing time each year for proper development. As a rule, players from other areas develop their skills more quickly and thoroughly because they can play all or most of the year outdoors. Dave Winfield, a first-round draft choice in 1973, is another notable exception.

Thomas carried his ruggedly handsome features on a 6'4" frame with the casual confidence most men wish they had, or pretend they do. Almost as casual is his lightning-fast locker-room wit, which ranges from funny to caustic. Thomas was the guy who told Cincinnati great Johnny Bench that putting player positions on the backs of jerseys was a super idea. "I play BENCH, too!" However, once you get past the good looks and verbal shrapnel, you find a man with a keen eye for talent who cares deeply about people—especially young people playing baseball.

Thomas believed Molitor needed representation and encouraged him to visit with me before the draft, suggesting that because of my close ties to the university and the community, as well as my experience in representing other professional athletes, I would be the best person for the job. In late May 1977, Thomas dragged Molitor and his father, Dick, an accountant with the Burlington Northern Railroad, to my office to discuss the matter of representation for Paul.

At that moment, my file of clients included zero baseball players. I'd considered representing Winfield back in 1973, but his college coach, Dick Siebert, had told me Winfield would never make the majors because of a hitch in his swing. I respected Siebert's judgment and never pursued talks with Winfield, since I presumed Winfield would be a lower draft choice who wouldn't need any initial help. As it turned out, Winfield was the fourth player taken on the first round by San Diego, but by then he already had an agent. Almost 20 years later, Winfield and his hitch are still torturing big-league pitchers.

There was no hitch to Paul Molitor, nor was there any competition to line him up as a client. He said he'd received calls from a couple of local attorneys but nothing more. Today, a college baseball player with Molitor's talent would need an unlisted phone number, but in 1977 agents were less numerous and less aggressive.

Molitor was well scrubbed, nicely dressed, articulate, unassuming, and he asked all the right questions in a polite manner. He and his father agreed to have me represent him. I was flattered.

Molitor grew up in St. Paul and went to a Catholic high school, where he starred in baseball and basketball. The St. Louis Cardinals drafted him after his senior season, but offered only a $4,000 signing bonus. Molitor and his family decided it would be best if he instead accepted a partial baseball scholarship from the University of Minnesota. He started at second base as a freshman and in his sophomore year was selected to captain the team. Though plagued by a shoulder injury during his junior season, he was named first team All American shortstop and led the Gophers to the 1977 NCAA College World Series in Omaha. We expected that he might be selected in the first half of the first round of the 1977 draft, and all of us were excited and delighted when he was the third player picked in the first round by the Milwaukee Brewers. No other player from the state of Minnesota has been selected this early.

Milwaukee had failed to sign its first-round pick the previous year, and the Brewers' incumbent shortstop was Robin Yount, baseball's Mozart. Yount had been a major league shortstop since the age of 18. He was only 21 in 1977, and it was unlikely that Molitor would be able to unseat him in the foreseeable future.

Ordinarily, the only significant term to be negotiated under a baseball contract for a newly drafted player is the amount of his initial signing bonus. Almost all drafted players are assigned to minor league clubs under one-year contracts, where they receive standard meager salaries. Several days after the 1977 draft, two Milwaukee representatives, scout Dee Fondi and club executive Tony Siegle, came to Minneapolis to meet with Paul Molitor, his father, and me. We were unable to reach an agreement on the amount of the signing bonus.

After the talks broke off, Molitor offered to drive Fondi and Siegle to the airport. I made a rookie mistake and allowed this airport shuttle. On the way to the airport, Siegle and Fondi expressed their disappointment to Molitor. They reminded him that he had assured them before the draft that he would turn pro if a reasonable signing bonus was offered. Paul felt guilty and was concerned about offending the club's representatives. They got to him, and I had to deal with the fallout from this private negotiating session.

For me, the lesson was obvious: Never allow your client and your counterparts to be alone under any circumstances. This gives the club's representatives an easy opportunity to negotiate directly with your unsuspecting and impressionable client. It's the old "end run." Veteran management warriors invariably take this opportunity to tell a young man that his agent is mistakenly overreaching. The novice is reminded that the club's offer is fair and generous, and will not be increased. Management is "disappointed" in the young man. Predictably the young, inexperienced athlete feels guilty, has doubts and fears about his future, is concerned about alienating the club's management, and wants to accept their offer. This is not a new strategy. Children commonly use it when seeking a favor from one parent after the other parent has turned them down. It was not the last time the Brewers would use an "end run" when dealing with Molitor.

Like any good coach, my job calls for me to defend against the "end run." I warn the player about the possible use of this tactic and its intended purpose. I caution him not to talk with management about the contract negotiations, and to report the details of any comments made by management to me. I also emphasize the importance of a united front in achieving a good result. When a young man is prepared for this tactic, it is not nearly as effective. This was my mistake with Molitor. He was not prepared for the "end run," and I allowed him to get into a position where the tactic could be applied. Since Molitor's airport courtesy, I have never allowed any of my clients to "talk contract" alone with any club representative.

A few days after the airport ride, the Brewers and Molitor agreed on a $77,500 signing bonus. As part of the agreement, I insisted on a guarantee that the club would invite Molitor to the major league spring training camp in 1978. This was highly unusual. Although we knew Molitor was a long shot to make the big club in '78, I wanted him to have the opportunity to be seen. You can't get dealt a straight flush unless you are in the game.

Experience is a valuable asset in conducting negotiations of any kind, but there are times when an inexperienced person with a fresh approach is more effective. In Molitor's case, an experienced baseball agent probably would not have had the gall to ask for a spring training look because it was unconventional. As things developed, we didn't get the signing bonus we wanted, but the spring training invitation proved far more important toward the professional career and long-range earnings of Paul Molitor.

My wife and I accompanied Molitor and his parents to Milwaukee for the contract signing. Molitor was introduced to the crowd at the Brewers' game, and after the game he toured the locker room and met some of his future teammates. Ever-unassuming, when Molitor met the 21-year-old Yount, he addressed him as "Mr. Yount." Teasing teammate Sal Bando tossed an outfielder's glove at Yount, a reminder that Molitor some day might be a threat to take Yount's shortstop job. Molitor reported to Burlington of the Single A Midwest League, completed the balance of the 1977 season, and was named the league's Player of the Year.

Not many players go from A-ball to big-league spring training, but we had an agreement. Molitor was with the Brewers and new manager George Bamberger when Milwaukee opened its Arizona camp in February of 1978. Molitor played well, but was given his minor league papers (Spokane, Triple A) when the final cut was made eight days before camp broke. Molitor was in the process of packing his bags when his roommate, Jim Gantner, approached him and said, "I ran into the general manager [Harry Dalton] a few minutes ago and he told me to tell you, 'Don't pack. Come back to practice tomorrow.'"

Yount, bothered by nagging injuries and frustrated by three losing seasons, had left camp claiming he was going to take up pro golf. When the Brewers opened their 1978 season at County Stadium in Milwaukee, Molitor was the starting shortstop. He'd played only 64 games of minor league ball and was less than a year out of Minnesota, but he was George Bamberger's star rookie infielder when the Brewers swept the powerful Baltimore Orioles in a three-game slugfest. In his first game, Molitor had 6 assists, 2 put-outs, 1 hit, and 1 RBI. The next day he had 3 hits, including a home run, and 5 RBIs.

"This kid's fantastic," Bamberger said. "I have never seen a kid in my life like him. He's really got a head on his shoulders. He looks like he's played the game for 10 or 15 years."

By the time Yount returned to the club four weeks later, Molitor had entrenched himself as a big leaguer. (He went on to play with Milwaukee for the next 15 years, before an emotional move to Toronto in the spring of 1993.) Yount reclaimed the shortstop position. Molitor moved to second base and won the Sporting News American League Rookie of the Year Award, hitting .273 with 30 steals in 125 games. In 1979 he played in 140 games and hit .322 with 33 steals and 88 runs scored, and earned a contract that would pay him $210,000 for 1980. He was extremely pleased with the new deal, and I reminded him that the poker face is the best face when you sign a contract—especially when you suspect there will be many future negotiations, probably with the same people.

Behind the masks, both Molitor and I were excited—so excited in fact that we couldn't wait to return to the hotel for the celebration of our first big contract together. As soon as we reached the hotel parking lot, he and I spontaneously hit the pavement and broke into a dance—two grown men doing the two-step together. I'm not sure who was leading, but it must have been quite a sight for Sun City's citizens.

But life isn't a dance through the parking lot. Perhaps Molitor had too much too soon. During the 1980 season I came to Milwaukee to watch Paul play and to spend a couple of days with him. He was living at the Astor Hotel in Milwaukee, so I stayed there also during my weekend visit. We returned to the hotel after a Friday night game together. The clerk at the front desk handed Molitor his usual telephone messages. There must have been 20 to 25 pink slips, most of them from young girls he had never met. At the ballpark, the pink slips came out in person and Molitor sometimes had to have the police bring his car around to the players' exit door.

I remember trying to leave County Stadium with Paul after a Sunday afternoon game against the Yankees. His car was about 150 yards from the stadium exit, but as we walked out of the park we were engulfed by a crowd of about a thousand people, most of them thrusting forward scraps of paper for Paul to sign. We weren't going to make it, so we retreated to the clubhouse and one of the deputy sheriffs had to retrieve Paul's car for him.

Paul Molitor is the kind of young man that a father would be happy to see his daughter bring home. He is handsome, well mannered, and articulate. He grew up in a large family and he's never forgotten his roots. In Milwaukee in the early '80s, he was everybody's All American. Jack Armstrong. In the flesh.

Living the life of a rock star, it was inevitable that Molitor would be introduced to drugs, and at an after-hours party in 1979 a couple of teammates got him to try cocaine. Cocaine usage among ballplayers in 1980 was widespread. Commissioner of Baseball Peter Ueberroth said he considered drug use the number-one problem facing the sport. Paul gave in to temptation because cocaine allowed him to escape temporarily from his image. It isn't easy being Mr. Squeaky Clean 24 hours a day, and Paul was burdened with the unrealistic expectations of family, friends, and baseball fans. His cocaine source was a 24-year-old sleaze ball named Tony Peters. Initially, Peters "favored" Molitor with cocaine without charge. Paul later described the feeling: "At first, cocaine stimulates you. Everything is speeded up. You're in the fast lane. You become more confident, outgoing, aggressive. Later you become more withdrawn." He soon began to suffer the side effects. He had trouble sleeping and eating. He became irresponsible and paranoid.

In 1979 and 1980 he used cocaine on and off, but never before a baseball game. Occasionally he went to the ballpark fatigued following a sleepless night. Cocaine was a comforting companion while Paul, lonely and depressed, was recovering from a rib injury that knocked him out of baseball for over three weeks during the 1980 season. Soon, cocaine became his first priority of the day. He had a need to use it often. He began to associate socially only with other "users." Unwittingly, I had been providing him with the funds to finance this expensive habit. All this led up to the scary Christmas episode at my home. It was then that Linda told him that he would either have to do something about his cocaine problem or lose her. Paul realized he was not only risking his relationship with Linda but his entire baseball career. He was addicted and afraid to ask for help.

He later told me, "Although I didn't seek treatment, I was actually desperate, crying out for God's help. I would literally pray to God on my hands and knees each day for forgiveness and to help me overcome the problem. I believe that God answered my prayers and gave me the strength to fight the addiction and finally to stop using cocaine."

Molitor stopped using cocaine that Christmas Eve at my house and has never used it since. He admits, however, that there are still rare moments when he feels a desire for the drug. Paul believes that it was God's plan for him to be a major league baseball player, but also for him to suffer through this cocaine addiction so that he could go forward with this experience to talk with other people to dissuade them from substance abuse. Molitor today often speaks at high schools about his personal experiences with the "Devil's drug." The kids listen because they know he's been there. He is also actively involved with pitcher Bob Welch, the 1990 American League Cy Young Award winner from Oakland (an arrested alcoholic), and Sterling Sharpe, the star wide receiver of the Green Bay Packers (a former steroid abuser), in a program called "STOP," which involves a presentation of videotapes warning of the dangers of chemical abuse.

Molitor was no longer a user when the season started in 1982, but there was still a price to pay. In 1983, Tony Peters was busted. Peters was indicted and charged with conspiracy to distribute cocaine and with income tax evasion. During the lengthy investigation, it was discovered that Molitor was one of Peters' clients. Molitor's white-bread image was threatened. He was contacted by the Milwaukee County Attorney's office, and "Mr. Clean" now had to "come clean." Reluctantly, the embarrassed star told me the whole story. He now was concerned not only about the negative publicity, but also about the possibility that he would be charged and convicted of a crime and that the commissioner of baseball might suspend him.

There was work to be done. My goals were to avoid criminal prosecution and suspension from baseball, and to preserve Paul's good name. We had to minimize the negative publicity that was almost certain to emanate from the Tony Peters prosecution. Negotiating with Larry Anderson, chief prosecutor from the U.S. Attorney's Office, Molitor and I agreed to meet in my Milwaukee hotel room with Anderson, an associate, and two federal investigators. We agreed to have Paul answer questions about his relationship with Tony Peters, details regarding his purchase of cocaine from Peters, and Paul's own usage. Molitor pledged to answer all questions truthfully. I had the right to oppose any questions that I deemed to be irrelevant to the investigation. In exchange, the prosecutors agreed to grant Molitor immunity from prosecution for any crime he committed by using or possessing the cocaine. In addition, it was agreed that the prosecutors would exercise their best efforts not to call Molitor as a witness during the Grand Jury hearings or the trial. Molitor was never charged and was not called to testify.

In 1984, Peters was convicted and sentenced to 22 years in the slammer for running a cocaine operation that authorities said grossed $17 million a year. Although most other major league baseball players who were users were not prosecuted, four Kansas City Royals were less fortunate. Willie Wilson, Vida Blue, Jerry Martin, and Willie Aikens all pled guilty to misdemeanor charges of possession of cocaine and each served three months in prison for the offense in 1983. Meanwhile, the baseball players' union negotiated new rules regarding the treatment of players who used drugs. Under these rules, Molitor and other users of cocaine were not suspended from baseball on condition that they subject themselves periodically to testing for substance abuse.

After he quit cocaine, but before it became public knowledge, Molitor enjoyed a spectacular 1982 season in which he played in all but two games, batted .302, had 201 hits (third in the league), stole 41 bases, and led the league with runs scored (136). He also played in his first (and so far his only) World Series, batting .355 with 11 hits, including a record 5 hits in Game 1.

Although Series' tickets were as scarce as hen's teeth, Paul came through with four in a prime location for the three games in Milwaukee. He was so popular there that when fans discovered I was his lawyer, they asked for my autograph. The Brewers lost the series in seven games. Paul allowed himself to wear the runner-up ring for one year, but then he took it off. He's waiting for a championship ring.

My client the World Series hero had completed five years in the major leagues and was now one year away from becoming a free agent and as such he would be free to sign with any other club. He had been named to the 1980 American League All Star Team and had played five different positions: shortstop, second base, center field, right field, and third base. At this point, I wanted to negotiate a long-term contract for Molitor to provide him with some security. With Molitor only a year away from free agency, the club was also interested in securing his services under a long-term contract rather than risking his loss a year later to another club. After some lengthy negotiations in February 1983, Milwaukee general manager Harry Dalton and I reached agreement on a five-year, guaranteed contract for $5.1 million, one of baseball's most lucrative contracts at the time. To celebrate the occasion, Paul, his wife, Linda, and I shared a $90 bottle of Dom Perignon champagne at the Pfister Bar in Milwaukee. It wasn't a dance in the parking lot at Sun City, but it wasn't bad.

In 1987, the last year of Molitor's five-year contract, he was sidelined for about six weeks during the first half of the season due to hamstring injuries. He was healthy by midsummer and on July 16 began a 39-game hitting streak that captured the attention of baseball America. It was the longest American League hitting streak since Joe DiMaggio's amazing 56-game streak in 1941 and is the seventh longest in baseball history. Molitor was pictured with his daughter, Blaire, on the front page of USA Today, and he was designated Person of the Week on ABC TV. The media coverage the last ten or twelve days of the streak was so intense that when Paul saw the stories on television, he said it felt like "an out-of-body experience," as though he were merely an impartial observer, not the Paul Molitor to whom the stories referred.

Molitor got into some rituals during the streak. Before the start of each game, standing in the dugout, he went through an elaborate high-five routine with teammate Rob Deer. When the streak reached 23 games, the club was playing the Chicago White Sox in Chicago. Deer was in the training room receiving treatment before the game and missed the "handshake." Molitor had gone hitless going into the ninth. Immediately before he stepped out of the dugout to take his position in the on-deck circle, Deer rushed over to Molitor to go through the routine. Molitor then strode to the plate and responded with a base hit to keep the streak alive. At the end of each game, reliever Dan Plesac would tell Paul, "The beat goes on." In the latter stages of the streak, the song was played in Milwaukee County Stadium when Paul came to the plate.

Molitor later said, "The pressure, although there, was not as intense as the pressure a player has in a big game during a pennant drive, the playoffs, or the World Series.

During this period, the team was doing extremely well. It picked up ten games in the pennant race, the crowds were big, and I was on a roll. I was having fun."

The streak was at 39 games when the Brewers were playing the Cleveland Indians at home in a scoreless tie game that went into extra innings. In the bottom of the tenth, with one out and a runner on second, Milwaukee center fielder Rick Manning, who had earlier been traded from opponent Cleveland, stepped to the plate. A hitless Molitor was up next. Manning came through with a sharply hit single to the outfield, scoring the runner from second. The Brewers won an exciting game 1–0, in dramatic fashion. Instead of the usual outburst of wild cheers, the normally partisan crowd fell silent. It was an eerie sensation. Manning (the hero) later said in the locker room that he felt like he had been traded back to Cleveland.

Molitor was saddened and disappointed by the end of the streak, but he also felt a great sense of relief. The day the streak ended, Paul was interviewed by Ted Koppel on "Nightline."

Although he played in only about 72 percent of the games that season, Paul batted .353 and led the American League in doubles with 41 and runs scored with 114. He also made a national name for himself, sold a lot of tickets for the Milwaukee Brewers, and put himself in a position to gain lifetime security. His timing was superb. On the heels of this stardust season, he became a free agent, free to sign a contract with any other major league baseball club. He was 31, healthy, and in the prime of his career. We were ready to strike the mother lode.

Unfortunately, no one was prepared for the free agent freeze out of 1987. The hints started dropping as soon as the season ended. After filing for Paul's free agency in November 1987, I didn't receive one telephone call or letter from any other major league club indicating interest in Molitor. How could this be? Molitor had just completed a half season of baseball without missing a game and had ended up with a .353 batting average. He'd stolen a career high 45 bases, had a 39-game hitting streak, been named to The Sporting News American League All Star Team, and had ended up eighth in the voting for American League Most Valuable Player. No other club wanted him? It was obvious that the owners had agreed not to bid for the services of other clubs' players. This collusion was clearly a breach of the agreement between the players and the owners, but that wasn't doing us any good in the winter of 1987–88.

My only alternative was to commence negotiations with Harry Dalton, the Brewers' GM. We quickly reached an impasse. Dalton's position was that Molitor was a great player when he played, but too often he was injured and unable to play. Thus, his value to the club was substantially diminished. The one blemish on Molitor's career has been his frequent stays on the disabled list. His medical chart includes almost every imaginable injury associated with baseball. Through the 1990 baseball season, Molitor missed over 400 games because of injuries, served 12 stints on the disabled list, and had nine surgeries to treat baseball injuries.

Paul has been hurt while running the bases, while running in the outfield before a game, in rundowns, and when struck by a ball thrown by his own teammate. The last straw came with six games remaining in the 1990 season. The Brewers had been mathematically eliminated from the pennant race, and Molitor (playing first base) collided with second-base teammate Jim Gantner while the two were chasing a pop fly to short right field. Molitor's right forearm muscle was severed, an injury doctors told him had never been suffered by a baseball player. He would need surgery to repair the muscle, but the prognosis for 1991 was excellent. When he received the news, Molitor broke down and cried. The accumulated frustration from so many injuries over so many years finally overcame him.

Although Molitor was a free agent, there were no other bidders and his salary could not be determined by an arbitrator because he had previously refused the club's offer to arbitrate. When negotiations are stalled, the skills of the negotiators are severely tested. Breaking the deadlock is perhaps the most important and difficult task. The positions of the parties become rigid, each side convinced of its correctness and unwilling to budge. Frustration and anger often follow. Patience, imagination, and control of emotions are required. The first step is to carefully analyze what differences exist between the parties and why they exist.

In this particular case, there was no dispute regarding the term of the contract, which was two years. However, there was a dispute regarding the amount of base salary to be paid Molitor for each of the two years. Dalton believed that Molitor, although a great player, was less valuable than other players with similar skills because he played in substantially fewer games. The previous four seasons he had played in only 376 out of a possible 648 games, an average of only 94 games a season. Dalton projected the past absences into the next two years of the contract. I conceded that Molitor had missed many games, but it was my belief that the disabling injuries would not necessarily recur in the future.

After identifying the reasons for the impasse, Dalton and I were able to close the gap by the use of performance bonuses based on the number of games Molitor played during the next two years of the contract. If he continued to miss as many games the next two seasons as in the past he would receive only one small bonus for playing in 81 games. However, in the event he was able to play most of the games the next two years, he would be handsomely rewarded. By looking closely at the needs and concerns of both parties we were able to come up with a solution that satisfied us both.

We agreed to the following bonus provisions for each of the two years of Molitor's contract:

    81 games—$50,000 bonus

    100 games—$100,000 bonus

    125 games—$100,000 bonus

    150 games—$100,000 bonus

    700 plate appearances—$100,000 bonus.

Performance bonuses can be used effectively to close the gaps in all kinds of negotiations. The concept is simple. If the performance of one party exceeds the expectations of the other party, the performing party is entitled to increased compensation. This concept can be used effectively in reaching agreement on the purchase price of a business (part of the purchase price is based upon the business's future earnings), an executive's compensation (company's profits), a TV anchorperson's compensation (ratings), or an author's earnings (book sales).

In Molitor's case, my assumptions proved correct. During the 1988 season Molitor played in 154 games, and in the 1989 season he played 155 games out of a possible 162. Consequently, he earned a whopping $350,000 in "games played" bonuses in 1988 and 1989, the largest amount of performance bonuses earned by any player in the major leagues either year. Meanwhile, in early 1990, an arbitrator ruled that the owners had been in collusion when they agreed not to bid on free agent players following the 1987 season. Arbitrators had previously found owner collusion in cases involving 1985 and 1986 free agents also. The owners and players agreed on a damage settlement in the sum of $280 million, to be divided among players who were effected by the collusion. Since Molitor was one of the top three or four players among the many free agents following the 1987 season, he will likely be entitled to a substantial award of damages.

Several months prior to the beginning of the 1989 season, I noticed an unusual trend. Many of the clubs were initiating discussions with their top players for extensions of existing contracts that would expire after the 1989 season. Normally one would expect these discussions to begin after, not before, the season when the player would become a free agent. Clubs had started talks with Kent Hrbek, Frank Viola, Jeff Reardon, Alan Trammell, Ryne Sandberg, Robin Yount, Wade Boggs, Ozzie Smith, Mike Scott, and others, all of whom would be free agents after the 1989 season. In each instance, the clubs were offering generous raises and guaranteed contracts extending two or three years beyond the 1989 season. The proposals were generally appealing to the players because their high salaries would continue several years beyond the 1989 season, regardless of how they performed in 1989. The players would also be protected in the event of a serious or career-ending injury during the 1989 season.

Molitor's contract was scheduled to expire after the 1989 season, but he would not be a free agent like the other top players. Since he had been a free agent in 1987, he could not become a "repeater" free agent for five years. After the 1989 season, Molitor had the right to go to arbitration on a one-year contract only if he and the club could not agree on terms. After the 1990 season, he also had the right to demand a trade—a questionable benefit. Since Molitor's alternatives after the 1989 season were not nearly as attractive as the other top players', he had less leverage in negotiations than they did.

I was vacationing in Florida in early March 1989 when I received an unexpected call from Paul Molitor from spring training in Arizona. Molitor told me that he had been contacted directly by the club's president and principal owner, Bud Selig, and its general manager, Harry Dalton, about a contract extension.

Allan "Bud" Selig is a successful businessman and former car dealer in Milwaukee. He loves Milwaukee and he loves major league baseball. Like so many other Milwaukee baseball fans, he was hurt, disappointed, and irate when the Milwaukee Braves years earlier had abandoned the city for Atlanta's warmer climes. Selig led the battle for the return of major league baseball to Milwaukee and finally succeeded when the Seattle Pilots were moved to the city. There were many lean years, but on the night Selig's Brewers finally became champions of the American League in 1982, a happy Selig was driving home after the game and observed the spontaneous celebrations throughout the city. He heard the cheers of the people and the horns honking. Overcome by emotion, he drove to the side of the road and cried. His fellow owners regard him so highly that when Baseball Commissioner Fay Vincent was forced to resign in 1992, they elected Selig to the top position in the restructured organization until a replacement could be found.

Typically, owners and ballplayers keep a comfortable distance. Selig and Molitor were different. Over the years, their relationship had grown into a close friendship. They enjoyed long talks and dined together with their wives. When Selig's daughter was married in the winter of 1991, Molitor was the only Brewer in attendance. Selig wanted Paul to become an executive of the club after his baseball career was finished. Paul was both flattered and interested.

When contract talks started in the spring of 1989, Selig suggested that Paul didn't need an attorney to negotiate the deal, and Paul was quite receptive to the idea. It was the "end run" all over again, 12 years later.

Paul contacted me and reported that he had met a couple of days earlier with Dalton, who had offered him an extension covering the 1990, 1991, and 1992 seasons at $1.8 million per season, plus some generous performance bonuses based on games played. I valued the proposal at about $2 million per year. Molitor and I were extremely impressed with this initial offer. After the 1989 season, the injury-plagued Molitor would be 33 years old and this guaranteed contract would cover him through age 36. Plus, he would be receiving a significant raise from his present $1.4 million base salary, regardless of what he did during the 1989 season. Molitor appeared tempted to immediately conclude the contract negotiations himself, but probably because of our close relationship, he extended me the courtesy of informing me of the developments.

Paul and I both knew that three of the top infielders in the game had signed new contracts within recent weeks: Cal Ripken, Jr., Alan Trammell, and Ryne Sandberg had all signed contract extensions through 1992 with average salaries of about $2.1 million per year. Molitor was in their class but didn't have their free agent leverage. Looking at the three-year, $6-million proposal, Molitor saw no reason to pay an annual six-figure (5-percent) fee to me for a simple review of the form contract. I couldn't blame him. Moreover, Trammell, a friend of Molitor's, had a few days earlier done his contract without an agent and had seemingly ended up quite well. Paul wanted my reaction. I gave Paul my standard response. "Let me give the matter some thought and I'll get back to you.

I learned a valuable lesson when I first began dabbling in the stock market. In 1959, I purchased 10 shares of Halloid Xerox (now Xerox Corp.) at $100 per share, or $1,000. The stock then suddenly took off, rising almost daily on high volume, and quickly reached $150 per share. It had obviously become overpriced. I sold it at $150 per share, showing a handsome 50 percent profit in a short time. After I sold, the stock skyrocketed past $200 per share, and then many times higher over the next eight years. A close friend in the investment business who was extremely astute cautioned me about the obvious. He pointed out that often when the price of a stock rises dramatically over a short period and it is an obvious "sell," this is the time to "hold" or buy more. "Smart money" often is buying the stock. When three people talking at a cocktail party are all certain that a stock is overpriced, politely excuse yourself to go to the nearest phone to instruct your broker to buy the stock. More often than not, it works.

Likewise, the initial Molitor offer looked too good to be true. It was similar to the amounts being paid to Trammell, Sandberg, and Ripken. It was only a first offer, and Paul wouldn't have the luxury of being a free agent after the season like the others. It was too obviously close to being an acceptable offer. Perhaps, I thought, the "smart money" (the owners) was bidding up the salaries for a reason. Maybe the owners knew something I didn't know. Maybe this was the time to hold and not the time to sell.

I find it helpful to have a healthy respect for the opposition, and I always operate under the assumption that my counterpart is smarter or more knowledgeable than me.

At least initially, I choose to believe my counterpart has a sound reason, rather than a mistaken belief, for making a proposal that appears to be surprisingly generous.

I was suspicious. However, it is one thing to be suspicious. It is quite another to persuade a close friend and long-time client not to close out the negotiations in "the ballpark area" of this seemingly fantastic first proposal on the basis of this suspicion. It was clear to me that my biggest challenge in the whole process was going to be persuading Molitor not to accept the deal without my involvement.

It was a tough sell. The player had a fair offer and a chance to put the matter behind him and avoid a six-figure legal fee. It was difficult for me to be objective because of my own self-interest, but my instincts convinced me that it would be a big mistake for Molitor to take this offer. In order to persuade Paul to accept my advice, I realized I would have to overcome Paul's legitimate concerns. It was time to negotiate with my client.

I assured Paul that his concern about the fee was legitimate. To eliminate the problem, I offered to allow him to ultimately determine the fee, if any, when negotiations were concluded. I placed him in a position where he had nothing to lose. Molitor accepted my proposal. I was back in the ballgame.

Paul's second concern was that the matter be concluded before the season started—in four weeks. Paul was concerned that another injury or a poor 1989 season would mean the offer would no longer be on the table. I promised to meet with Paul in Phoenix in a few days, and also to start discussions with Mr. Dalton at the same time, with a view to concluding the agreement as quickly as possible. It behooved me to improve the offer. If I recommended acceptance, I would have nothing to show for my efforts. How could I justify any fee?

In retrospect, the Brewers' first offer was too high. It was close to what they intended their final offer to be. A first offer should not be the best or final offer, or close to it. A negotiator should allow significant room for negotiation for several reasons. It's important that your counterpart ends up looking good. Only then can he comfortably recommend a deal. If your first offer is the best offer, your counterpart is placed in a position where he can't justify his value by accepting it. He hasn't done anything for his principal. He hasn't obtained any concessions or improvements and can't show that the final deal is any more favorable due to his efforts or involvement. He must establish a reason for existence.

Upon returning from vacation, I immediately flew to Phoenix to meet with Molitor and then Dalton. Usually, I try to avoid traveling to another city to conduct negotiations. Like most sports teams, I have found that competing "on the road" is a definite disadvantage. You invest substantial time and money in the trip, while your counterpart expends none. You meet in surroundings that are unfamiliar to you and comfortable to him. You raise your client's expectations as he is anxiously awaiting a report on the meeting and is hopeful that you will have reached an agreement. If there is no agreement, he is disappointed. You risk a great deal, while your counterpart risks little. You find you are reluctant to leave the city without a deal because it then appears that you have failed, and under these circumstances you are more prone to compromise to conclude a deal. The other side has the advantage all the way.

The alternatives are conducting the negotiations by telephone, meeting on "neutral" ground, or agreeing that the meetings will be alternated between your city and your counterpart's city. Negotiations by telephone are often adequate, especially if you are acquainted with the other side; if not, a personal meeting initially is helpful. It gives you an opportunity to study your counterpart, observe his demeanor, his facial expressions, and tone of voice. Sometimes careful observation of your counterpart during face-to-face meetings can be revealing. Some people have certain nervous traits, like clearing their throats, wiggling their knees, lowering their voice, or looking away from you. I look for a lump in the throat, twiddling thumbs, or a tapping foot. If a person is nervous when he makes a proposal, he usually fears that you won't take it seriously. These offers can safely be rejected. Better offers will follow.

My purpose for the trip to Phoenix was twofold. My primary goal was to meet with Paul personally, merely to reassure him that we should not hastily conclude the negotiations at this level. The other purpose was to start negotiations with Dalton to reduce Paul's anxiety.

Ordinarily, my job is to negotiate a contract for the player that pays him his "present fair market value," that is to say, pay similar to that earned by comparable recently signed players. However, when a contract extension is involved, a new factor is introduced into the equation. Will the fair market value be much higher a year later and, if so, is it worth the risk to wait a year? In our case, the club's offer came close to reflecting Molitor's present value, but what would his market value be one year hence when the extension took effect? In addressing this consideration, I concluded that there was a good chance Paul's value would be substantially higher because the "smart money" was offering too much money now. I wasn't going to sell Xerox too cheap a second time. I wanted to see a few more cards, a few more contracts signed perhaps during the season, to see which way the wind was blowing. Besides, in the back of my mind I was thinking that I still needed a raison d'être.

I knew the contract was not "ripe" for negotiation. It wasn't the right time yet; however, since I had to make a counterproposal, I set my sights high.

I met with Dalton in the stands at the ballpark during a pre-season game and submitted a counterproposal of $7 million for three years. He ridiculed my offer and suggested that it was so out of line that it would not be dignified by another counterproposal. Dalton spent only a few minutes with me discussing the matter, making short shrift of my visit. Later, as I was leaving the game, I bumped into Bud Selig. He had talked with Dalton and scoffed at the $7-million proposal. I had not expected an agreement, but I had hoped to come away with some slightly improved counteroffer to show Paul some progress. The club's total rejection created the impression that my trip to Arizona had been a failure, which is precisely why I do not like to "play on the road."

Dalton and I had quickly reached an impasse because he was unwilling to make a counterproposal and I refused to negotiate with myself by making another proposal. If one makes a proposal that is rejected and no counterproposal is provided, it is extremely imprudent to make a second lower proposal. If you negotiate with yourself, your counterpart won't take any of your proposals seriously.

I had to devise a "game plan" to deal with this impasse. Neither side was willing to make further proposals, and Paul was eager to have the matter resolved. After considerable reflection, I decided to apply my favorite concept, the KISS principle—"Keep it simple, stupid." My plan was to await the outcome of the club's pending contract negotiations with Robin Yount and then grab a similar contract.

Too often, people tend to look for complicated solutions to complex problems. I follow KISS whenever possible. A very strong case could be made for Molitor's contract to be close to Yount's. Most baseball experts would agree that Robin Yount was the club's most valuable player, but Molitor was considered a close second. The club had initiated discussions with both players prior to the 1989 season for three-year extensions of their contracts, both of which were expiring after the 1989 season. Unlike Molitor, Yount had the leverage of becoming a free agent.

Selig negotiated only the Yount contract. Dalton negotiated the others. Selig had described Yount as "The Franchise," and since Yount had been ably represented in the past by his brother, Larry (a real estate developer), I felt there was a strong likelihood that Yount would end up with a lucrative contract. Yount and Molitor had ended up with similar contracts in the past. The best strategy for us was to stand in the on-deck circle while Yount took his turn at the plate.

When the public reads about high salary demands of athletes, the players are often perceived as greedy. Molitor is far from greedy. Over the years he has given freely to his family members and numerous charities, and recently gave $100,000 gifts to the parochial school he attended and to the University of Minnesota. He refused recognition for his contributions. Molitor in 1989 simply had a strong desire to be paid fairly in relation to other players, particularly his own teammates. By waiting until Yount signed his contract, Molitor would know that there would be a fair relationship between their respective contracts.

This strategy had two possible drawbacks. First, in view of Paul's history of numerous injuries, would he be willing to accept the risk of another serious injury during the 1989 season while waiting for Yount to sign a contract? Second, at the end of the 1989 season, Yount would be a free agent, but Molitor would not. The club could make a distinction on that basis.

Several times during the 1989 season I contacted Dalton to inquire about the status of the Yount negotiations. His answer was always the same. He knew nothing about the negotiations except that Selig was handling them, the parties were close to an agreement, and the proposal was similar to that offered Molitor. He would always add that the one contract had nothing to do with the other, especially since at the end of the 1989 season Yount would be a free agent and Molitor would not. The usually calm Dalton soon became irritated when I continued to question the status of the Yount contract. To me, this was the tip-off that I was on the right track. At mid-season, I asked Molitor to check directly with Robin Yount. Yount told Molitor that he and the Brewers were miles apart. Someone was not being truthful. I was staying the course, but Molitor was becoming increasingly uncomfortable.

We were gambling. A word about risk: Risk-taking requires courage and a knowledge of the odds. If you play safe, you'll never attain lofty heights. To succeed, you must fail. This is the price you occasionally pay to get top results. Earlier in my career, a wily trial lawyer told me, "Show me a trial lawyer who never loses a case, and I'll show you a trial lawyer who settles too cheap." It is appropriate to take risks, but they must be carefully calculated. An athlete's career is fragile. It can be snuffed out at any time. An injury can end his career or reduce his skills to the point where he is no longer competitive at the major league level. If the worst happened, Paul would lose the $6 million offered him for 1990–92. Moreover, there was always the chance of an off year. If so, maybe the club would only want to offer a one-year contract at reduced pay. Fortunately for us, through the first half of the season, Yount was having an excellent season and Molitor a good one.

In early August I received a telephone call from Paul indicating he was very eager to get the contract resolved. When I probed further, I discovered that Selig had talked directly to Paul. The club was making another "end run," and this time, the strategy was extremely effective because of the close friendship between Paul and Selig.

Molitor was torn. On the one hand, he was told to rely upon my advice—the Yount strategy—to be paid fairly in comparison to Yount. His pride required it. On the other hand, he had developed serious guilt feelings about rejecting a $2-million-a-year contract guaranteed for three years. It was more money than he had ever dreamed of earning in a lifetime of baseball and so high in comparison to what non-athletes make. He also felt he had cheated his boss in the past because of all the games he had missed due to injuries. In addition, he had heard rumors that the club might be forced to move from Milwaukee to a larger, more profitable metropolitan area because of financial problems. He would then be putting one of the nails in the Milwaukee coffin, something he did not want to do to Selig or to Milwaukee.

Selig had assured Paul that he was talking almost daily with Larry Yount and that they were "close to a deal." I persuaded Paul that we should not accept the $6-million contract until I had met with him in a few days in Milwaukee. Although ostensibly the purpose of the trip was to continue negotiations with Dalton, the time was still not ripe for negotiation. We'd be ready only after Yount agreed to terms. Serious negotiations before that would be of no value. My job was to persuade Paul to stay with the game plan. I wanted Paul to complete the season, which had only two months remaining, and to await the Yount contract. He agreed to hold off. I did meet with Dalton, primarily to prove to Paul that no progress could be made now, and Dalton obliged by refusing to budge from his previous offer.

Many lawyers and sports representatives take the position that the representative has a duty to disclose the proposals to the client, inform him of the relevant facts, and provide him with a recommendation. If the client then wishes to reject the recommendation and to accept the proposal, so be it. In theory this is a reasonable approach, but I don't buy it. This practice produces bad results, and often the client later discovers this and blames the representative for allowing it to happen. I believe the representative should do everything within his power to persuade the client to follow the representative's recommendation. The judgment of a good representative on this subject is usually far superior to that of the relatively young and inexperienced professional athlete. This is the very reason the professional athlete has a representative. He needs the advice of a more objective, experienced, and trained adviser. Although the player certainly has the right to make the final decision, it's ill advised when it is contrary to his representative's advice, and it's the representative's responsibility to fight not to allow it. One reason some representatives often allow the players to "call the shots" is that fighting for the additional 10 to 20 percent in benefits that makes an average contract a good one does not increase their fee significantly. Thus, it is not worth the risk should the advice to the client later prove to be wrong. If the client makes the decision, his representative is off the hook.

On September 5, 1989, Linda Molitor left this message for me with my secretary:

"Paul wants to talk to you today. He wants to sign the contract as offered." I called Paul in Anaheim and persuaded him to finish the season.

Paul had a sensational September and finished hitting .315, with 84 runs, 56 RBIs, and 27 stolen bases. Yount had a sensational season. He ended up hitting .318, with 101 runs, 103 RBIs, and 21 home runs. He was later named the Most Valuable Player in the American League for the second time in his career. We had picked the perfect stalking horse.

I was feeling pretty good about our strategy, right up until November 27 when Linda left this message for me: "Pigs end up being slaughtered." We were a divided house, and Dalton and Selig probably knew it.

At about the same time, baseball's free agents started signing fat, new contracts. Collusion was over, the wallets were open, and the dollars were flying. Pitcher Mark Langston got a five-year deal with California for $16 million. Pitcher Bryn Smith got a three-year deal with St. Louis for $6 million. Kevin Bass, coming off a season during which he suffered a broken leg and played in 87 games, signed a three-year, $5.2-million deal with the Giants. Rickey Henderson and Kirby Puckett signed multi-year contracts for $3 million a year. Suddenly, Molitor's $2-million-a-year proposal for three years looked puny.

The clubs had correctly anticipated in March that salaries for free agents would soar after the 1989 season. Salaries that had been artificially controlled were rising dramatically now that bidding was competitive and market forces were allowed to work freely again. As usual, the "smart money" was right.

I told Paul that I planned to be at the annual December baseball meetings to be held in Nashville early that month. These meetings were usually attended by all of the clubs' general managers, owners, managers, and administrative people. It was also an opportunity to negotiate player contracts. Paul urged me to complete the negotiations at the baseball meetings, regardless of whether Yount's contract had been signed. He suggested I assume that Yount's contract provide for $3 million a year in compensation for three years. This, I knew, was the wrong approach. There was no need to make an assumption. The season was over, there was no longer any risk of injury or an offseason, and Yount would likely sign by a January 8 deadline. I was unwilling to assume anything about the Yount contract, but to placate Paul I had a brief visit with Dalton in Nashville. His position remained unchanged, even though new contracts were running 25 to 50 percent higher than those awarded to players with similar ability before the 1989 season began. The market value of the same players had increased dramatically since March. All I had to do now was to stick with my game plan and wait for Yount.

Although the salaries were escalating through the roof, Dalton had only imperceptibly improved upon his March offer to Molitor. I knew why. The club knew our ranks were divided, that Molitor was a soft touch, and that he was calling the shots. I had the feeling I was playing poker and my opponent could see all the cards in my hand.

On December 19 Robin Yount, the 1990 American League MVP, reportedly agreed to terms on a new three-year contract with the Brewers for $9.6 million. He didn't sign a contract. He agreed to terms. His annual salary now ranked first, along with Mark Langston, among all major league players.

The time was ripe for negotiation. In fact, there is no more perfect example of a time when a contract is ripe for negotiation.

A few days after Yount agreed to terms, Molitor and I had the important meeting at my house that turned negotiations around.

Paul was not eligible for free agency, but he had the right to and did file for salary arbitration. Under salary arbitration, the best that could happen would be a one-year contract, something neither of us wanted. We needed details of the Yount pact. I called the baseball players' union. Ordinarily, the union has details of a player's contract within 72 hours after the contract has been agreed upon. However, in the Yount case, the union advised me that for some reason the terms of the contract were not provided to them. Upon checking further, the union representatives were informed that although there was an oral agreement, a written contract had not yet been signed. This was highly unusual. The club's line was that "a few unimportant details had to be worked out before the contract could be signed." Although the terms can usually be verified by direct contact with the player's representative, in this case that was not possible because Larry Yount had no loyalty to the union. He represented only his brother, no other players.

Something was fishy. I began to wonder if Yount's new contract could be even fatter than the three-year, $3.2-million-per-year salary reported in the newspapers. I was legally entitled to know the details, but only when the contract was signed. I chose to resume negotiations only when I had the details on Yount's contract.

On January 22, over a month after an oral agreement had been reached on the Yount contract, I telephoned Dalton to inquire about its status. Our arbitration hearing was coming up in February. I told him that since I didn't have the details of the Yount contract, the only proposal I could make would be that Molitor's contract be identical to Yount's. Dalton said the "holdup" on Yount's contract was due to the negotiation of an agreement regarding previous outstanding loans made to Yount by the club and a bank. Dalton continued to claim that he knew nothing about the terms of the Yount contract because it had been negotiated by Selig. It seemed incredible to me that one of the top general managers in baseball, Harry Dalton, did not know the terms of Yount's contract. I didn't believe it then and I don't believe it now. Dalton did, however, take the position that Yount's contract was not comparable to Molitor's because among other things Yount was a free agent and Molitor was not.

A week later, Dalton called and said Selig had informed him that Yount's compensation package was indeed "about" $9.6 million over three years as reported in the newspapers. I inquired about any additional benefits, and Dalton informed me that Selig had told him there were none. It had been more than six weeks since the Yount contract had been announced and still there was no formal, signed written agreement.

Dalton had something else to tell me. The Brewers were prepared to offer Molitor a three-year pact worth over $8.7 million, or more than $2.9 million per year. This was almost 50 percent higher than the previous offer, and it would make Paul one of the highest paid players in the game.

It was a little sudden. Paul and I surmised that this change of heart was related in some way to the Yount contract terms, which had not yet been disclosed. I decided to probe further. I asked Paul to contact Yount directly, and if necessary Robin's brother Larry, to obtain the exact details of the contract. I agreed to press Dalton for more details. Two days later, Paul reached Robin, but Robin told Paul that Larry was busy working on the matter, that Robin was not familiar with all the details, but that Paul could contact Larry. I could not believe that Robin wouldn't know the basic terms of his own multi-million-dollar contract—perhaps his last contract in baseball.

Paul then contacted Larry Yount. Well coached by me, Paul asked all the tough questions. Larry assured Paul that there were no benefits in addition to the three-year, $9.6-million contract that was reported in the newspapers, except that some substantial part of the compensation was to be deferred. Paul said Larry was evasive regarding the amounts of the deferments and the effective rate of interest, if any, to be paid on the deferments. I told Paul I was totally unsatisfied with the Younts' response. I became even more suspicious.

Later that same day, Harry Dalton "coincidentally" called me, indicating that he had talked again with Selig, who had told him that the contract was as previously disclosed but that he had more details. He said that there were substantial deferments at an unknown interest rate, which I later discovered to be 11.5 percent. Then came the shocker. Dalton nonchalantly mentioned that the club had granted to Yount an option for a fourth year (1993) at $3.2 million also. I was stunned. This was an unbelievable concession. Yount was guaranteed a fourth season (during which he would turn 38) at $3.2 million. Moreover, since the fourth year was at Yount's option, if he was still playing well after the third year and salaries continued to climb during that three-year period, he could wind up with an even higher salary for the fourth year. Conversely, if age reduced his skills or injury prevented him from playing the fourth year, he would still receive the $3.2 million. Heads Yount wins, tails the club loses. Yount had ended up with the best contract in baseball at the time, and the key ingredient had not been disclosed.

I understood fully why Dalton and Selig had wanted to conceal the "details." Their major concern probably was a demand by Molitor, one year younger than Yount but with a long history of injuries, for a guaranteed fourth year on his contract. Also, I suspect there was some kind of an agreement between Selig and the Younts regarding confidentiality of the fourth-year option and the rich deferment interest. My suspicion is that Dalton finally "fessed up" on the afternoon of February 1 in response to pressure from both Robin and Larry Yount to do so. Molitor had asked both Younts earlier that day about the contract terms, and each probably felt very uncomfortable about "stonewalling" Paul. The timing of the telephone calls would be too much of a coincidence otherwise. I now also understood why the signing of the Yount contract was delayed so long—to keep it from the union, to keep it from us.

Molitor was hurt by these revelations. Selig and Yount had been his close friends over the years. It appeared at best they were less than candid, at worst they knowingly deceived him.

I was looking at things from a business perspective. Though the Brewers' new offer was generous by any standard, it paled in comparison to Yount's blockbuster pact. Selig and Dalton's lack of candor could not be ignored. I felt their deception could be used to our advantage. My hope was that their embarrassment would result in an even more favorable contract. I insisted upon a meeting with Selig and Dalton in Milwaukee immediately to air our grievance. I met with them on February 8. Paul was not present. I outlined our complaint, and predictably, Selig exploded. He became overly defensive, a sure sign of his guilt. He denied any deceit, steadfastly clinging to his previous assertion that the Yount contract was really only for three years, in spite of the fact that Yount had an option for a fourth year. He argued the insignificance of the fourth year by pointing out that it was not firm but only at Yount's option, and that Yount was the kind of person who would not exercise the option if he was no longer playing at the major league level. This was an absurd attempt to defend the indefensible.

It turned out that the 37-year-old Yount had a so-so 1992 season (the third year of the contract). During the off-season, the Brewer's new general manager, Sal Bando, expressed the opinion that Yount would probably have attracted a one-year, $1-million, guaranteed contract for 1993 as a free agent. Yount wisely decided not to test the free agent market but instead, in effect, exercised his right to play the 1993 season at $3.2 million. The "worthless" option turned out to be worth $2.2 million.

Selig also indicated that the 11.5 percent interest paid to Yount on deferred salary over the years was more of an accommodation by Yount to the club than the reverse. He claimed the club was in need of the funds and would probably have to pay a bank higher interest. I told him that Molitor would like to do the club the same favor by accepting deferred payments at 11.5 percent interest. Selig had no choice but to voice no objection to that suggestion.

Backed into a corner, Selig ranted and raved about the total lack of leadership provided by Molitor and Yount during the 1989 campaign. He suggested that the Brewers' poor record was due in part to the failed leadership of the club's two top players. He referred to them as "wimps" and "greedy ballplayers." He pointed out that while the club was going bad in 1989, the two players sat alone on opposite ends of the dugout, sulking and silent, instead of providing leadership and enthusiasm. He said that our suggestion that he deceived us was an attack on his honesty and integrity that might irreparably damage his close personal relationship with Molitor. Under the circumstances, he said, it was perhaps best if Molitor was traded. I agreed. I was not about to backpedal.

Dalton said little—just enough to indicate to Selig his complete support. Selig, of course, suggested that all of the details of the Yount contract, including the fourth year, had been disclosed to us a few days earlier and that if he was trying to conceal the facts, why would such a disclosure have occurred? There is no question in my mind that the disclosure occurred only because the Younts, being pressured by Molitor for the facts, in turn pressured Selig to make the disclosure.

I proposed either a trade, a one-year contract at $3.2 million with an announcement by Molitor that at the end of the season he would exercise his right to request a trade, or a contract similar to Yount's. If no agreement could be reached, Molitor would go through with the scheduled arbitration hearing two weeks hence, and regardless of the outcome, we would announce that he would request a trade at the conclusion of the 1990 season. Although a trade would not benefit Paul, I knew it would provide good leverage. If Paul was traded the full story would come out and the Brewers' fans would be outraged. The club could not risk such a reaction. To soothe hard feelings, I told them that it was not Molitor's position that they were dishonest. I explained that there was a "perception that we were misled," and that we wanted an explanation. Selig demanded a statement of Molitor's position.

When I met with Molitor over lunch after the meeting, he reacted in typical

Molitor fashion. He was forgiving, one of his many endearing traits. He was more than willing to give Selig the benefit of the doubt and authorized me to advise Selig that he accepted Selig's explanation that no deceit was intended. Paul later told me, "I'm convinced that Selig did not intend to deceive us and that he honestly interpreted the Yount contract to be for three years at $9.6 million dollars." Their close friendship remained intact.

Four days before the scheduled February arbitration hearing, Dalton and I reached agreement on a three-year, guaranteed $9.1-million contract for Molitor. Now that the basic terms had been resolved, I approached Dalton about the possibility of including those lucrative deferment payments at the 11.5 percent interest rate to be paid to Yount. Dalton informed me that Selig had talked with the comptroller and had been advised that granting deferments at that high an interest rate would not be in the club's best interest. I reminded Dalton of the earlier conversation I had had with Selig in Dalton's presence about how advantageous it was for the club to loan Yount money at 11.5 percent interest. Selig had characterized the loan as a favor to the club from Yount. Apparently Selig wanted no further favors from his players.

"Harry," I said. "Certainly you recall that conversation, don't you?" There was a long pause on the telephone. Dalton then said, "No, I really don't remember that."

Molitor's annual salary placed him sixth among all major league baseball players before the 1990 season. It was over $9 million, $3 million more than the $6-million contract Paul had been so eager to accept a few months earlier. But this time, we didn't feel like dancing in the parking lot or clinking glasses of Dom Perignon at the Pfister Bar. The circumstances had soured the joy of the moment. Molitor and I refused to make comments to the media applauding the contract or praising the club for its generosity.

I have always had the highest respect for Harry Dalton and Bud Selig, but my intelligence was insulted by Dalton's continued insistence that he was kept in the dark regarding the details of the Yount contract even after an agreement had been reached and by Selig's assertion that Yount's option was initially not disclosed because it had no value. On the basis of my past experience with them both, I chose to believe they were honorable men who had made a mistake. However, they did deceive us, and they should have admitted it and apologized.

In April 1990, shortly before the baseball season began, Molitor called me and said that Yount may not have known much about the terms or status of his contract when he talked to Molitor. Paul concluded that maybe it was only Larry Yount who misled him, and even Paul could not honestly find a way to justify Larry's deception. I didn't believe this scenario for a minute, but Paul has always had a very forgiving nature and perhaps it was best that he reached those conclusions. He and Yount are still good friends and have never discussed the matter.

In accordance with our agreement made in March, Molitor had no obligation to pay me, but in December 1990, he told me my fee on this contract would be the same as it had always been—5 percent of his earnings. Business is business, but friendship is something else. Paul has been a close friend for many years, and I think I know him very well. To me he's still "Jack Armstrong, the All American Boy."

Is an agent worth the money? Let's look at Molitor versus Tiger shortstop Alan Trammell. These two players are quite comparable. Like Molitor, Trammel came up in the late '70s and, at the time of this comparison, both had played for only one team. The two players' skills and personalities are comparable, and there's little doubt that Trammell meant as much to the Tigers as Molitor did to the Brewers.

Trammel has negotiated his own contracts most of his career. In an article in *The Sporting News* in September 1980, it was reported that Trammell had negotiated a new seven-year, guaranteed contract for an estimated $2.8 million without an agent: "Allan Trammell didn't like the thought of salary arbitration again next winter. He said the process upset him last winter. The idea of handing a chunk of his earnings over to an agent was another troubling prospect."

Sounds simple. Trammell may have thought it was simple and he did avoid paying a "chunk of his earnings to an agent," but the larger question is whether it pays to be represented in contract negotiations by a qualified representative who charges a percentage fee.

The schedule below reveals the career earnings of both Molitor and Trammell from 1978 through 1992.

MOLITOR/TRAMMEL COMPENSATION COMPARISON

Year	Molitor	Trammell
1978 base salary	$21,000	$21,000
1979 base salary	$65,000	$65,000
1980 base salary	$210,000	$130,000
1981 base salary	$320,000	$230,000
signing bonus		$120,000
1982 base salary	$360,000	$280,000
negotiated performance bonuses	$75,000	
1983 base salary	$700,000	$330,000
signing bonus	$300,000	

Year	Molitor	Trammell
negotiated performance bonuses	$75,000	
1984 base salary	$900,000	$350,000
1985 base salary	$900,000	$400,000
negotiated performance bonuses	$50,000	
1986 base salary	$1,100,000	$450,000
prorated signing bonus	$60,000	
1987 base salary	$1,200,000	$500,000
prorated signing bonus	$60,000	
1988 base salary	$1,400,000	$900,000
signing bonus		$600,000
negotiated performance bonuses	$375,000	
1989 base salary	$1,400,000	$1,000,000
negotiated performance bonuses	$350,000	
1990 base salary	$2,100,000	$1,800,000
signing bonus	$1,000,000	
1991 base salary	$2,900,000	$2,200,000
1992 base salary	$3,100,000	$2,400,000
Totals:	**$19,021,000**	**$11,776,000**

Molitor has earned over $7 million (or 61 percent) more than Trammell. In 1990, Molitor, two years older than Trammel, signed a $9.1-million contract for the same three-year period (1990–92) that Trammell earlier agreed to be paid $6.5 million for. Molitor's attorneys' fees through 1992 were approximately $950,000. The fees of course include a number of other legal and financial services as well as negotiating the contracts. Nevertheless, after payment of the fees, Molitor's earnings have exceeded Trammell's by over $6 million, or over half as much as again as Trammell made through 1992.

Maybe there is something to that old adage that "An attorney who represents himself has a fool for a client."

There is an update to the Molitor story. In 1990, Paul and I assumed that we were working on his last contract. At the end of the 1992 season he would be a 36-year-old free agent. Most athletes that age are collecting pensions. With his injury history, it was even more likely that he would be heading out to pasture.

Although Molitor was the club's third baseman when he signed the contract in 1990, the aggravation of previous injuries prevented him from putting mustard on the long throw to first base. Consequently, at the beginning of the 1991 season, Paul was converted to a designated hitter and part-time first baseman. Since that time he has defied the calendar. Neither the Ignitor's power at bat nor his speed on the bases declined during the 1991 and 1992 campaigns. Indeed, he seems to be getting better with age.

In 1991, Molitor played in 158 games, batted .325, scored 133 runs, and had 75 RBIs. He led the league in runs, hits, and at bats. In 1992, he played in 158 games, hit .320 (fourth best in the American League), scored 89 runs, and had 89 RBIs. At this point, Paul and the legendary Willie Mays are the only players in the history of baseball with a .300 average, 300 steals, and more than 150 career home runs. Those are the numbers of an All Star, not an over-the-hill jock struggling through his last contract.

Since Molitor was a free agent, under baseball rules if the club did not offer Paul salary arbitration on a one-year contract on or before December 7, Molitor as a practical matter could no longer play with Milwaukee, and if he signed with another club, Milwaukee would receive no compensation from the other club. If Milwaukee did offer salary arbitration by the deadline, Molitor could accept or reject the offer by December 19. If he accepted, he could not sign with any other club, but would return to the Brewers. If the parties failed to reach agreement on a new contract, an arbitrator would determine his salary for the 1993 season. If Molitor did not accept the arbitration offer by December 19, he could nevertheless sign a new contract with the Brewers on or before January 8, or he could sign with any other club. If he signed with another club, the Brewers would be entitled to compensation. The compensation was one or two high draft choices, depending primarily upon the player's ranking.

Despite public assurances that re-signing Molitor was one of the club's top priorities, the Brewers seemed to be dragging their feet in the negotiation process.

In fact, it wasn't until November 25 (about seven weeks after the season had been completed, and only 13 days before the December 7 deadline) that Paul and I first met with Bud Selig and Sal Bando. Sal had replaced Harry Dalton as the team's general manager the previous year, and he had warned us that this initial meeting was called primarily to discuss the Brewers' financial difficulties, and not to engage in contract negotiations. When we finally met, the meeting was focused on the club's dire financial straits, and Selig concluded the meeting by brushing us aside with a plea for "imaginative" negotiations—a euphemism for taking a big pay cut. Both Bando and Selig made it clear that the club would not offer salary arbitration to Molitor. They apparently felt that Molitor, whose 1992 salary had been $3.1 million, would accept and the club would get burned in arbitration for over $4 million. If this was the club's highest priority, I was wondering how management was tackling their other priorities.

The Bud Selig that I observed during our meetings was not the same man who in previous years had used all his energy and wisdom to successfully re-sign Molitor and Yount. This Bud Selig was disinterested. When Baseball Commissioner Fay Vincent was dethroned in 1992, Selig became, in effect, the acting commissioner. As a result, he seemed to be more focused on the many problems that were besetting the game as a whole, perhaps even hoping to become baseball commissioner himself. It appeared to me that Selig had already decided that the club was unwilling to pay Molitor anywhere near his market value, and the excuse was going to be their red ink.

Meanwhile, I had received a phone call from Pat Gillick, general manager of the World Champion Toronto Blue Jays, inquiring about Molitor's availability. Gillick and I had developed a friendship after we met in 1990 when we were on opposite sides of the table during negotiations on a contract for Chris Weinke, their second-round draft choice.

I have always found a good relationship, although not imperative, can be helpful to both sides, and our friendship made it easier for us to explore the possibilities of a Molitor-Toronto marriage.

In contrast with our meetings with the Milwaukee brass, the tone of our meeting with Gillick and Toronto's President Paul Beeston was upbeat. Most of the talk revolved around Molitor's great value as a player and how much he could help the team. Money was not mentioned; neither was Toronto's 41-year-old designated hitter, Dave Winfield, who was also testing the free agent waters.

At the baseball winter meetings in Louisville that started on December 4, Bando made me an offer. An extremely astute baseball man, he was direct and honest. Although he recognized Paul as a great player, he viewed him as a risk on a contract for more than one year because of his age and ailments, and he believed that Paul was worth significantly less than the $3.1 million he had earned in 1992 because he was now primarily a designated hitter.

Bando offered $2.3 million for 1993, with $1 million paid during the season and $260,000 a year for the next five years without interest. The club also wanted an option on Paul's services at $2 million for 1994. If it didn't exercise the option, it would pay him $200,000. Their final offer was inadequate and late in coming.

Back in Milwaukee, the pressure to re-sign Molitor was mounting. A strongly worded editorial in a local paper called for the club to move quickly. The "Molitor watch" had begun, and the headlines were telling. On December 4, the headline was "Molitor rejects team's first offer," On December 5, it was "Brewers make Molitor another offer." And finally, on December 7, it was "Final seconds ticking down on Molitor era." Molitor occupied a special place in the hearts of Brewers' fans, and the public responded predictably with an outpouring of calls to radio talk shows and to the club's offices supporting his return.

Milwaukee's front office chose to describe the offer as a one-year, $2.5-million contract, which was misleading. In reality, it had a value of about $2 million. The only way Paul would actually end up with $2.5 million was if he was a complete bust in 1993. If he had a typical Molitor season in 1993, he would be obligated to play the 1994 season at $2 million, far below his market value. The two-year contract would be for $4.5 million, but since the payments were strung out over time, the present value would be a lot less. I realized then that Milwaukee was not serious about re-signing Paul and was, for all practical purposes, out of the picture. However, Milwaukee still looked like an obvious bidder to the outsiders, and it was important that this appearance be maintained.

Fortunately, the Toronto people were ready for some serious talking. A few days earlier, the club had balked at Winfield's request for a guaranteed three-year contract for $12 million. Gillick preferred Molitor over Winfield. Molitor's potential slot on the team was now open, and it was clear that Toronto was willing to pay to fill it. After several sessions, Toronto's guaranteed contract offer had reached three years and was in excess of $10 million dollars. Another meeting was scheduled for December 8.

Meanwhile, although I had written the Brewers off, at Bando's urging I agreed to meet with Bando and Selig two and a half hours before the December 7 midnight deadline as a courtesy. Although an agreement with Toronto was almost certain at this time, as a precaution, the Blue Jays meeting was rescheduled to take place before the meeting with Bando and Selig.

It was vital that any agreement with Toronto be made then. If Milwaukee failed to offer arbitration by midnight as they had repeatedly promised, I would lose what appeared to be my only other serious bidder and my main leverage with Toronto. If the Brewers did offer arbitration by the deadline, the Brewers would pick up Toronto's two top draft choices for the next season. At that point I didn't care about an offer of salary arbitration.

At the meeting with the Toronto representatives, agreement was reached on a three-year guaranteed contract for $13 million dollars, plus an extra $250,000 if the Brewers didn't offer salary arbitration. It would be the largest guaranteed contract ever for a designated hitter, and also for a player over 35. The disparity between the two offers was astounding and I was elated.

Now came the tough part. I had to meet with Bando and Selig at the eleventh hour to talk about a contract for Molitor, when I already had an agreement with Toronto. I couldn't tell them anything until I had their final answer on the salary arbitration matter. At the start of the meeting, they asked me what it would take to keep Molitor in Milwaukee. I tried to be vague. If my number was too high, it would reveal I had received a large offer elsewhere, which would prompt them to offer arbitration. If it was too low, it could be accepted. Then I would really be in trouble. I'd have contracts with two clubs.

After a brief caucus, in which Bando and Selig apparently concluded that Paul had received a substantial offer from another team that he would accept, they decided to offer salary arbitration after all. If they had to lose Molitor, at least they would look good in the eyes of the Milwaukee fans by appearing to have fought for him. There went our $250,000 bonus. They would also pick up Toronto's two highest draft picks.

Moments later, I told Bando that we had already struck a deal with the Blue Jays. He was relieved. The Toronto numbers were so large that Sal could claim Milwaukee's financial position did not permit them to come close.

Although Molitor was delighted with his new contract, he was hurt by the way Milwaukee had handled the negotiations. Had the club come up with a reasonable offer, he would have been prepared to stay in Milwaukee for much less money because he felt that was where he belonged. Paul felt the club's rhetoric about re-signing him was misleading, and he resented the last-minute offer of salary arbitration. We had both been assured that no such offer would be forthcoming. It seemed to him to be no more than a grandstand play designed to curry favor with the fans and to pick up two draft choices. He and I both agreed it was not motivated by a desire to re-sign him.

The December 8 Milwaukee *Sentinel* announced: "Molitor becomes a Blue Jay—$13 million deal stuns Brewers and ends fifteen-year career here." Paul was not mentally prepared to leave Milwaukee. He had played his entire career there, was a full-time resident, and felt a strong loyalty to the baseball fans and people of Milwaukee. He received close to 100 letters from fans who were disappointed and outraged to see him go. A comment from one of them says it all: "The Brewers will never be the same without you. It's truly the end of an era." At a press conference on December 9, a teary eyed Molitor said his good-byes.

Winfield ended up accepting a two-year, guaranteed contract for $5.2 million with Minnesota, a figure Toronto would have exceeded, according to Gillick.

Like Gillick, and unlike Bando, I am convinced that Molitor is not yet a fading star. In spite of his age, I believe he will continue to produce All Star numbers that will help Toronto to future championships.

The Molitor move can be characterized as a win/win/win/win situation.

Toronto was happy because it added a superstar to its team, while at the same time weakening its closest competitor.

Molitor was happy because if he couldn't play for Milwaukee, he wanted to end up with a top contender. He was also rewarded with a record-breaking contract.

Milwaukee was happy because it had pared its payroll and had picked up a couple of high draft choices, while sending the message to its fans that it was working on their behalf.

The Toronto fans were happy at the prospect of being treated to some great entertainment by one of the top players in the major leagues.

Unfortunately, not everyone won.

Ask the Brewers' fans. For them, December 7, 1992, like Pearl Harbor, is a day that will forever live in infamy.

9

KENT HRBEK, THE HOMETOWN HERO

THE NAME HRBEK MEANT NOTHING TO ME when my friend George Thomas, the University of Minnesota assistant baseball coach, called me in late June 1978. I made a practice of scouring the sports pages daily, but there wasn't much mention of this big kid from Bloomington, and when his name was printed, one could only assume it was either an abbreviation or a typographical error.

On that fateful day in '78, Thomas explained that Kent Hrbek was an outstanding first baseman on the Bloomington Kennedy High School baseball team in suburban Minneapolis, and that Hrbek had been drafted in the 17th round of the June 1978 draft by the Minnesota Twins. He also told me that Kent had accepted the University of Minnesota's offer of a full baseball scholarship. Thomas indicated that Hrbek was having a difficult time making a decision between college and turning pro. He'd recommended that Hrbek and his father, Ed, seek my advice. I told Thomas that I would be happy to meet with the Hrbeks to discuss the matter, but wondered aloud why I would possibly want to represent a 17th-round draft choice.

Thomas said, "Because, in my opinion, Hrbek could be another Winfield or Molitor." Both players were already stars in the majors.

It was hard for me to equate this vowel-wanting young man with Winfield and Molitor. Hrbek had been overlooked by each of the 26 major league clubs in the draft on each of the first 16 rounds. At least 416 players had been selected ahead of him.

Knowing that only about six out of every 100 players who sign pro contracts ever make it to the major leagues, and that only one out of every 10,000 high school athletes ever plays in the pros, Hrbek's odds of "making it" were extremely slim. But I had a great deal of respect for Thomas's judgment. I agreed to see the Hrbeks.

A few days later, the 18-year-old, 6'4", 220-lb. Hrbek lumbered into my office for the first time. Hrbek was born and raised in the shadow of Met Stadium, the Twins' old outdoor ballpark in Bloomington. He could see the stadium lights from his house. He used to go to night games because he could get in for a buck. He was pretty happy to have been drafted by the hometown team. Accompanying him to my office for this first meeting were his father Ed Hrbek, a 49-year-old employee of Minnegasco, and Thomas. After a few minutes of polite conversation Thomas left, never to return. The Hrbek meeting was to be the first step in what turned out to be one of the most gratifying personal and professional relationships I have had.

It took me only a few minutes to realize that Hrbek's first love was baseball and that he really wanted to play professionally. He would have attended college only as a step towards big league baseball. But there was serious doubt about whether I could negotiate the significant signing bonus that would make it worthwhile for Kent to turn pro immediately. If he opted for college, he would not be eligible for the draft again for three years. I was doubly pessimistic because, under the ownership of the penurious Calvin Griffith, the Twins had a reputation for being particularly stingy. Their standard bonus for a 17th-round draft choice was about $1,000.

Hrbek provides us with a case study in the inexact science of baseball scouting. At this hour he's a former All Star, a two-time World Champion, and one of the highest-paid players in Twins history. But he'd probably be just another aging, overweight guy with nothing more than high school stories of glory days if not for the observations and persistence of a man who worked in the Twins concession department. Clyde "Smoke" Teawalt lived in Bloomington and worked under Calvin Griffith's brother, Jimmy Robertson, when the Twins were playing at the old Metropolitan Stadium. Smoke spotted Hrbek's talent while watching his own son play against Hrbek in high school competition. The pro scouts had shown no great interest in Kent, but a month or two before the draft, Smoke persuaded Robertson and brother Calvin to come to the next game to see the big slugger. They liked what they saw. Calvin through the years has been the subject of much ridicule, but he knows baseball talent.

"I saw him swing that bat," Griffith remembered. "I said, 'Hell, he's got power.' That was it. You had to like him, the way he hit the ball."

After Hrbek was drafted, Smoke Teawalt and veteran scout Angelo Giuliani followed Hrbek like process servers. They lobbied management almost daily, pressing them to sign the local prospect. Hrbek's bargaining position was weak and the scholarship offer was attractive. I agreed to represent the Hrbeks, but the relationship had to be concealed to avoid conflict with the NCAA rule providing for loss of college eligibility for student-athletes who hire agents. If Hrbek lost his eligibility, he lost any possible leverage he would have in negotiations with the Twins because he would have lost the alternative of attending college. In late June, the Twins offered a signing bonus of $5,000, which was rejected. As the negotiations progressed during the late summer, I was amazed that the Twins had increased the signing bonus offer to $20,000. In early September, I came out of the closet to personally meet at the Twins' offices with Calvin Griffith's son, Clark, the Twins' negotiator.

Clark Griffith was 36 years old and, unlike his father who attended college only briefly, Clark was a 1966 graduate of Dartmouth College, New Hampshire. When I walked into his office with the Hrbek file under my arm, Clark said, "What's a big-shot downtown attorney like you doing representing a 17th-round draft choice?" The $30,000 signing bonus we finally agreed upon is no doubt one of the highest ever paid to a 17th rounder. My fee was only $500, but the time proved to be well spent.

Hrbek began his pro baseball career in the fall of 1978. In 1979 he played for Elizabethton in the Appalachian League (a Single A league, the lowest level), batting .203 with one home run. In his third year, 1981, he still was playing Single A baseball.

Life in the minors could be harsh. Players traveled to road games sometimes for many hours in hot, crowded buses. Salaries were meager, around $500 a month. Modest living accommodations usually had to be shared with several other players. Money was so scarce that Hrbek almost cried after dropping a dozen eggs on the floor in front of an angry teammate with whom he shared expenses.

In mid-August 1981, I was reading *The Sporting News* when I noticed an article about Hrbek. He was tearing up the California league. He was batting .379 with 27 home runs, 111 RBIs, and was leading the league in a number of categories. The Twins at the time had not yet found a replacement for Hall of Famer first baseman Rod Carew, who had defected to the California Angels as a free agent in 1979. The Twins were floundering near the American League West basement when Kent was called up to join them in New York City for a game against the Yankees. This was quite a leap. He was bypassing Double A and Triple A baseball.

Later that night, I turned on the TV set to watch Hrbek's big-league debut in Yankee Stadium. The game was tied at the top of the 12th inning when Hrbek strode to the plate. The Twins' pitching coach, Johnny Podres, had just told him, "Kid, it's getting late. I need a cocktail." Hrbek launched a long home run into the right-field bleachers, the same depository that received home-run balls off the bats of Yankee immortals Babe Ruth, Lou Gehrig, Roger Maris, and Mickey Mantle. Suddenly, George Thomas's prediction didn't seem so absurd. Hrbek was a major leaguer at the age of 21.

Hrbek is not the only late-round draft choice who has defied the odds to become a star in the major leagues. Consider some of the other superstars ignored during the 27-year history of the draft:

Nolan Ryan—10th round, 1965, Mets.
Dave Parker—14th round, 1970, Pirates.
Dave Stewart—16th round, 1975, Dodgers.
Andre Dawson—11th round, 1975, Expos.
Ryne Sandberg—20th round, 1978, Phillies
Don Mattingly—19th round, 1979, Yankees.
Orel Hershiser—17th round, 1979, Dodgers.
Jose Canseco—15th round, 1982, A's.
Bret Saberhagen—19th round, 1982, Royals.

Among the players who weren't drafted at all are Kevin Mitchell, Bobby Bonilla, Jeffrey Leonard, Frank White, Bruce Sutter, Jeff Reardon, Tom Herr, Bob Ojeda, Claudell Washington, Brian Downing, and Dan Quisenberry.

I wish I had been in New York with Kent when he made his major league debut. Sentiment isn't the only reason. Prior to the game, Howard Fox, Calvin's chief lieutenant, explained correctly that Kent could not play in the major leagues until he had signed a major league contract. Hrbek quickly signed the form contract placed in front of him. The contract provided that he would earn the customary minimum salary under his first contract, $33,500, for the balance of the 1981 season. In the heat of the moment, Fox had also slipped a second contract in front of Hrbek, one that covered the 1982 season at the same minimum major league salary. I discovered the 1982 contract when checking with the Twins in December about a new 1982 contract. Fox's trick was legal, but it was wrong. This is one of the reasons why young players need representation. Howard Fox would not have pulled this stunt if I had been in the room with Kent Hrbek that day.

In 1982, Kent's first full year in the major leagues, he finished second in balloting for Rookie of the Year. Hrbek was beaten by Baltimore shortstop Cal Ripken, Jr., a future MVP. Kent batted .301 with 92 RBIs, had a 23-game hitting streak, was the only rookie on the 1982 American League All Star Team, and made it all the way to the cover of *Sports Illustrated*. He did all of this despite playing with a heavy heart. During the 1982 season, Hrbek's father, Ed, died of A.L.S., or "Lou Gehrig's Disease," at age

53.

Kent and his father were close. It was a huge loss. In 1986, Kent and I started the Kent Hrbek Celebrity Golf Tournament to raise funds to help with the battle against "Lou Gehrig's Disease" in memory of his late father. Each year golfers pay a substantial fee to play with Twins players and other well-known local pro athletes during an open date in the baseball season. Kent Hrbek's wife, Jeanie, and my secretary run the tournament which since its inception has raised hundreds of thousands of dollars to help combat this dreaded disease. My close relationship with Kent developed as much from our common struggle to succeed in this endeavor as from our successful business relationship.

In the spring of 1983, we were not able to reach a contract agreement with the Twins, and since Hrbek had been playing in the major leagues less than two years, the ballclub exercised its right to renew Hrbek's contract at the club's own figure. Hrbek was paid $85,000, an amount lower than that paid to Cal Ripkin and the other top first-year players. Hrbek had no leverage because he was still a year away from arbitration rights. He accepted the situation, but both he and I resented the mistreatment. I've never understood why teams dig in like this with young players. It always costs the ballclub in the long haul.

In April, after the 1983 season had started, I received word that Mr. Griffith wanted to see Kent and me at his office in the Metrodome. I had only met Griffith casually in the past and was looking forward to getting acquainted with this legendary character. As Kent and I entered Calvin's office, I was impressed by the colorful baseball memorabilia that adorned the walls. There were pictures of Calvin and famous people from his days when the team was the Washington Senators before the move to Minnesota in 1961. There were pictures of Calvin with President Eisenhower and with Vice-Presidents Nixon and Humphrey. Other photos included Calvin with Billy Graham and with Ted Williams. But his most cherished items were Gold Glove awards given to him by former players Earl Battey and Jim Kaat, and a Silver Bat award given to him by Tony Oliva. Calvin and I negotiated a one-year contract for Kent for $110,000. This pact replaced the $85,000 contract unilaterally imposed in March. Kent and I were satisfied.

However, what stood out most in my mind from that meeting was not the negotiation of the contract or the impressive memorabilia, but the image of Griffith. The 66-year-old owner was overweight, disheveled, and he seldom smiled. He had a perpetual scowl on his face. He struck me as a tragic, pitiful figure, a man alone with his millions and his fame. He told us how pleased he was to be living in Edina (perhaps at that time the only suburb with cable TV), because his greatest pleasure was watching cable television each evening. At the time, Calvin was living alone, estranged from his wife, Natalie, from whom he was later divorced. His conflict with his only son, Clark, had escalated to the point where they were no longer talking. He was embittered by the rising baseball salaries and the resultant loss of his top stars to other clubs, whose owners (unlike Calvin) had successful businesses outside baseball to provide them and their families with large incomes. He complained that he could not survive the financial losses and was being driven from baseball, which was his life and the sole source of income for his family. I pictured him in his Edina home, sitting alone behind a television tray, eating dinner, and watching ballgames. It made me a little sad.

At the conclusion of the 1983 season, Hrbek had played more than two years in the major leagues and became eligible for salary arbitration. I was unable to reach agreement with the Twins on a new contract, and Hrbek and I flew to New York for the arbitration hearing. One hour before the scheduled hearing, Fox and I reached agreement on a salary of $375,000 for one year. This was cause for celebration. I suggested we include my brother, Howie, and a friend, Ahmad Rashad, who both lived in New York City. I recommended we have lunch at the world-famous "21 Club," a celebrity hangout with average food and extraordinary prices. Hrbek got stuck with the bill (about $275) for the one cocktail and hamburgers each of us had. Although Hrbek's salary is almost $3 million a year now, he still complains about how he got suckered into paying the bill.

Hrbek had one of his best years in 1984. He batted .311 with 27 homers and 107 RBIs and finished second to Tiger reliever Willie Hernandez in voting for the American League's Most Valuable Player award. We were in an excellent position to obtain a substantial raise either by agreement or through salary arbitration. The figure we submitted to salary arbitration was $1.1 million. The Twins' offer was $650,000. The difference was larger than any previous gap between clubs and players since arbitration began.

In previous contract negotiations, I always compared Hrbek to Cal Ripken, Jr., and Wade Boggs, because these three were the top players among the group that became major leaguers in 1982. Boggs, the perennial American League batting champion, was headed for arbitration at around the same date and was asking for $1 million. If Boggs won or settled above the mid-point before our hearing, our chances of winning would be improved. Of course, if he lost we were in trouble. I jockeyed to position our hearing date two days after Boggs's. Meanwhile, we kept talking and one day before the Boggs hearing was scheduled I was able to negotiate a five-year, guaranteed contract for approximately $6 million, but I couldn't find Kent to get his approval. I went ahead anyway. I later discovered he had escaped to the seclusion of an ice-fishing shack,

Scott Studwell of the Minnesota Vikings played more games than any linebacker in the history of the NFL other than Ted Hendricks. Thanks to a contract renegotiation, or in General Manager Mike Lynn's words, a contract "extension," Studwell earned more in his last two seasons of football than he had in the previous ten years put together.

On January 15, 1992, Minnesota Vikings' tight end Steve Jordan strolled into the Vikings' office to pick up his $100,000 "Super Bonus" for three consecutive years in the Pro Bowl. A fixture at tight end for Minnesota, he is one of the highest paid tight ends in the NFL.

Showing off a prize catch, I stand flanked by fishing buddies Dave Vriese and George Thomas. If Thomas hadn't dragged Paul Molitor and Kent Hrbek into my office years ago, I might not be a sports attorney today.

In 1992, after 15 years with the Milwaukee Brewers, Paul Molitor, my first $4-million man, bid a tearful farewell to the city, the teammates, and the fans that he loved. He was Toronto-bound. (Milwaukee Journal Photo)

Some general managers are difficult to deal with. The Twins' Andy McPhail, however, is a class act. Here we jointly announce Kent Hrbek's $14-million contract with the Twins in 1990. (AP Photo)

Jim Eisenreich is a living example of what perseverence can bring. Here he proudly displays the 1989 Kansas City Royals' MVP Award, which he won by beating out the likes of Bo Jackson.

Below: Nobody has ever accused Kent Hrbek of failing to appreciate good food and drink. Here we are in a Munich beer hall on a trip to Germany in 1990.

Kent Hrbek has used his hero status in Minnesota to help others. Here I am with my wife, Schatzi, Kent's wife, Jeannie, and Kent at the annual Hrbek Celebrity Golf Tournament, which Kent and I started in 1986 to raise money to combat A.L.S., the disease that took the life of Kent's father.

Paul Molitor became one of the Milwaukee Brewers' most popular and productive players. After the 1992 season, he and the legendary Willie Mays were the only players with a .300 average, over 300 steals, and more than 150 career home runs. (Milwaukee Journal Photo)

perfectly content to allow me to make the decisions. The headline in the Minneapolis *Star Tribune* the following day read: "Kent Hrbek, now a $6-million man." Hrbek had become by far the highest paid of any of the professional athletes ever associated with any team in Minnesota. Generally I am opposed to long-term contracts, but this one was guaranteed and likely to outstrip inflation, which it did, primarily due to club collusion on salaries.

The 1987 baseball season was one of everlasting joy for all fans of the Minnesota Twins. There would be another championship four years later, but the defining hours of the Twins franchise came when the Twins won the sixth and seventh games of the 1987 World Series in the Metrodome. Every Upper Midwesterner had a Homer Hankie, and the Twins were carried by thumpers named Kent Hrbek, Kirby Puckett, Gary Gaetti, and Tom Brunansky, plus pitchers Frank Viola, Bert Blyleven, and Jeff Reardon. The '87 Twins won the AL West, beat the Tigers in five games in the ALCS, then faced the St. Louis Cardinals in the World Series. It became the first World Series in which the home team won every game, and the din from the Dome still rings in the ears of those who were there.

I will always remember Game 6 in '87. St. Louis led the series three games to two. In the second inning the Twins were trailing when Hrbek was picked off second base. It seemed as if a hundred neighboring heads turned in unison with icy stares directed at my wife and me. I felt I was being held personally responsible for the miscue. Then, in the sixth inning with the bases loaded, Kent walked to the plate with the Twins leading six to five. He glanced upward and said, "Well, Pops, this one's for you." He crushed the first pitch for a grand slam. As pandemonium broke loose, these same neighbors deluged me with pats on the back and words of congratulations. For a brief moment I had the euphoric feeling that I had hit the ball. Hrbek later told me, "I was so ecstatic that I wanted to run around the bases a second time. In a matter of innings I went from the low point to the high point in my career."

It was that kind of year, the kind of year that would have made Kent's father very proud.

Hrbek managed to hang onto the ball he caught for the last out of the seventh game even through the wild celebration with his teammates in the field that followed. He later gave that ball, and the balls he caught for the final outs in the division-winning game in Texas and the American League championship game in Detroit, to his manager, Tom Kelly.

At the conclusion of the 1988 season, Hrbek had only one year left on his five-year contract, but in February 1989 the Twins began to show some interest in negotiating a new contract that would extend beyond the 1989 season. If Hrbek were allowed to complete the 1989 season without a new contract, he would have the right to become a free agent, the right to leave the Twins. Kent was eager to get a two-year extension for 1990 and 1991 before the 1989 season started. At Kent's urging, in mid-February, I submitted a two-year, $4-million proposal to Andy MacPhail, the Minnesota Twins general manager.

MacPhail, then only 38, comes from one of baseball's most famous families. His father, Lee, was the general manager of the Baltimore Orioles and the New York Yankees, and was president of the American League. His grandfather Larry was general manager of the Cincinnati Reds, and was part-owner of the Brooklyn Dodgers and the New York Yankees. Andy was assistant general manager of the Houston Astros from 1982 until he joined the Twins in August of 1985.

Andy looks more like a young college professor in his 20s than a baseball executive. He's highly intelligent, well organized, and logical when negotiating player contracts. He is firm but fair, and the discussions are always carried on at the highest level. He doesn't become excited or emotional, nor will he attack you personally as some of his colleagues are prone to do.

MacPhail indicated that he thought a two-year contract in the amount of $3.75 or $3.8 million would probably be approved by the club's owner, Carl Pohlad. Thus, we were only a couple of hundred thousand dollars (or 5 percent) apart at the beginning. It appeared that the matter could be concluded quickly and easily. Fortunately for Kent, it didn't happen. Less than 10 months later, I negotiated a five-year, guaranteed, $14-million contract for Kent with the Twins at the December baseball meetings. Although these numbers aren't mind-boggling now, at the end of 1989 the total amount of Hrbek's contract was second among all of major league baseball players only to pitcher Mark Langston, signed by the California Angels for five years at $16 million. In a *Sports Illustrated* article at that time about the big contract signings, a writer wrote, "If there was an MVA (Most Valuable Agent) for the meetings, it was probably Simon, the agent for Hrbek, the Twins' first baseman."

This is how it happened.

Hrbek's teammate Frank Viola, the Twins' ace pitcher and 1988 American League Cy Young Award winner, also a free agent at the end of the 1989 season, was engaged in contract negotiations. My preference was to await the outcome of the Viola negotiations in the hope that a megabuck contract would set a precedent for us. One day before the 1989 Home Opener, Viola's negotiations with the Twins broke down. MacPhail had offered a "take it or leave it," three-year contract for $7.9 million. Viola and his agent rejected the offer, and sharp words were exchanged. Upon the advice of his agent, Viola issued a statement to Twins' fans on Opening Day, thanking them for their support and kindness, but telling them he would not return after the season was over. He intended to test the free agent market. Viola and his agent claimed that the offer was "an insult." Predictably, Viola and his agent were portrayed as unreasonable and greedy. Public opinion was overwhelmingly on the side of the Twins.

One fan said, "The day Frank Viola can save a life (AIDS cure, cancer cure) is the day he's worth eight million." Another said, "At my present wage ($35,000 per year) it would take me 225.7 years to make what Frank Viola was offered."

Hrbek was mad. In the *Star Tribune* he said, "I always felt me and Frank were good friends. He was the best pitcher I ever saw on the mound, and it was great to play behind him, but if a guy on my team says before the start of the year that he doesn't want to play with us, he's not my idea of a team player."

Unfortunately for me, Hrbek also talked publicly about his own situation, saying, "I'm playing for the Twins next season. There is no doubt about that. There might be a minor difference in what they want to give me, but I'm not going to rape them and they aren't going to rape me. I'd feel lucky. I'm comfortable with my situation. I could be a jerk and say if this guy gets $80 then I deserve $75. But I'm happy with what they are paying me this year, and I will be next year. . . . I think I have a good relationship with the Twins, and I think they have a good relationship with me. Sure, I might lose a couple of dollars because I want to stay here, but I don't give a damn."

When I read those statements from Hrbek in the newspaper, I cringed. Hrbek had made it clear he was going to remain in Minnesota and money was not his primary concern. Now no other club would even waste its time making an offer to Hrbek after the season was over. Moreover, if any other club did make Hrbek a good offer, the Twins wouldn't take it seriously. Without a serious competing offer, I would have no alternative, and thus no leverage. Kent's refreshing honesty had placed me in a difficult position.

Although Hrbek was anxious for me to continue talks with the Twins, I had other ideas. As a result of the Molitor negotiations, which were occurring at the same time, I had recently developed a large dose of suspicion about seemingly generous offers from clubs. Moreover, it was obvious to me that MacPhail and Pohlad were in no mood to talk in the wake of the bitter Viola negotiations. (Viola signed, but was traded within the year.) The best time to talk is when your counterpart's mind is most likely to be open to your suggestions and ideas. MacPhail couldn't be expected to be in the right mood to talk contract when he was still smarting from the Viola experience. Unfortunately, MacPhail became even less interested in mid-May when Hrbek, diving for a ball, suffered an injury to his shoulder that disabled him until July. During that period, I had many sleepless nights thinking about the two-year, $3.75-million offer that I had insisted Kent pass up. Fortunately, Kent made a full recovery and played exceptionally well after his return.

Near the end of August, MacPhail's interest was revived after observing Hrbek's return to his previous form. By this time, a large number of top free-agents-to-be had already signed two- or three-year extensions through the 1991 and 1992 seasons. Top players comparable to Hrbek, including Howard Johnson, Von Hayes, Ozzie Smith, Alan Trammell, Lou Whitaker, Ryne Sandberg, Wade Boggs, and Dwight Gooden, had signed for $2 to $2.1 million a year. This pattern was unusual. Usually, free agents wait until their final season is completed and then test the free agent market. Apparently, this year the players and their agents had decided that the offers were too good to pass up. Although I was obviously swimming against the current, I was still waiting.

It seemed to me that an interesting situation could develop for Hrbek as a result of these signings. Unlike in previous years, there would now only be a few top unsigned free agents after the 1989 season: Robin Yount (Milwaukee outfielder), Nick Esasky (Boston first baseman), Ricky Henderson (Oakland outfielder), Mark Langston (Montreal pitcher), Mark Davis (San Diego pitcher), and Jeff Reardon (Minnesota pitcher) were the most prominent. I wanted Hrbek to join this elite group.

My hope was that if there was competitive bidding (no collusion) by the clubs for the few remaining free agents, the salaries could escalate dramatically. However, to placate Kent (who was eager to have the matter resolved), I went through the motions of meeting with MacPhail. I also raised the ante by demanding a third year. MacPhail balked at the new demand because of the club's concern about Hrbek's physical condition (primarily his weight) and his tendency to miss games because of injuries. MacPhail pointed out that while the years were going by, Hrbek each year was playing fewer games due to injuries. The GM believed that these injuries were due to his excessive weight and poor conditioning.

None will dispute that Hrbek at 6'4" and listed at 250 lbs. is overweight and an avowed "couch potato." Hrbek makes no bones about the fact that he doesn't like to run or engage in weight lifting or other extensive year-round conditioning exercises. He looks like a slo-pitch softball slugger, and he's been seen eating a Snickers bar while working on an exercise bike.

"No one on this team has a worse work ethic in warm-ups than I do," Hrbek admitted. "While the others are stretching, I'm hiding out on the runway."

Hrbek is a throwback to the great ballplayers of bygone years. He has a large appetite for good food and beverage. Although he is aware of references to him as "The Whale" and similar uncomplimentary descriptions, he has never made a serious effort to lose weight or to be in top condition. He has always told me: "I don't buy the complaints and criticism. I'm happy with my performance, I'm happy with the way I am, and that's good enough for me."

Kent is a realistic man with plenty of common sense, but he may have a blind spot when it comes to his weight. His performance is probably not now affected by his weight, but unlike Kent, I suspect that ultimately his career will be shortened.

Kent not only eats and drinks likes the old-timers, but while he is playing baseball, there is usually a pinch of snuff between his left lower lip and his teeth and a lump of leaf tobacco expanding his cheek. He said, "Sometimes I like to mix it with bubble gum. It gives it more texture."

After the 1989 season was finished, in early November 1989, MacPhail finally offered for the first time a three-year, guaranteed contract at an average of $2.1 million a year.

By this time, I was elevating my goal. In 1989, Kent had batted .272 with 25 home runs and 84 RBIs in 109 games. Through his career, he had a lifetime batting average of .290, with 201 home runs and 724 RBIs. Under the baseball rules, Kent could become a free agent after the baseball season, but only if he elected to do so in writing within two weeks after the end of the World Series. Kent was not interested in exercising this option because he wanted to remain with the Twins and he was very concerned about the adverse publicity that would follow such an election. He was particularly sensitive to the reaction following the Viola uproar. I knew that it would be impossible to get Hrbek a top contract if he did not opt for free agency. Without this election, he would have no right to contract with any other club, and thus we would have no alternative when negotiating but to sign with the Twins. The importance of finding an alternative cannot be overemphasized.

Hrbek and his wife, Jeanie, were about to leave town for a one-week cruise in the Caribbean when I urged Kent to authorize me to file the paper requesting free agency. I had to persuade him of its importance and promise him that I would handle the matter with the media with the greatest discretion and delicacy and that there would be no negative repercussions. I pointed out that he had taken the risk of playing a full season without a new contract, and now that he had survived the season without a disabling injury or a "bad year" he should take advantage of his free agent status. I also told him that if he allowed me to file for free agency, I would have the matter concluded by Christmas. I knew this would appeal to him. Because of the unpleasant nature of important negotiations, most people want them to be concluded quickly. This provides a big advantage to those of us who have infinite patience. At my urging, Hrbek reluctantly authorized me to file for free agency but warned me: "I don't want a Viola situation."

When Hrbek returned from his trip a week later, he was pleased to find there was no backlash or negative publicity following his filing. In mid-November, Hrbek kiddingly called the office and asked my assistant, "Am I still employed?"

Although Hrbek had filed for free agency on November 9, none of the other clubs were indicating any interest in him. I wasn't surprised, given his previous pronouncement that he would remain a Twin. I decided I would have to take steps to change this perception or Hrbek would have no choice but to accept the Twins' offer. I decided to take the offensive and contact some of the clubs that I had learned were in need of a first baseman, and I found in each case that the club was operating under the assumption that Hrbek had no desire to leave Minnesota. I assured each club that Hrbek would leave Minnesota if there was a significant disparity in the offers, but that if the offers were close, he would remain a Twin. I also made it known that the Twins' offer at this time was substantially below the fast-rising market.

Often it's necessary in negotiations to be very active in keeping the other side informed. The outlook for a successful conclusion is not promising if the other side does not have the information it needs, and you have to be aware of what the missing pieces might be and be ready to provide them.

In late November, Atlanta and Seattle were the first clubs to indicate an interest. Free agent players began to sign new contracts, some with their present teams and others with new clubs, but all in amounts larger than anyone had dreamed.

Hrbek's teammate Kirby Puckett, although not a free agent, had signed a new three-year, guaranteed contract with the Twins for $3 million a year. Puckett had just completed an incredible 1989 season, batting .339 with 45 doubles, 9 home runs, and 85 RBIs, and he was the first player in baseball history to make $3 million annually.

Kevin Bass, the Houston outfielder, signed with San Francisco for three years for $5.25 million; Nick Esasky, Boston's first baseman, signed with Atlanta for three years for $5.7 million; Bret Saberhagen, the star Kansas City Royals' pitcher, obtained a contract extension over three years from 1991 through 1993 at $8.9 million. Ricky Henderson, the Oakland superstar, signed a four-year, $12-million contract; Tony Pena, the St. Louis catcher, left for Boston for a three-year, $6.4-million contract; Bryn Smith, a pitcher from Montreal, signed a new three-year, $6-million contract with St. Louis; and Pascual Perez left Montreal to sign a new three-year contract for $5.7 million with New York several days after the Thanksgiving weekend. The free agent market was hot. Salaries were skyrocketing. My assessment had been correct, although I must admit, I certainly had not anticipated salaries would rise this high.

The new salaries were proof of the basic, simple concept I learned in Beginning Economics at the University of Minnesota about supply and demand. The supply of top free agent baseball players available to other clubs was small because so many potential free agents had signed prior to or during the 1989 season. Thus, there was greater demand for the few remaining top players, and as a result, the price had increased.

Through Jim Kaat, another client and friend, I learned that 36-year-old Keith Hernandez, who had been released by the Mets, had been offered approximately $2 million to play the following season for another club. If a player released by his club is worth $2 million to another club, what is Hrbek worth? This new information confirmed my suspicions that the market was rising to a new level. Any previous collusion among the clubs with respect to bidding for free agent players had disappeared. Moreover, the clubs were better able to afford the new player contracts because of their lucrative new television contract with CBS Sports and ESPN. Under those contracts, the TV revenue per club had increased from $7 to $14 million a year per club starting in 1990.

Bill LaJoie, Detroit's general manager, contacted me on November 28 inquiring about Kent's interest in leaving the Twins. I told him what I'd told everybody else, that Kent's strong preference was to remain with the Twins and if the Twins' offer was reasonably close to that of any other offer, Kent would opt to remain a Twin. However, I offered encouragement by explaining that at this point, the Twins' offer was clearly below the present market.

LaJoie asked, "What kind of contract are you looking for for Kent?"

I was in uncharted waters. No one had a feel of what the market was. It seemed that salaries were limitless. I desperately wanted to avoid making the first offer. I told LaJoie I had no proposal in mind, but would be receptive to an offer. LaJoie said he could go as high as $7 million–plus for three years. Had I been compelled to make the first proposal to him, I wouldn't have dared to ask for that much and the negotiations would have been botched.

This exchange is a terrific illustration of the importance of attempting to avoid making the first proposal. I told LaJoie I would get back to him, but two days later he called again to offer a $2.7-million-per-year contract for four years. He told me his owner, Tom Monaghan, the Domino's Pizza king, was serious and determined to build a winning baseball team. He certainly had my attention now. Twenty minutes later he called again, upping the offer to four years at $3 million a year before I could respond to the previous offer. I was stunned. I told him we would talk further at the December baseball winter meetings. I promised LaJoie confidentiality regarding the source of the offer.

The annual baseball winter meetings were scheduled for Nashville from December 2 to December 7. It was clear to me that this was the perfect setting for me to conduct and conclude my negotiations on behalf of Hrbek. I had been working on the Hrbek contract for ten months, but I sensed that the matter was now for the first time ripe for negotiation. I decided I would not leave Nashville without a contract for Kent Hrbek with some major league baseball club.

Before I left for Nashville, I met with Hrbek to talk about my plan. He emphasized again that he did not want the negotiations to become a repeat of the Viola situation. No acrimony. Hrbek loved Minnesota, the people, the fans, and the Twins. To hear Hrbek talk about it, you'd think he was the head of the local Chamber of Commerce. Hrbek would rather bowl and ice fish in the dead of a Minnesota winter than lie on a beach in sunny Florida. I remember once leaving a Minneapolis restaurant with him one winter day. As we walked out the door, we were greeted by a blast of arctic air. Hrbek's wife, Jeanie, remarked that she could hardly wait for spring training. Kent said, "The cold doesn't bother me. I guess I'm one of the few guys who loves it here in the winter!"

Kent Hrbek wanted to stay home.

As our meeting concluded, I was flabbergasted when Kent expressed concern that if I was too difficult with the Twins, the Twins would find another first baseman to replace him and he'd be out of a job. In fact, the Twins' alternative would have been the reserve first baseman Gene Larkin, who was coming off a horrible year, hitting .267 with only 6 home runs and 46 RBIs, or Paul Sorrento, the club's Triple A first baseman, a good prospect who was an excellent hitter but a poor fielder with concrete hands. For a player with his credentials, Kent was surprisingly insecure. It was the first time I had heard him express any doubts about his abilities.

I did not want to tarnish my credibility and integrity by misleading Detroit or any other interested clubs. I had to walk a thin line about Kent's reluctance to move. I arranged to meet with Andy MacPhail and his partner, Bob Gebhard, the Twins' vice-president of personnel, in Nashville on Saturday night, at which time I presented them with a brief, concise letter:

"Dear Andy:
Another major league baseball club has made an unsolicited offer to pay Kent Hrbek a guaranteed $3 million a year for four years. Kent wants to remain a Minnesota Twin if possible, and thus would accept a competitive offer from the Twins."

I was well acquainted with and had a high regard for MacPhail and Gebhard, so why the letter? Because so much was at stake. The letter served two purposes. First, the letter clearly and unequivocally set forth our position so there was no room for misunderstanding. It eliminated the possibility of ambiguity. Second, it insured that our position would be transmitted to the decision-maker, owner Carl Pohlad, without shading or equivocation by a nervous underling. MacPhail and Gebhard were stunned. If true, the Hrbek offer was the same $3 million per year given to the Twins' top player Kirby Puckett two weeks earlier, but in addition, was for four years rather than three.

I told MacPhail I couldn't tell him who had made the offer. He said the money was so large, it would be Pohlad's decision. He asked how Pohlad would know if I was being truthful. Good question. I offered to take a lie detector test. MacPhail and Pohlad apparently decided it was unnecessary and that they could rely on my credibility. Without credibility, the competing offers would have been of no value in negotiations with the Twins. Credibility can only be established by a reputation over the years for honesty, which is one reason why deceit or bluffs are poor negotiating practices in the long run.

On Monday, December 4, MacPhail offered a three-year contract at $2.7 million a year, a dramatic increase from the previous offer of $2.1 million a year. It was still a long way from Detroit's four-year, $3-million-a-year package, however. MacPhail and I had lunch together that day but did not talk business. We were both glum and agreed that it was unlikely that the Twins and Hrbek could reach an agreement that would be anywhere close to the competing offer. Pohlad was coming to town the following day and he would take over the negotiations.

A negotiator should always try to determine who will be making the decision on the other side. Once this is discovered, every effort should be made to hold talks directly with the decision-maker. Something is lost in the translation when your counterpart carries the message back to his boss.

A new development occurred that evening. I met with Seattle's general manager, Woody Woodward, and a principal owner, Jeff Smulyan, a young, aggressive Indianapolis businessman who was determined to build a winner in Seattle and had recently acquired the club for nearly $76 million. Much to my surprise, Seattle matched the Detroit offer of four years at $3 million a year. Now there were three bidders. I had an insurance policy.

Early Tuesday morning on December 5, I was invited to meet the Detroit people. General manager LaJoie was unable to attend the meetings, but the club's top executive, Jim Campbell, and its legendary manager, Sparky Anderson, were present. Detroit upped its offer to five years at $3.1 million a year, or $15.5 million. This contract would make Hrbek the second highest paid player in major league baseball, second only to Mark Langston, who had just signed a five-year, $3.2-million-a-year contract with the California Angels. Anderson was highly complimentary of Hrbek and pointed out that Hrbek and George Brett were the two best left-handed hitters he had ever seen in Detroit's baseball park.

Late that afternoon, I contacted Woodward of Seattle to advise him of the new five-year, $3.1-million-a-year offer. He upped the Seattle offer to five years at $3 million a year.

Up to this point, although there had been widespread coverage of the lavish salaries being offered to the few top free agents, no mention had ever been made of the Hrbek saga. I decided that the chances of meeting my goals would be enhanced if there was widespread media coverage of the bidding war that was taking place for Hrbek. Moreover, if the baseball fans in the Upper Midwest were made aware of the danger of losing Hrbek to a higher bidder, there would be pressure on Pohlad to make a competitive offer. I was somewhat handicapped, however, because of my intention to honor my pledge to keep the source of the competing offers confidential.

Jon Roe, a Minneapolis *Tribune* sportswriter, was covering the meetings from Nashville. Roe and I were long-time acquaintances who had mutual trust and respect for each other. I decided it was time to leak the details of the Hrbek saga, and I wanted Roe to have the "scoop" because of our past friendship but also because I presumed that the story would receive maximum coverage in Minnesota if he alone had the story. Hrbek was an extremely popular figure in Minnesota, a local-boy-made-good who drank beer, joined a winter bowling league, and loved to hunt and fish. Success had not spoiled him. Minnesota could relate to the "Big Guy."

The situation was great for Roe. He alone had the details on the Hrbek story, which began to receive national coverage. Sitting with me before lunch on Tuesday, it dawned on Roe that no other person had confirmed the veracity of the story. Finally, when his discomfort over this realization became too great, he asked cautiously, "Simon," he said, "there is honor among thieves, isn't there?" Jon and I were using each other to the fullest. He alone was writing about the details of the Hrbek negotiations to the exclusion of every other newspaper in the country. Now he wanted to know if I was telling him the truth or merely using him to enhance my negotiating position. I reassured him. The next day, the *Star Tribune* sports page headline was "Twins face a tough task retaining Hrbek."

The timing was perfect. On the day that Carl Pohlad was arriving in Nashville, the Minneapolis *Star Tribune* headlined a Hrbek story with "Hrbek eyeing market. Twins facing competition." The gist of the story was that Hrbek had substantially higher offers from two other clubs, that I had set a deadline for Wednesday, December

6, regarding a decision, and that if the Twins weren't reasonably competitive, Hrbek would sign with another club.

I set a Wednesday deadline because I wanted to strike while the iron was hot. With three mind-boggling offers, the situation was ideal, and I didn't want to run the risk that one or more of the clubs would withdraw.

If one sets a deadline, it must be done carefully and in a manner that seems to be reasonable to the various bidders. The deadline must be perceived as one that gives the bidders a fair and reasonable period of time in which to conclude the negotiations; otherwise, the deadline can easily be interpreted as an ultimatum. Ultimatums do not permit room for maneuvering or "face saving." An ultimatum produces a certain defiance on the part of the counterpart, which substantially reduces the likelihood of a successfully negotiated settlement. In the Hrbek instance, it was reasonable to set the deadline for this day, because Wednesday was the day most of the top officials from each of the clubs were leaving.

On Tuesday afternoon, December 5, I was taking a mid-afternoon nap in my underwear when suddenly I was awakened by a knock on the door. Half asleep, I groggily asked who was there. I thought I heard the response, "Carl Pohlad." I assumed it was one of the "wise guys" at the meetings playing a prank on me. More awake, I asked a second time. This time when Carl identified himself I recognized his voice.

I had met Carl before. My impression was that he was a very straightforward, likable person with a pleasant temperament, low-key and with a nice sense of humor. He didn't take himself too seriously, although he was listed by Forbes as the fifth wealthiest person in the state of Minnesota in 1990.

I had been waiting since Saturday to talk to Pohlad. I leaped to my feet and, without opening the door, asked Carl if he could return in five minutes. He indicated he would, and then I dashed into the bathroom and splashed some cold water on my face to accelerate the wake-up process. I wanted to feel and look wide awake and alert, and to remove the cobwebs from my brain. Carl probably would have been shocked if he had known how relaxed I was. Five minutes later when Carl knocked again, I was awake, dressed, and ready to receive him.

When Carl entered, he indicated he was staying in the room next door. There were 1,891 rooms in this hotel, the seventh largest in the country, and Carl Pohlad's room was right next to mine. My telephone was situated on a desk next to the wall separating our rooms. I was constantly involved in telephone conversations of a most sensitive nature with my office, Hrbek, Jon Roe, and other clubs. If the Twins had been privy to any of these conversations, it would be like playing poker with a person who saw every card in your hand. I was concerned that somehow Mr. Pohlad or other club representatives had devised a way to eavesdrop on these conversations. This was, of course, total nonsense, but nevertheless at the time I was worried. I was paranoid. After Pohlad left my room that day, I initiated important conversations regarding the Hrbek matter from the pay phone in the lobby. If I was called in the room, I wouldn't discuss important details with anyone. I even went to the lengths of devising code language when communicating with my secretary at my office. "Deep Throat" was the Detroit Tigers and "the other guy" was the Seattle Mariners.

Sitting in my hotel room, Pohlad expressed dismay and shock at the escalating baseball salaries. He complained that he had never been involved in a business before where he had so little control over runaway salaries. He appeared genuinely depressed about the Hrbek situation. He had an especially high regard for Kent, both as a player and as a person, and wanted to go the extra step to re-sign him, but from a business standpoint he couldn't justify a five-year, $15-million contract or anything close to it.

Carl indicated that he had purchased the Minnesota Twins baseball club five years earlier to save the club from being relocated to St. Petersburg, Florida. He said that although he had had great pleasure in owning the club, including the memorable World Series victory in 1987, it was not a good investment and was becoming worse by the day. He said most of the years he owned the club it had sustained losses and with the rising salaries, the losses would increase. He said that although many clubs were profitable, the clubs like the Twins in the smaller population markets with much smaller local TV revenue were losing money. He said he could not continue to sustain these losses. It was not good business.

I countered by explaining to Carl that I was not guilty of contributing to the rising salaries. I never took a gun into negotiations. My job was merely to do the best I could for my client. I indicated that if the Twins' offer was reasonably close to that of the competition, frankly Kent would opt for the Twins.

I also pointed out that Kent's market value had been supported not by one but by at least two other clubs, one of them from a smaller market than the Twin Cities, and that one could certainly argue that he should be paid his market value. I also argued that although the club may have sustained losses in most of the years Pohlad had owned it, that he had acquired the club five years earlier from the Griffith family for approximately $32 million and that, according to my research, the Seattle club had recently sold for $76 million and the Twins had a present market value in the neighborhood of $95 million. Thus, I indicated that his present "profit" on the purchase of the franchise had far exceeded the aggregate amount of the losses over the past five years. When Carl countered that $95 million was really theoretical and that he would never be able to sell the franchise for that amount, I politely disagreed.

On August 3, 1990 (eight months after our discussion), the major league base-ball offices announced that two new National League expansion franchises would soon be awarded, with the clubs to begin playing in 1993. The price of the expansion franchises? Ninety-five million. In addition, a new club would need $25 to $35 million for start-up costs and player salaries. If a new franchise with no players or other assets costs $95 million, the existing Minnesota Twins franchise should be worth at least that much. On August 6, 1990, the Montreal *Gazette* reported that a Miami group had offered $117.4 million for the Montreal Expos with the intention of moving the team to Miami. The offer was rejected because the owners wanted the club to remain in Montreal. It was reportedly sold several months later for $86 million to a group who promised to keep the club where it was. In 1993, *Financial World* magazine valued the Twins' franchise at $95 million.

In the hotel room, I informed Mr. Pohlad that earlier that morning, I had met with one of the bidding clubs, which had increased their offer from a four-year, $3-million-a-year contract to a five-year, $3.1-million-a-year contract. Thus, the total package "on the table" from one of the clubs was for five years, at a total of $15.5 million.

After much discussion, Pohlad implied that if Hrbek would accept the contract, the Twins would agree to pay him a shocking $3 million a year for four years. He shook his head in disbelief and said that if Hrbek accepted this contract offer, to be fair he would have to voluntarily add a fourth year at $3 million to Puckett's $3-million-per-year contract.

Pohlad was leaving for Minneapolis the following afternoon. I told him I intended to make a decision before he left. I also told him that the fifth year was extremely important to me because of Kent's age and his questionable physical condition. A guaranteed fifth year became critical.

That evening the annual Baseball Banquet, including a dinner and a program that featured the Oak Ridge Boys as the entertainment, was being held as the grand finale of the meetings. Each of the clubs had reserved a couple of round tables for ten to seat their personnel. Shortly before dinner, Pohlad indicated he would not be able to attend the banquet but urged me to join the Twins as his replacement. Under the circumstances, I was most reluctant to do so, but I didn't want to offend Pohlad, so I accepted.

I called Kent from the lobby pay phone to update him. By this point, Kent seemed numbed by the "boxcar" offers from the competing clubs and told me that he was leaving the matter entirely in my hands. It was solely my decision to make. He was relieved, however, that the matter was going to be concluded the following day because he was being swamped with telephone calls. The contract negotiations were dominating the sports news in the Twin Cities area, and it was difficult for him and his wife to leave their home. I gave him one final pep talk. I urged him to communicate with no one and to bear with me for one more day—24 hours. Above all, I didn't want him talking with any representative of the Twins. I feared that some caller could influence his decision at this sensitive stage in the negotiations. It was agreed between us that I would contact him the following day at approximately noon at a bowling alley. Of course. We were weighing offers of $15 million and Kent was going to be bowling.

That evening I arrived late to the banquet in the great ballroom. I finally located the two Twins' tables amidst the filled banquet hall. I observed there was only one unoccupied seat available—the one next to the Twins' manager, Tom Kelly. As I had expected, the situation was awkward. I was very uncomfortable. It had been a mistake to accept the invitation. I left early and returned to my room to touch base with my wife in Minneapolis. She described to me the furor in the Twin Cities area and said that the news was dominated by the Hrbek story.

I have made a number of difficult decisions during the course of my career, but it seemed as if this would be the most difficult of all. The decision would have a major impact upon the life of another person who was not only a client but also a close friend about whom I cared a great deal. It would also have a major impact upon the club and the community. I was a member of the Twin Cities community, as well as a great sports fan. I knew Kent Hrbek well, what he liked and what he disliked. I had a long-standing relationship with Andy MacPhail and Carl Pohlad. Hrbek had a strong preference to stay with the Minnesota Twins. One of his stronger suits was his loyalty. Yet, the additional year (the fifth year offered by Seattle and Detroit) at approximately $3 million a year was critical: Kent would be 33 years old at the end of the fourth season and, because of his weight and physical condition, if he wasn't under contract there was a strong possibility that he wouldn't be offered a new contract. As I anguished over the decision, I felt very lonely. I wished I could have had someone else to talk to about the matter. I finally decided that Kent was going to Detroit if the Twins didn't come up with the fifth year. I knew I wasn't going to win any popularity contests in Minnesota, but I had to call it the way I saw it. I had made the toughest decision of my life. Now, I could rest easy.

It was almost 11:00 P.M. when I was startled by a knock. When I opened the door, I found it was my dinner partner, Tom Kelly. I invited him in. "T.K." is a sincere, honest, no-nonsense man with sound values and good character. He said he would be brief. He knew the decision was forthcoming tomorrow.

T.K. began to tell me that Kent Hrbek had a unique opportunity. Kent was in a position to show the youth of America, who looked up to him, that his decision in this instance would not be based solely upon money but on more important factors like loyalty, and that Kent was willing to take less to stay where he belonged, where he would be happiest. In the middle of his comments, he broke down. He began to cry. He could talk no further. As he hurriedly walked from the room without further comment, I gave him a knowing nod.

I met with Pohlad for breakfast early Wednesday, but neither of us ate much. The hang-up of course was the fifth year. I broke the news to Pohlad that I had to have it. Later that morning, Pohlad and MacPhail came to my room to offer a compromise: a fifth year, conditional on Kent's performance during the fourth year. If Kent played in 100 games the fourth year, there would be a fifth year. This was progress, but I rejected the offer.

I contacted Kent at the bowling alley at noon. I updated him on the situation, but as usual, Kent's only response was, "You're the boss. You make the business decisions. I hit the fastballs." He told me that while he was bowling he couldn't be reached or disturbed, but that he would be back at his home about 4:00 P.M. and I could contact him then.

Pohlad was leaving for the airport in an hour, and Pohlad, MacPhail, and I decided to give it one last shot. Pohlad simply couldn't assume the risk of a fifth year unconditionally; I simply couldn't give up the opportunity for a guaranteed fifth year at over $3 million. I had only one remaining approach. MacPhail had left the room briefly to attend other business. I pointed out to Carl that if he didn't sign Hrbek, he would lose a valuable asset. On the other hand, if he signed Hrbek, even if it was a five-year contract, there was a strong likelihood that he could trade Hrbek and get a player of equal value in return. I pointed out that at least two clubs were willing to assume a five-year contract on Hrbek. My point was that he would be in a better position if he signed Hrbek with the right to trade him, because he could get something of equal value in return, than if he just let him go. Pohlad seemed persuaded by this argument but then correctly pointed out that my previous proposal included the right by Hrbek to veto any trades. Under his last contract, Hrbek could list 13 clubs to whom the Twins could not trade him. At that point, I decided to take a significant gamble.

For the first time, I agreed that Kent would waive his right to veto any trade, if he could exclude six of the other 25 teams from a trade during the term of the contract. Pohlad and I had found a way to break the impasse. The compromise would reduce Pohlad's risk because, at least for two years, Kent could be traded to 19 other clubs. After that, under baseball rules, Kent couldn't be traded because he would be a ten-year veteran with the last five years with the same club. I was willing to take the gamble that Kent wouldn't be traded in exchange for the fifth year of the contract and the opportunity to continue to play in his home town.

Three years later, I would have reason to be thankful that I had insisted on the fifth year in the contract. Coming off a successful season in 1991, when the Twins bested Atlanta in the World Series, in 1992, an injury-plagued Hrbek had his worst of 11 seasons. It would not have been a comfortable situation to be in had Hrbek's contract been for only four years.

After concluding the deal with the Twins, I personally visited briefly with Jim Campbell, president of the Detroit Tigers, and a few minutes later with Woody Woodward, the general manager of the Seattle Mariners. I expressed my appreciation to each and told them that although the Twins' offer did not equal their offers, it was reasonably close. I reminded them that I always had said Kent would remain with the Twins if their offer was "reasonably close." Both were disappointed but quite understanding. Campbell indicated he would have no objection if I disclosed that Detroit was one of the two serious bidders. It was my impression that Mr. Campbell wanted the Detroit fans to know that the club was making every effort to sign top players, which of course was true.

In the excitement, I had almost forgotten to call Hrbek. It was now approximately 4:00 P.M., the time Hrbek had said he would probably be home. When I called, all I got was his answering machine. I decided it was time to play some mischief on Hrbek. I merely left a message that I had called and had made a new deal for him—no details, no team, no terms, no explanation. I hoped he would get the message before he heard it on the radio or television.

Later in the day, I was in my room talking on the telephone when Hrbek tried to reach me. Hrbek later told me that the hotel receptionist had advised him that the line was busy. When Hrbek had asked if the phone call could be interrupted, the receptionist replied only if it was an emergency. Kent paused and said: "For me it's kind of an emergency."

Hrbek was thrilled. He had the giant long-term contract and he could stay home in Minnesota. The following morning, I returned to Minneapolis, where I was greeted by my wife, my secretary, Hrbek, and his wife, Jeanie. The celebration began. Corks popped and the champagne was flowing right at the gate as we greeted each other with hugs and kisses.

That day, while going through the mail, I noticed a note scrawled on the outside of an unopened envelope addressed to me. It said, "Thanks for keeping Kent a Twin—Mailman." I had never met the postman, but his sentiments expressed the feelings of most Minnesota fans.

The Hrbek contract was another example of the win/win situation. The Twins had re-signed their star first baseman to a contract for 10 percent less than the competing club's offer and with the right to trade him. Hrbek ended up staying where he wanted to, in Minnesota, with a five-year, $14-million-dollar contract, $10 million more than the two-year, $4-million-dollar contract he had been willing to accept nine months earlier. Although Detroit didn't end up with Hrbek, it was able to show its loyal fans that it was making every effort to sign top-flight players from other clubs and to build a winning franchise. After losing Hrbek, the Tigers signed a forgotten first baseman named Cecil Fielder who'd been hitting homers in Japan. In 1990, Fielder hit 51 home runs, the highest in the majors, and for three consecutive years (1990–92), he led the majors in RBIs.

MacPhail publicly thanked Hrbek for accepting $1.5 million less than was available elsewhere to remain with the Twins. Kent Hrbek was a hometown hero for accepting the Twins' contract of $14 million dollars. Only in America.

Randy Bush, the Twins' outfielder who started with the Twins in 1982 with Hrbek, approached me at Kent's surprise 30th birthday party in May of 1990 with a smile on his face and asked me a question to which he expected no answer: "I have asked Hrbek several times how he could land a contract with the Twins for a 'gizzilion dollars,' and have everyone in Minnesota thank him and think he's a hero for doing it. He always gives me the same answer: 'Ask Simon.'"

Homer Hankies and record decible sounds returned in 1991 as the Twins bested Atlanta in the World Series. The thrill for Hrbek was marred by the aftermath of an incident involving Hrbek and Atlanta Braves' outfielder Ron Gant.

In Game 2, Gant singled to left, rounded first base, and then scrambled back safely just ahead of the throw to Hrbek. Gant and Hrbek came into contact. Gant ended up off the base, Hrbek tagged him, and the umpire called Gant out. A furor followed with the irate Gant claiming that Hrbek had pushed him off the bag, while Hrbek and the umpire maintained that Gant was off the bag as a result of the collision. The incident caused a lot of fallout, and Hrbek, his mother, sister, and wife all received death threats from some nut case. This was no laughing matter. The family members were scared, and the FBI was called in. During the games in Atlanta, Jeanie Hrbek was always under surveillance by the FBI. Although Kent felt uneasy in Atlanta, he raised his arms in defiance when he was greeted with 50,000 boos following his introduction in the next game. Notoriety sometimes comes with a high price tag.

The 1992 season was a bummer for Kent. A dislocated left shoulder in spring training disabled him for a month. A few months later the season ended the way it began when Hrbek hurt his right shoulder in a home-plate collision in late August. He had shoulder surgery in mid-September. In the interim, Kent had his worst season in the majors, hitting .244 in 112 games with 15 home runs and 58 RBIs. To make matters worse, during the offseason when Kent and I met with Tom Kelly and Andy MacPhail at Andy's request, T.K. called Kent on the carpet for fading during the second half of the 1992 season, suggesting it was due to poor conditioning. During the offseason, Kent worked harder than ever before on his weight, conditioning, and rehabilitation of his shoulder following surgery. Kent is a fun-loving guy, and is one of the few athletes I have ever known who looks at baseball strictly as a game to be played for fun. Neither the 1992 season nor the following offseason were fun for Kent. If the game ceases to be fun, Kent will walk away from it regardless of how much money he leaves behind. He knows there are plenty of lakes and streams yet to be fished, and plenty of birds and deer to be hunted. Either way, this is one time that the long-term, guaranteed contract paid off.

10
DAN "MR. TEAM SPIRIT" GLADDEN

HIS GIVEN NAME IS CLINTON DANIEL GLADDEN III, which suggests high tea, impeccable grooming, trust funds, and Little Lord Fauntleroy.

Dan Gladden is none of the above. In a baseball locker room, his name is "Wrench," a name given to him by former Twins' teammate Kent Hrbek. Like an auto mechanic, Gladden gets dirty playing baseball. "Wrench" is his trademark. The license plate on Dan's car reads "WRENCH," and his wife proudly wears a gold medallion wrench given to her by Dan.

When Dan was six years old, while playing with some of his brothers and friends on a family outing, he chose the wrong way back to the family campsite. It was late afternoon on a cool November day, and young Dan was hopelessly lost in California's Portola State Park. He walked aimlessly for half an hour, then attempted to cross a creek by walking on some logs. He slipped and fell into the cold water, breaking his arm in the process. Cold, wet, scared, and hurting, he pushed on. He found a spot next to some big logs, where he curled up for the night. Meanwhile, his frantic family enlisted the help of the park rangers, who sent out a search party that included 75 prisoners from a nearby minimum security prison. In the morning one of the prisoners found Dan.

Dan Gladden is one tough guy. He is a survivor.

Gladden played college baseball at Fresno State College in Fresno, California. In

June 1979 he became eligible for the baseball draft. A Los Angeles Dodgers' scout told him that if he hadn't been taken by the 11th round, the Dodgers would draft him. Gladden made arrangements to track the draft at a college booster's office in Fresno. During the two and a half days the draft was conducted, Gladden listened and waited at the booster's office. Almost 700 players were picked, but Gladden's name was not called.

He shook off the disappointment and drove to Visalia for a tryout involving about 100 players. Two were selected. Not him. He went to a similar tryout at the Oakland Coliseum. More nothing. After several weeks, his booster friend talked with Bill Thompson, the general manager of the Single A Fresno Giants. Thompson agreed to give Gladden and another college player a look because of their local appeal. Each day for five days they took batting practice and infield grounders. Thompson asked Chili Davis, one of the Giants' blue-chip prospects, which of the two local players should be given a contract. Davis recommended Gladden. Davis has never let Gladden forget it.

Gladden, an infielder, was later asked by the Giants' general manager if he could play outfield. Gladden insisted that he could, although he had no clue how to play the position and had no outfielder's glove. Coincidentally, Chili had an extra glove in his personal inventory, which he gladly sold to Gladden for $20. To this day, Gladden still demands his money back from Davis.

Gladden defied the odds by making it to the San Francisco Giants. He got in a couple of games in 1983, played over half the 1984 season in the "bigs," and finally made the majors full time in 1985.

He was always a competitor, always combative. While playing for San Francisco, he and teammate Jeff Leonard raged in the batting cage before a game at Cincinnati. Their wives, who were close friends, were riding together in an automobile listening to the game on the radio when the fight was reported. After a brief moment of awkward silence, both women broke out laughing.

Gladden is a winner and a terrific teammate. He won't tolerate those who don't think "team" first. He was traded to the Twins after the 1986 season and became the regular left fielder for the World Champions of 1987. It was Gladden who got the Twins off to a great start in Game 1 of the World Series against the St. Louis Cardinals by hitting a grand slam that landed him on the cover of *Sports Illustrated*.

He's never lost his fire. During the 1988 season the Twins again were in the heat of a division pennant race. The Twins were losing to Boston's Roger Clemmons on a hot summer night at Fenway Park. In the top of the fifth, the Twins had narrowed the gap to 5–3, with two outs and runners on second and third. Manager Tom Kelly decided to pinch hit Kelvin Torve for second baseman Steve Lombardozzi. A disgusted Lombardozzi returned to the dugout where he angrily threw his helmet and bat toward the bat rack, grabbed his glove, and started heading for the club house. Gladden, sitting at the other end of the dugout, called out, "Hey, Lombo. Where are you going? Don't you think you should stick around and pull for your teammates to do well? We've got a chance to win this game." Lombo paid no heed, and continued his march.

The Twins later tied the game, but lost on a three-run homer by Todd Benzinger in the bottom of the ninth. When Gladden entered the club house, he saw Lombo sitting in the trainer's room showered and dressed in his street clothes, filing his fingernails. Gladden was really steamed. He confronted Lombo. "Hey, why didn't you stay and cheer on your teammates?" No response. A few minutes later, Kelly approached Gladden and said, "Hey, Dan, the Boss [GM Andy MacPhail] is flying back with us tonight. Don't make a scene." Dan obliged.

The following morning when Dan responded to a knock at his door, he was surprised to find Lombo standing there. When Dan asked Lombo what he wanted, he was told to step outside. They went at it. Lombo got the worst of the brawl and ended up with a black eye and a banged-up face. Gladden had a broken finger. Dan shrugged off the injury and ended up with two hits that night.

Gladden had such a thirst for victory that when he was in my office before the 1991 season started, he said he would offer Hrbek $25,000 out of his own pocket if Hrbek would peel off some poundage and keep it off during the season. I admired Dan's team spirit but didn't want to be the messenger carrying the offer to Kent. Gladden contacted Kent directly and offered him $25,000 if he checked in at spring training at 230 lbs. or less. When Hrbek declined, Gladden persisted. "I'll pay you $25,000 if you come in at 235 lbs. or less, and you pay me $1,000 for each pound over 235 you weigh each month of the season." Hrbek wouldn't go for it.

Gladden used several agents earlier in his career, but always he was disappointed. He decided to represent himself before the 1990 season, and shortly before the 1989 season ended worked with MacPhail on a two-year contract that would pay him $650,000 in 1990 and $1.05 million in 1991. Unfortunately, Dan's timing was off. The market began to increase dramatically two months after he made the deal. Kirby Puckett became baseball's first $3-million man with a three-year contract for $9 million. It was the start of a new wave of salary escalation. Dan decided to hire someone else to represent him the next time around.

Gladden approached me, and in 1990 we set up a December meeting at a local bar/restaurant to discuss my possible handling of negotiations for his next contract. I walked in about 10 minutes late, looked around, but there were no signs of Gladden.

The only person I spotted was a blond with shoulder-length hair sitting alone at the bar. After sitting 20 minutes on a bench waiting for Dan to appear, I decided to call his home. His wife, Janice, assured me that Dan had left on schedule. As I stepped back into the waiting area I saw Gladden stepping down from the bar stool—the same stool I thought had been occupied by a blond lady. I decided it was best not to mention this to Dan.

Gladden is strong-willed and says what he thinks. He wanted to remain a Minnesota Twin. He really liked the team, the players, and the fans. His wife and family loved the area. Dan would be a free agent at the end of the 1991 season, but he didn't leave me many options. If you don't have options, you don't have leverage. If you don't have leverage, you don't get as good a contract.

The 1991 season was going to be a critical one for Gladden, especially since he would turn 35 a year later. Unfortunately, his batting average dipped to .247, 25 points below his lifetime average, and his power numbers were down. Hrbek made a good case for his teammate: "Gladden is probably the best fielding left fielder I have ever played with, even though he doesn't have the strongest arm. But when it comes to 'crunch time', he is the man who makes it happen."

For Gladden and the Twins, crunch time came in the bottom of the tenth inning in the seventh game of the 1991 World Series between the Twins and Atlanta Braves. Gladden led off with a "broken bat" short fly ball to left center field that dropped in for a hit. To everyone's surprise, Gladden tried to stretch the single into a double and slid into second safely. A few minutes later, he was perched on third with one out and the bases loaded. He scored the winning run on a Gene Larkin fly ball over the head of a drawn-in left fielder.

I asked Dan, "When did you decide to stretch the single into a double?" He said, "I was going for two all the way. You have to go full blast towards second from the minute you hit the ball. You can't wait to see if you're going to make it or where the ball is. The first base coach doesn't give you a signal one way or the other. You're on your own."

Regardless of Gladden's big-game potential and intangible values, when I talked with MacPhail in late November 1991, he candidly told me that the club intended to go with Pedro Munoz, a good young prospect, as their regular left fielder. If Gladden was willing to accept a reduced role as a defensive specialist at a commensurate salary for a one-year contract, MacPhail said he would be happy to discuss the matter further.

So far, not so good. Gladden wanted to play regularly and only for the Twins; the Twins wanted to use him as a defensive specialist and cut his $1.05-million salary substantially. It didn't sound like a good match to me.

Gladden filed for free agency. MacPhail made it absolutely clear to me that the club was not going to offer him salary arbitration. This made perfect sense, because an arbitrator would almost certainly give Gladden a raise in salary. An award would be based in part on his performance last season and over his career, but other criteria would include the Twins' record and their attendance. Of course, the Twins won the World Series and their attendance record was the second highest in club history. The Twins would lose their right to pick up a draft choice as compensation if Gladden signed elsewhere, but since Dan was only a C-rated player, the lost draft pick would be between the second and third round, not a first-rounder. The Twins wanted to halve his pay, commensurate with their plan to reduce his playing time.

In early December, when I talked specifics with MacPhail, he told me the best he could do for Gladden would be a one-year contract at $550,000, plus some performance bonuses based on games started. Of course, there was no plan to start Gladden, so these bonuses would likely not be attainable.

I was in Minneapolis facing a serious dilemma. If December 7 came and went without a salary arbitration offer by the club as MacPhail promised, Gladden's days as a Minnesota Twin would be over. His heart was set on staying with the Twins, but neither of us was willing to accept a one-year contract with a 50-percent pay cut. If salary arbitration was offered and Gladden didn't accept by the December 19 deadline, he could nevertheless agree to terms with the Twins on or before January 8.

I have known MacPhail for a long time. There was no doubt in my mind that when he said "no salary arbitration," he meant it. I was really under the gun. I had only a few days left to make a deal with the Twins. The club wouldn't budge, and my man was off in Hawaii at a meeting of player reps and union officials. After giving the matter some thought, I finally came up with an idea that might work for both the Twins and Gladden. Two days before the deadline, I contacted MacPhail and proposed that the club formally offer Gladden salary arbitration on condition that Gladden promised on the QT not to accept the offer. MacPhail and I trusted each other and agreed—subject to Gladden's approval.

The scheme would give both sides another month in which to assess the situation and try to work something out. If the arbitration offer wasn't made, the club would get no draft pick if Gladden signed elsewhere, and Gladden couldn't re-sign with the Twins. It was another case of teaching the horse to fly. I was trying to buy time, but I also knew we'd benefit from the appearance of salary arbitration for Dan with the Twins. If some other club did become interested in Gladden between December 7 and the December 19 deadline, it would be pressured to quickly come forward with an offer before Gladden accepted salary arbitration. Only the Twins would know Dan had already rejected the offer.

I called Gladden in Hawaii, eager to tell him about my innovative agreement with MacPhail. I presumed his approval would be a mere formality, but after giving it some thought he told me that he was not in favor of the idea. I was stunned. Gladden explained that he was convinced that MacPhail would offer salary arbitration.

I had to talk sense into Dan and it wasn't easy. He was getting bad advice from a member of the Players Association who misunderstood a rule regarding draft-choice compensation. It is important not to play the game unless you know and understand all of the rules—knowledge of obscure regulations can be the difference between success and failure. I told the individual in question to butt out, then talked to Dan's wife and encouraged her to have Dan trust my judgment. We wore him down, and finally Dan approved the strategy. I couriered a letter to MacPhail indicating that if the club offered salary arbitration, Gladden would reject it. The following day, the Minnesota Twins offered salary arbitration to Dan Gladden. To outsiders, it appeared that Gladden had until December 19 to accept or reject the offer.

I contacted a number of general managers by telephone, selecting the clubs that seemed to me would have the greatest need for Gladden. Among them was Detroit's GM Jerry Walker, who indicated he would be talking with his people in the next day or two. He seemed interested.

Now it was time for me to pack my bags and head to Miami Beach for baseball's annual winter meetings. I needed to be where the action was if I wanted to make something good happen for Gladden. After my arrival, I telephoned representatives of clubs that might have an interest in Gladden. Unfortunately, no one was breaking down my door to sign him. Gladden, a man of his own strong convictions and ideas and not one to sit idly by, was drowning me with a steady flow of ideas about which clubs I should contact. I still considered Detroit a possibility. The club's top outfielders the past season had been Rob Deer, Milt Cuyler, Pete Incaviglia, and Lloyd Moseby. Moseby and Incaviglia were free agents whom the Tigers apparently had no interest in re-signing. Tony Phillips, an excellent utility player who also played the outfield, was more valuable as an infielder. Gladden's great attitude and aggressive style of play could be appealing to Tigers' manager Sparky Anderson.

Since I hadn't heard back from Walker, I decided to phone Anderson. I caught him as he was on his way out the door. I dropped Gladden's name, and he immediately warmed to the idea. He said he would talk with Walker, who made these decisions. I had a hunch that Sparky had a lot of input, too. Walker contacted me the next day and agreed to give me an audience. The meeting went well. As we parted, he said that he would get back to me with a definite proposal the following day. I never heard from

Walker. The rumor mill had Detroit pursuing free agent outfielder Dave Winfield. I bumped into Walker in the lobby a couple of days later, but he barely acknowledged me. I left Miami with a nice tan but no deal.

Gladden was a good player, but he was turning 35, coming off a so-so season, and because of the rising salaries many of the clubs were going with younger players. Some of the GMs told me they liked Gladden very much, but their club was set in the outfield. Some were being polite; others were turned off when I mentioned a $1-million contract. I returned to my office on December 12. Often, free agent players and clubs cut deals on new contracts on or immediately before December 19 because it is the deadline for player acceptance of club salary arbitration offers. Accordingly, I had planned a family trip with my wife, son, and daughter for one week on the island of Aruba starting December 20.

It was around this time, as word leaked out that Gladden might not be returning, that I was surprised to discover a spontaneous groundswell of support to keep Dan a Twin. In many ways, Gladden was not merely a ballplayer but a part of the soul of the club. His intense competitiveness made him the people's choice, from the lunch-bucket crowd to the highbrows. The local media created a stir on his behalf, but so did ordinary fans. I found myself being approached in elevators and on the street by strangers who valued his intelligent and aggressive style of play, and who wanted him to stay in Minnesota. I decided that if all else failed, Dan's popularity could help to influence the Twins' decision.

Waiting for a possible last-minute telephone call from Walker was difficult. However, for me to call Walker to force the negotiations would have been a mistake. Making the first move in situations like this may satisfy your curiosity, but it's harmful. It signals to the other side that you are eager to make a deal and probably have no other good alternatives. The more you push, the weaker your bargaining position becomes and the more the other party backs off. I bit my lip, and waited and hoped. I was helpless to do anything else.

December 19 arrived without any word from Walker or anyone else. According to news reports, Detroit was still pursuing Winfield. The following morning I was leaving town, and the baseball world would know that Dan Gladden had not accepted salary arbitration. Our cover would be blown. Any club interested in Gladden would know that Gladden had lost his leverage with the Twins and would quickly figure out that the Twins' offer would likely be substantially less than the sum an arbitrator would have awarded.

I was at my office late in the afternoon tying up some loose ends in preparation for my vacation. Suddenly, out of the blue came the long-awaited telephone call from

Jerry Walker. He explained, "I didn't get back to you because our group decided to pursue Dave Winfield. Thirty minutes ago I was informed Winfield decided to sign with Toronto. We'd like to sign Dan Gladden before the salary arbitration deadline."

Good negotiators not only assess the strengths and weaknesses of their own position but should also attempt to evaluate their adversary's position as well. The leverage pendulum is determined by the comparative strength or weakness of both. For example, you may have greater leverage either because the other party is unaware of your weak position or because they believe you are aware of their position of weakness.

In this situation, Gladden had no offers from any other club and in a few hours it would be clear that he had no right to salary arbitration and thus any leverage with the Twins was out the window. But Walker was not aware of my weak position because it appeared that Dan had the right to accept salary arbitration, and Walker was in the dark about any other offers I may have had. I also surmised that Walker and Detroit fans had to be disappointed about the last-minute loss of Winfield to Toronto. In addition, there were only a few top free agent outfielders that year, and several (including Otis Nixon and Dan Pasqua) had already re-signed with their clubs, leaving slim pickings. I concluded that Walker was dealing from a position of weakness. On the basis of outward appearances, Walker probably figured he could pry Gladden away from Minnesota only if he offered the 35-year-old a guaranteed, two-year contract for at least as much as the amount of an arbitration award for Gladden for one year.

When Walker asked me about my position on the term of the contract, I was prepared. I confidently asked for a guaranteed, two-year contract. Walker agreed, and after a couple of telephone calls in which we exchanged offers and counteroffers, we settled on a guaranteed, two-year contract for $1.05 million for 1992 and $1.15 million for 1993. The much larger contract and the opportunity to play regularly for Detroit outweighed Dan's strong desire to remain a Twin.

But wait—the ecstatic Gladden wanted one minor concession: an exception to Sparky's policy against long hair. Forget it, Dan! I wasn't going to press my luck. The contract was four times the Twins' offer and it was also guaranteed. As far as I was concerned, if Sparky wanted him to shave his head, he'd shave his head.

The day after Dan agreed to terms with Detroit, he talked with Sparky. Sparky told Dan he had only one rule and that was that the players had to be "sharp upstairs." Gladden got the message, but he wasn't happy. The day before he was to report for 1992 spring training, he had his hair cut short by his Minneapolis hairstylist, Shelly Young. Shelly put some of Dan's hair in an envelope and wrote a note to Sparky: "Dear Sparky: My name is Shelly Young, and I am Dan Gladden's barber. I have cut his hair short, but he has a difficult time allowing other people to cut it for him. If the length of his hair is a problem for you, I will fly down and cut his hair again, but at the expense of the Detroit Tigers."

If the Twins had not offered salary arbitration pursuant to our agreement, Dan would have been a benchwarmer for the Twins with commensurate pay.

Gladden's teammate, reserve utility infielder Al Newman, was in the identical situation, but got a different result. As with Gladden, MacPhail was willing to offer Newman salary arbitration if Newman agreed to reject it. Newman didn't accept MacPhail's proposal. As a consequence, he was finished as a Twin and ended up with a contract with the Texas Rangers for only $175,000. The Twins had planned to offer Newman in excess of $300,000.

The morning after the contract was signed, I headed with my family to Aruba for the great escape. At a press conference that same morning, Gladden said his good-byes with a tinge of sadness. After five years that he described as "the five greatest years of my life" with the Twins, Dan walked away with two World Series rings.

It was hard to escape the news of Gladden's departure. In fact, it followed me out of the country. On the first morning of my vacation, I picked up a copy of *Aruba Today*, the island's small daily newspaper, only to find the back-page headline, "Detroit Gladdens Dan." The distance, in miles, from my client didn't separate me from either his triumph or his slight disappointment. The article noted that, despite the generous terms of his new contract with the Tigers, Gladden was upset about the Twins' emphasis on his declining statistics. "There is more to this game than statistics," he said. "You bring more to a club than just numbers." Sparky Anderson, and legions of devoted fans in Minnesota, couldn't have agreed more.

11

JIM EISENREICH AND A LESSON IN COURAGE

ON JANUARY 10, 1991, NEW ENGLAND'S BASE-
ball junkies gathered for a quick fix at the annual Boston Baseball Writers Association banquet. The evening marked the presentation of the first annual Tony Conigliaro Award for Courage and Determination to Overcome Adversity. Jim Eisenreich, the Kansas City Royals' outfielder, stepped to the podium to accept the award. Jim is one of my guys, and I was extremely proud of him.

Tony Conigliaro was born and raised in the Boston area, and realized a boyhood dream when he broke into the major leagues with the Red Sox in 1964 at the age of 19. In 1965, he slugged 32 homers to become the American League's youngest home-run champ. He was the youngest player in big-league history to hit 100 homers, but his life changed forever on the night of August 18, 1967, when he was beaned by a Jack Hamilton fastball. The pitch shattered Conigliaro's left cheekbone and left him legally blind in his left eye. He was never the same hitter and retired for good in 1975 after several aborted comebacks. He was working on a second career as a television sports-caster when he was struck by a massive heart attack in the winter of 1982. He slipped into a coma and never regained consciousness. He died in February of 1990.

Jim Eisenreich was born and raised in St. Cloud, a small town 50 miles from Minneapolis. He comes from a modest background. His father was a counselor at the St. Cloud reformatory for wayward juveniles. His mother was busy raising Jim, two older brothers, and a younger brother and sister. Somehow they made ends meet. Jim went to the local college, St. Cloud State, and in 1980 was drafted by the hometown Minnesota Twins. He's an avid fisherman and hunter, and he loves to play baseball. He's quiet and stoic. With his short answers—"Yep" and "Nope"—he reminds me of Gary Cooper. The major leagues have not changed him one bit.

The full Eisenreich story is far from over, but much of what has happened to Jim has never been told.

Up until the age of seven or eight, Jim's life was quite normal, but then he began experiencing eye tics. Sometimes, the rapid involuntary blinking lasted all day. A year or two later, he noticed that he was also making grunting and sniffling noises. It sounded as if he was clearing his throat. Constantly. Sometimes, the voice tics were loud. It was embarrassing. Jim's father took him aside and sternly questioned him about why he was making all these loud sounds. Jim broke into tears, explaining, "I don't know why I'm doing those things, but I can't help it." His father took him to see the family physician in St. Cloud, who told Jim's parents that their boy perhaps was hyperactive and looking for attention. He prescribed Valium. Poof! Like magic, all the tics stopped. So did everything else. Jim was so zonked out from the Valium that nothing twitched. He barely moved. The doctor wisely discontinued the Valium, and the tics returned.

When Jim was about 11, the blinking, head jerking, shoulder twitching, and strange sounds got worse. This time, his physician admitted him to the local hospital for evaluation. The first thing he said to the doctor was that he didn't like school "because the teacher gets mad at me" and the kids in school "didn't play with me too much because my head jerked all the time." A neurologist was called in to examine him and found nothing wrong. He diagnosed the problem as "nervous tics."

Jim ended up seeing a shrink on a weekly basis. At each session they would play darts and other fun games. More often than not, Jim won. After a number of months of "game playing," the doctor concluded there was nothing wrong with Jim's thought processes or with his concentration. He pulled Jim's father aside and said, "Maybe he'll outgrow it." By now Jim was marked as an oddball, and most of his neighbors and classmates wanted nothing to do with him. The one exception was a quiet, withdrawn neighbor named Mike Lauer, who became Jim's friend.

In addition to the tics, Jim began to develop some strange habits. He found himself touching every drawer in the kitchen to be sure it was completely closed. He always put his left shoe on before his right shoe. Whenever he was in an automobile, he made a point of observing the license plates of each of the cars on the road. He often had the urge to wash his hands. He couldn't control these impulses. Jim knew there was something wrong, but he was convinced he wasn't crazy.

Jim encountered difficulties at school. He had a short attention span. He sometimes overheard groups of girls in the halls talking about how weird he was. Boys in his class taunted and mimicked him. In junior high school, his uncontrollable grunting became so loud and so distracting that one teacher mercifully allowed him to observe the classes from a video room situated at the back of the classroom. During this same period, a football coach lashed out at him in front of the team, mocking Jim's mannerisms and yelling, "What is all this ugh, ugh, ugh?"

When Jim received the sacrament of Confirmation, he struggled to suppress the eye and voice tics during the hour and a half ceremony. It was a brutal inner battle and when the ceremony finally ended, Jim was soaked with sweat.

A particularly disturbing incident occurred one day in his early teens when Jim was playing ping-pong with his buddy Lauer in Lauer's basement. Suddenly, they were startled by a loud bang at the basement window. They looked up to see a group of his neighborhood "friends" pounding on the window while taunting and mimicking him. Jim was crushed. Today, when Jim-the-hometown-hero returns to St. Cloud, some of these same "friends" suck up to him. He has forgiven them, but the incident remains indelibly etched in his mind.

Like all young people in school, he underwent the usual school medical examinations and periodically trekked to the family doctor for a checkup. One school nurse who examined him used to say, "You've got the tremors." That was as close as anyone came to uncovering Jim's problem.

With no outside help from doctors, Jim accepted his condition. He maintained a positive attitude, while hoping and praying that the tics would go away. His true salvation was sports. He was a good athlete and the field of play neutralized some of his weaknesses. Most of his teammates accepted him. When Jim went to college, the skinny 140-pounder played junior varsity baseball his freshman year, and as he grew he developed into an outstanding hitter on the varsity squad. When he wasn't playing baseball, he was hunting or fishing with Lauer.

St. Cloud State was not exactly a pro baseball factory. Major league scouts needed help from Rand McNally to find the place. But on a tip from Jim's coach, Dennis Lorsung, veteran Twins' scout, Angelo Guiliani, decided to take the one-hour ride from Minneapolis. He liked what he saw, so he came back a few more times to watch Eisenreich play. Scouts judge baseball talent on the basis of five criteria: running, hitting, hitting with power, fielding, and throwing. Eisenreich did them all well. He was a complete player. In 1980, Minnesota drafted him in the 16th round.

Jim quickly grabbed the $2,000 signing bonus and was headed for Elizabethton, Tennessee, to join the Single A club for rookies. Jim was 21 and had never been away from home before. Early on, his new manager told his 25 wide-eyed rookies that only two, maybe three, on average, ever made it to the big leagues. Among his teammates, only Richard Yett pitched some for Minnesota and Cleveland, and catcher Jeff Reed was a backup catcher for Cincinnati and San Francisco. Jim ended up being voted the Most Valuable Player of the Year in the rookie league. Not bad for a 16th rounder. The next season, the Twins promoted him to their higher level Single A club at Wisconsin Rapids. He played so well that he was invited to spring training with the major league team in 1982. At age 21, he had made the jump all the way from Single A to the majors. He was elated.

His elation was short-lived. During spring training that year, when he would step up to the plate, ticking away, he sometimes observed manager Billy Gardner and pitching coach Johnny Podres trying to contain their laughter. Yet, Gardner recognized Jim's talent. "Eisie has the best stroke on the team," Gardner said then. "We're rushing him from Class A, but some guys don't need much time in the minor leagues. Al Kaline never played in the minors." Al Kaline and Jim Eisenreich mentioned together. Pretty impressive company for the rookie.

On Opening Day 1982, Jim Eisenreich was the starting center fielder. But unbeknownst to anyone except Jim, his tics had become more severe and frequent in recent months. The vocal tics continued, and now there was upper body twitching, and neck and shoulder twisting.

Despite the increasing tics, he was hitting .310 in 20 games, when on April 30 he began hyperventilating and twitching so severely out in center field that he had to be replaced in the fifth inning. The same scenario occurred in the next two home games. Then it was on to Fenway Park in Boston. When he took his position in center field, he was unmercifully heckled and mocked by some of the bleacher fans. The twitching and hyperventilation worsened. His body was jumping and moving visibly. The embarrassment became intolerable. He walked off the baseball field in the middle of the inning. He could take it no more. He wasn't angry with the fans. He was angry with himself because he couldn't control the tics.

The Twins moved on to Milwaukee. Jim was on the field for pregame batting practice, but didn't even make it to the cage before he suffered a repetition of the previous night. Back to the clubhouse he went. This time, however, he suddenly had difficulty breathing. It was a bad reaction to a medication the team physicians had prescribed for hyperventilation. His teammates had to rip his clothing off and he was rushed to a nearby hospital, accompanied by teammate Mickey Hatcher. At the hospital, Jim remembers being given two shots with a long needle to sedate him, but he was so hyperactive the medication didn't work well. After Eisenreich and Hatcher hailed a taxi to return to their hotel, the agitated Eisenreich kiddingly turned to the driver and said, "You probably think I'm going the wrong way."

Randy Bush, the Twins' reserve outfielder, was Eisenreich's roommate at the time. Bush, then also a rookie, recalled that the word from the Twins' officials was that Eisenreich's problem was stage fright. After those road games, he tried to reassure Eisenreich.

He said, "Jim, you can run, throw, hit. You can do it all. I can't do any of it. If you're nervous, I should be in a straight jacket. Just relax." Jim responded, "I don't want to go to the ballpark anymore. It's no fun."

The flight from Milwaukee to Minneapolis was horrible. The tics were uncontrollable. He thrashed about frantically. He wasn't playing in front of a large crowd, so the official explanation was that the latest bout was due to a fear of flying. At one time or another in the past week, his problem had been described as stage fright, a nervous disorder, an anxiety attack, a flying phobia, or a mental disorder. Take your pick. It was none of the above. Confused? Jim was frightened.

Upon his return, he was admitted to the psychiatric ward at a Minneapolis hospital where he was seen by a psychiatrist, psychologist, neurologist, psycho-pharmacologist, you name it. The psycho-pharmacologist, a psychiatrist who specializes in the effects of drugs on the mind and behavior, was called in as a consultant. He talked with Jim, examined him, and then said emphatically, "You have Tourette's Syndrome." When Jim questioned the diagnosis, the dogmatic doctor looked him in the eye and said, "I'm an expert. I wrote a book on the subject. I am certain you have Tourette's Syndrome." He was right. He recommended a medication called Haldol to help control the tics.

Jim was not devastated by the diagnosis. He had never heard of the disorder, but he was relieved. After a 16-year struggle, at least he had finally learned what his problem was. He wasn't crazy after all.

Tourette's Syndrome is a neurological disorder caused by a chemical imbalance in the brain. More than 200,000 people in the United States have it. It is characterized by multiple involuntary tic movements, the most common being eye blinking, shoulder shrugging, facial twitches, and head, arm, or leg jerking. In addition, the victims may be unable to control vocal sounds such as throat clearing, grunting, or sniffling. Some involuntarily utter obscenities. Often people mistakenly believe this occurs with all victims. Fortunately, Jim was not cursed with this problem. There is no cure for Tourette's Syndrome, but certain medications can control the tics. Sometimes there are major side effects from the drugs, including severe depression and drowsiness.

The tics increase under stress. They can sometimes be controlled for short periods but then become much more severe when later released. In addition, many of those suffering from Tourette's have a short concentration span and ritualistic or obsessive-compulsive behavior. This explained Jim's strange habits. Many undiagnosed victims have doubts about their sanity. Fortunately, Jim was not one of them.

The condition has commonly been misinterpreted to be a psychiatric problem. It is not. It is a physical disorder, genetic in origin.

Unfortunately, the treating doctor at the Minneapolis hospital wasn't completely convinced. His discharge diagnosis included "Adult Adjustment Disturbance" and "Anxiety Neurosis with Hyperventilation." Translation: This guy is upset, nervous, and breathing heavy. I don't know why, and I'm not sure the psycho-pharmacologist does either.

The doctor prescribed a medication, but not Haldol, the one most commonly used for Tourette's and the one that had been recommended by the psycho-pharmacologist. The Twins' medical staff weren't convinced either and sent him to a hypnotist. He was also placed on the disabled list.

Jim remained in Minneapolis that summer, hoping to return to baseball. He spent time going to doctors, getting biofeedback therapy, and seeing his hypnotist. Initially, the drugs helped control the tics but made Jim so drowsy he couldn't play baseball. The doctors recommended he cut back on the dosage, hoping his drowsiness would be reduced so he could resume his career. Unfortunately, after the cutback, the tics returned with a vengeance. When Jim attempted to drive from St. Cloud to Minneapolis for doctor visits, the tics were so severe that he was thrashing about uncontrollably in the car. Sometimes fearful motorists would pull off the road; others broke into laughter. Finally it reached a point where his father had to drive him to the city. It got so bad that he couldn't eat dinner at the table with his family, and he chose to eat alone in the basement. The twitching and hyperventilation had become so severe that the food was falling out of his mouth when he ate.

He was unable to rest, he was losing weight, and, as he described it, he was a "nervous wreck." He landed back in the psych ward in September 1982. At this point, his doctor unequivocally accepted the Tourette's Syndrome diagnosis and put him on Haldol. Jim began to improve, but the Twins' medical staff was not convinced.

Jim returned to the team in spring training 1983, refreshed and eager to play ball. The new medications were working better, but he still had some grogginess. When the curtain went up for the 1983 regular season, Eisenreich again was patrolling center field on Opening Day in the friendly confines of the Metrodome. However, during each of the first two games, he became so terrified that he would have to endure a repeat of the previous year's nightmare that he spontaneously began crying in the outfield. After those two games and a total of seven at bats in 1983, he retired. The club recommended he change hypnotists. He did. He had already seen five or six hypnotists and biofeedback therapists. Apparently all of them had the same goal: to relax the patient so that he was more responsive to the power of suggestion. The similarities ended here.

One hypnotist was convinced Jim's problems stemmed from a "negative birth experience." He suggested that Jim, a non-swimmer, be submerged in a large tank of water, breathing only through a snorkel tube, while he questioned Jim about his birth. Jim passed.

Another turned on strobe lights in a darkened room at the beginning of each session, and spent almost the entire 60 minutes of each session repeatedly telling Jim that he was a good player, he could play 15 more years, and make lots of money. Jim would sit quietly thinking, "What are you talking about? When are we done? I drove an hour and 15 minutes each way for this?"

In 1984, Eisenreich gave it another try. He returned to spring training with the Twins. The prescriptions were working better but he still wasn't quite right. He continued to tinker with the dosage. For the third straight year, on Opening Day he was the starting center fielder for the Twins. After a couple of games, Gardner inexplicably benched him. Jim couldn't believe it. Not now, not after the meds were starting to work. On May 8, the Twins called up a no-name player who had only played in 224 professional games in the minor leagues, and inserted him in center field. The replacement's name was Kirby Puckett. After two months, Jim had only played in 12 games with 32 at bats. Club officials wanted to send him down to the minors for more playing time. Eisenreich refused. "I'm ready to play here," he said. He was stubborn. It was a mistake, Eisenreich later admitted. He voluntarily retired on June 4, 1984. The headline in the Minneapolis morning *Star Tribune* the following day read, "Eisenreich leaves—this time for good."

He went home to St. Cloud and played amateur baseball or softball almost every night of the week during the summer. He worked part-time at an archery shop to keep busy and to earn a little spending money. He had plenty of time for fishing and bow hunting. A big evening on the town was hanging out at Sammy's Pizza Joint. He was comfortable, but the dream to play major league baseball did not die.

He was glad to be done with the doctors, shrinks, hypnotists, biofeedback, group therapy, and new medicines. After two years of experimenting with different dosages of Haldol, he found the right combination. The tics were under control and he wasn't groggy.

Several months before the 1985 spring training, Jim received a call from Twins' club president Howard Fox who asked him if he would come back but start in the minors. Eisenreich said he definitely would. He was excited, and he began to work out daily to get in shape. He had high hopes. But then a week before spring training started, another club official called him to tell him the Twins didn't have any plans for him. Fox had been overruled. This happened again in 1986. Jim was crushed.

His break came in 1986 when a college teammate and friend from St. Cloud named Bob Hegman was hired by the Kansas City Royals for a front-office job after playing seven years in their minor league system. Hegman heard from his parents in St. Cloud that Jim was batting a scorching .625 for the St. Cloud Beaudreau Bar team in a State Amateur League. Hegman checked it out, then he and Eisenreich talked on the phone, and Jim indicated an interest in trying pro baseball again. Hegman told Jim that he could not talk with Jim about an employment opportunity until he had been released. While Eisenreich asked for his release from the Twins, Hegman went to Royals' GM John Schuerholz and recommended that the Royals sign Eisenreich.

Eisenreich headed off for the Twin Cities in late September carrying a letter requesting his release. When he arrived at the Metrodome he delivered the letter personally to the new general manager, Andy MacPhail. The Twins released him. Twenty-four other teams passed on him, and the Royals signed Eisenreich for one dollar. It may have been the best dollar the Kansas City Royals ever spent.

In 1987 Jim started the season in Kansas City's Double A Memphis farm club and burned up the league, hitting .382 in 70 games. By the middle of the season, he was back in the "bigs." He finished the year with the Royals. While his rookie teammates from 1982—Hrbek, Laudner, Gaetti, Brunansky, Viola, and Bush—danced on the Metrodome floor as World Series champs in October of 1987, Jim felt happier than any of them. He was back in the major leagues living his dream.

Prior to the 1988 season, Eisenreich asked me to represent him. During the meeting, I asked him about his "nervous disorder." He quickly pointed out it was a neurological disorder and one that had nothing to do with nervousness. It's an important distinction and I had made the same mistake as so many other people.

In 1989, Eisenreich played the full year for Kansas City, batted .293 with 33 doubles, 27 stolen bases, 59 RBIs, and played excellent defense. He was named the Royals Player of the Year over George Brett and Bo Jackson. However, being named the Royals' MVP in 1989 was only the second best thing that happened to him that year.

When I asked Jim what was the best thing that ever happened to him in his life, he didn't hesitate for a second. "My wife and my daughter."

In his entire life, Jim had one or two dates before he met Leann. He wanted to date, but there had been too much rejection. He couldn't help but remember how the school girls had shunned him in his youth. In this instance, however, a friend of a friend had lined up a blind date for lunch in June 1989. Leann, a 21-year-old native of Kansas City, didn't follow professional baseball and had never heard of Eisenreich. She was a college graduate with a degree in accounting and was also a competitive roller skater. When Leann's friend explained that Eisenreich was a professional baseball player, Leann decided to scope him out the next time the Royals were on TV.

When Jim and Leann parted after their lunch date, Jim gave her his telephone number and asked her to call him if she was interested in seeing him again. A clever move for a person who had suffered enough rejection for two lifetimes already. He later said, "After lunch I was a nervous wreck. More nervous than I had ever been in any baseball game."

During the lunch, Leann noticed Jim's hands were shaking through the entire meal. When Leann reported back to the matchmaker she said, "He was very sweet and wasn't arrogant like many ballplayers, but the guy was so nervous he shook like my grandpa." The matchmaker responded, "Haven't you read the articles in the newspapers about Jim Eisenreich and his Tourette's Syndrome?" Leann had not, but she began to read up on Tourette's Syndrome.

After a couple of days passed without word from Leann, Jim could wait no longer. The hell with rejection, he had to find out if she was interested in seeing him again. He telephoned and left a message. Leann called back at 1:30 A.M. Yes, she was interested. Jim invited her to a baseball game. The romance blossomed, and they married during the 1990 season. Mike Lauer and Bob Hegman were there, and so was I. It was a very happy occasion. Jim even wore a tuxedo. The supreme sacrifice. Their daughter Lauren was born in May 1991.

Jim's miraculous comeback was not without financial reward, but the money didn't change him. In February 1990, Jim and I were in New York for salary arbitration and had just concluded an agreement with the Royals at the Waldorf Astoria Hotel on a $450,000 salary for the 1990 season. It was his first big payday, so we decided to celebrate at a fancy restaurant nearby. We swaggered in without a reservation. Eisenreich was clad in blue jeans and an old flannel shirt, and I was anything but dressed up. The maître d' winced but decided to accommodate us. During the long walk to our table, we caught disapproving glances from the well-dressed patrons. I turned to Jim with a sheepish grin and said, "You can't judge a book by its cover. Some of these people think we can't afford this place because we aren't wearing our dress clothes." Jim responded in earnest with a satisfied grin, "They'd really be upset if they knew these were my dress clothes." In 1991 his salary was up to $950,000.

From a financial standpoint, 1991 would be Jim's most important year. After this season, for the first time, he would be eligible for free agency. He started the season as the regular left fielder under manager John Wathan. Brian McRae patrolled center field and Danny Tartabull held down right field. George Brett was manning first base, and newly acquired free agent Kirk Gibson was the designated hitter. In mid-May, Wathan was fired and replaced by Hal McRae, a former Royals' great who had never been a manager before. At about the same time, Brett (age 39) was recovering from some nagging injuries, so he pushed to become the designated hitter, replacing Gibson. McRae was then forced to make a choice between Gibson and Eisenreich in left field. At the time, Eisenreich was hitting .300 and doing the job in the field. Gibson was struggling at the plate, playing ineffectively in the outfield, and suffering from persistent shoulder and knee injuries. Picked up by the Royals as a free agent at the beginning of the season, he had cost the club a lot of money. His two-year, guaranteed contract averaged $1.85 million a season and was sprinkled liberally with performance bonuses. Eisenreich was earning half the money.

McRae's choice should have been easy, but politics intervened. Much to everyone's surprise, he went with Gibson. At a private meeting at the end of the season, McRae explained that the front office didn't want to be embarrassed by benching Gibson after shelling out big bucks for him. Eisenreich had to take one for the team. Ouch. McRae added, "If it had been my decision, you know who would have been playing left field." Contrary to the popular belief of most sports fans, sometimes the best players aren't picked to play.

The Gibson decision didn't escape criticism from the pundits. It evoked this comment from USA Today baseball writer Mel Antonen on October 1, 1991: "Except for the huge financial free agent investment, it is difficult for me to see why Kansas City allows Kirk Gibson to play in the outfield ahead of Jim Eisenreich, a .300 hitter who can cover more ground on defense and is fundamentally sound in all phases."

Jim played only periodically the balance of the '91 season, but ended up hitting .301. Gibson finished at .236. Before the regular 1992 season started, Gibson was traded to Pittsburgh when Kansas City agreed to pay part of his salary, and shortly thereafter he was unconditionally released. A much healthier Kirk Gibson made a remarkable comeback with the Detroit Tigers in 1993 as a designated hitter.

In December 1991 I was at the annual major league baseball winter meetings in Miami, hoping to lock in a three-year, megabuck contract for Eisenreich that would put him on Easy Street the rest of his life. It could be his last contract. One club in addition to Kansas City was interested, but while I was negotiating with K.C. officials daily, the other club went from warm to cool. The day before the meetings ended, I met one last time with the Royals' people and they made me their best offer: a three-year, guaranteed contract for $5,250,000. I was told that the offer was "only on the table for the balance of the day."

I'd heard that one before, many times. Nice try. I'd never had a club pull an offer before. I wasn't going to fall for that old ploy. Kansas City's outfield was decimated. The club was going to lose its top slugger, right fielder Danny Tartabull, to a higher-paying club through free agency. That was certain. Brian MacRae, the son of manager Hal MacRae, returned in center field, but Kirk Gibson, who had manned left field in 1991, was washed up due to injuries. Since Jim could play both left field and right field, and the club had to fill not one but two outfield spots, we were in a strong bargaining position. Kansas City's offer would be there later, and if not Jim could always fall back on a one-year contract with the Royals through salary arbitration and become a free agent again at the end of the 1992 season. Jim went along with my recommendation to reject the offer. That's why he hired me.

Then came the bombshell. Kansas City announced a major trade with the New York Mets. The Royals traded infielder Bill Pecota and superstar pitcher Bret Saberhagen to the Mets for third baseman Gregg Jeffries, outfielder Kevin McReynolds, and Keith Miller. Miller, primarily a second baseman, had also played the outfield. MacRae immediately announced that Miller was going to occupy the left field position for the Royals with McReynolds in right and MacRae in center. I was stunned. Eisenreich was the odd man out. The two jobs had been filled in one fell swoop. I had no advance warning of the impending trade. The Eisenreich offer was not only "off the table" but the other interested club had traded for an outfielder and was out of the picture. No other bidders surfaced in the next two weeks, so we accepted salary arbitration offered by the club by the December 19 deadline. This process provides only for a one-year contract, not guaranteed, with the salary to be determined by an arbitrator.

Shortly before the hearing date, we settled for $1.65 million for one year, but with no guarantees. Jim wouldn't be in the bread line but it was a far cry from the guaranteed, three-year deal I had rejected.

My favorite song is "The Gambler" sung by Kenny Rogers. Sometimes during a critical point in intense negotiations, I can hear Rogers' voice reminding me, "You've got to know when to hold 'em, know when to fold 'em, know when to walk away, know when to run." In retrospect, the offer was a fair one, and in not grabbing it, I made an error in judgment. It was time to fold 'em and walk away, and I was holding 'em.

I feel badly about it, in particular because it's Jim. Jim has suffered a string of disappointments throughout his life. He has been let down by so-called friends who taunted him and made life miserable for him as a youth; by well-meaning doctors who misdiagnosed him for years; perhaps one could even argue by his parents for not being aggressive enough in seeking other medical help during his adolescence; by the Twins' officials for giving up on him; and now perhaps by his lawyer for giving him bad advice. Eisenreich never looks back, though. He's very forgiving. He looks ahead.

The $1.65 million was not guaranteed, and the club could cut Eisenreich at any time during spring training with only the obligation to pay him between $275,000 and $400,000 in severance pay, depending upon the date of termination. Termination was a frightening thought for me. That would have been a financial disaster, yet it was more than a possibility.

During the preseason, manager MacRae stuck to his guns. The starting outfielders were Keith Miller, Brian MacRae, and Kevin McReynolds. No platooning. "Eisie," a .300 hitter in 1991, would be the benchwarmer, euphemistically described as the utility or role player. Under baseball rules, if the player isn't released by March 31, his entire salary is guaranteed for the season. Another veteran teammate, Kevin Seitzer (the third baseman) was in a similar position. MacRae had announced plans to start Jeffries at third base. Seitzer had fallen out of favor with MacRae, although he had been Kansas City's regular third baseman for several years. His 1992 salary was as hefty as Eisenreich's.

During spring training 1992 I nervously scoured the sports pages early each morning, searching for information on Eisenreich's progress. Was he playing? Was he hitting? Was he injured? Each day up until the March 31 deadline was a mini-crisis. If Eisenreich got the "pink slip" before March 31, I would never be able to forgive myself.

During spring training, clubs were trimming their payrolls, and for the first time I noticed good players were being released. The Yankees cut Alvaro Espinoza, Pittsburgh released Bill Landrum, and Cincinnati dropped Ted Power. Then came the worst: Seitzer got the ax from Kansas City and ended up with approximately $400,000 in severance pay rather than the $1.6-million contract. Clubs were now paring their rosters to the 25-man limit, not adding players. Seitzer was one of the more fortunate ones. He caught on with Milwaukee, albeit for the minimum salary of $109,000. At least he had an opportunity to continue to play the game. Others who were released were less fortunate and ended up in the minor leagues. Would Eisenreich be next? Would any other club be interested at this late date? If a top player like Seitzer got his walking papers because of his high salary, why not Eisenreich? The two were in almost identical situations.

Fortunately, during spring training, Eisenreich was hitting over .400 and leading the team in hitting. The pressure was mounting as the end of March approached, yet Jim never mentioned the possibility that he'd be cut. The last several days of March were agonizing. I was on vacation in Florida, hoping that each time the telephone rang it wasn't Eisenreich with the bad news. The March 31 deadline passed. Eisenreich was safe. My relief was indescribable. We had dodged another bullet. This was "old hat" for Eisenreich.

Kansas City won only one of its first 17 games. Jim was on the bench for most of this disaster. Near the end of the losing streak, I called the club's GM, Herk Robinson, the first time I'd ever done such a thing. Jim opposed it. I said, "Herk, for Christ's sake, you're paying Jim $1.65 million to sit. Meanwhile, your team has won one out of its first 15 games. Play him or trade him." He said he was meeting with McRae and Jim's situation would be discussed. Jim hadn't complained when he was benched in favor of Gibson, or when K.C. pulled its offer in Miami in December 1991, so I wasn't surprised he didn't complain now. He was accustomed to adversity and disappointment. He accepted his lot and he never bitched about it.

MacRae's experimental lineup was trashed two days later. The weak-hitting second baseman, Terry Schumpert, was banished to the minors and was replaced by Keith Miller, who most baseball people knew never could play the outfield and should have been installed at second base at the beginning. Eisenreich replaced Miller in the outfield against right-handed pitchers, platooning with Gary Thurman.

Every morning during the 1992 regular baseball season, my routine was the same. The first thing I did was to scan the sports page to see what kind of a night Eisenreich had had. Was he playing? Did he do well? Did he suffer an injury? How many runs or RBIs? I suffered through a sudden drop in his batting average to below .250 during early August when he went 2 for 20 while playing with a rib injury. The following 30 days that the rib injury sidelined Jim seemed like an eternity. He ended the season batting .269, but again was used only as a role player. He didn't put up the numbers he had in 1991.

Each day I hoped that Eisenreich was playing well enough and stayed healthy enough to give me my "last at bats," a chance to redeem myself from striking out in the last negotiation. I won't rest easy until I do. Time may soon be running out for the 33-year-old. But the fat lady hasn't sung yet. Jim had done his job. Now it was my turn to step to the plate.

In early December of 1992 I returned to the baseball winter meetings, this time in Louisville, Kentucky. I was there panning for gold for Eisenreich, a free agent again. I struck gold, but it was for Paul Molitor on a three-year, $13-million, guaranteed contract with Toronto. Unfortunately, I had no such luck with Jim.

The market conditions for Eisenreich had changed dramatically in that one year. Jim, now 33, was coming off a so-so year, unlike the 1991 season when he hit over

.300. This year, the market was flooded with 26 other free agent outfielders, compared with only a handful (Bonilla, Nixon, Tartabull, Pasque, Boston, and Gladden) a year earlier. Clubs were beginning to pare back their payrolls in preparation for the almost certain decline in TV revenues after the 1993 season. I knew that the basic economic principle of supply and demand would wreak havoc with the salaries of most free agent outfielders. I anticipated that there would be exceptions only for superstars like Bonds, Puckett, Carter, Sierra, and Dawson.

I made lots of calls during my three-day stay, but either my messages were not returned or I was told, "Don't call us, we'll call you." I watched with envy and disappointment in the press room each day as releases were posted regarding outfielder free agent signings. Meanwhile, my telephone was silent. Not one ring. Before I left the meetings, I even looked into possible baseball opportunities for Jim in Japan, but nothing was available there.

Christmas was not merry for the Eisenreich family. By that time, the crop of free agent outfielders had been picked over, leaving only Eisenreich, Tom Brunansky, Kevin Bass, Hubie Brooks, Stan Javier, Chris James, and Herm Winningham unsigned. To make matters worse, the most recent signees included Joe Orsulak, Darryl Boston, Lonnie Smith, and Willie Wilson, all comparable to Jim. Each was taking a big pay cut.

I began to wonder if this was the end of Jim's career. I knew in my heart that he could still play the game well, but my opinion didn't matter. It appeared to me that all of the clubs had filled their needs for outfielders, and I was powerless. I could empathize with a teenage girl, waiting desperately by the phone for an invitation to the high school prom. All I could do was hope that the telephone would ring one day soon.

After the first week in January, it looked as if my worst fears would be realized. Three more outfielders, most considered to be of inferior ability to Jim, signed one-year contracts. Houston signed Chris James and Kevin Bass to one-year minor league contracts for $500,000, the lowest yet, and the contracts weren't even guaranteed. At the same time, California signed Stan Javier for $600,000. Neither club had even contacted me about Jim. The downward salary spiral was continuing. Now the pickings were really slim. Eisenreich, Brooks, and Winningham. The outlook remained bleak.

Throughout the ordeal, Eisenreich never lost his sense of humor. Over the holidays, I was contacted by a representative of the Professional Baseball Writers of the Greater Philadelphia area. The group wanted to honor Jim with its Most Courageous Athlete award at an upcoming annual banquet. When I passed the news on to Eisenreich, he quipped, "I don't need an award. I need a job."

Fortunately, the phone finally rang a few days later, not once but twice, and I got

Eisenreich his job. Atlanta and Philadelphia, the unexpected bidders, had both appeared to be set in the outfield, but each was looking for a left-handed "role" player. Philadelphia won the bidding skirmish with a better offer—a contract for $600,000 for one year, plus some attainable playing-time bonuses that could earn Jim as much as $200,000. Better yet, the contract would be guaranteed, a first for Jim. Although the contract wasn't what we had wanted or hoped for initially, it wasn't bad under the circumstances.

Needless to say, I'll be scanning those Philadelphia box scores early every morning during the baseball season. All the same questions will flash through my head. Is he playing? Is he hitting? Is he healthy? Jim will be a free agent again at the end of the 1993 season. I'll be riding the emotional roller coaster with him all the way. Neither Eisenreich nor I will quit. True to form, Jim will be playing his guts out for the Phillies. I'll be back at the next round of baseball winter meetings, hustling for another contract for Eisenreich.

Jim's battle with Tourette's is ongoing. The medications help control but do not eliminate the symptoms. In every visiting stadium, the bleacher jockeys are still on him, heckling and taunting him when he takes his position in the outfield. It seems like the tics sometimes return if he's not concentrating on something when he patrols the outfield. So often in between pitches he has found it helpful to sing his favorite country music songs. He is often bothered by the bright lights in stadiums, a reaction experienced by many people with Tourette's Syndrome, who have greater sensitivity to loud sounds, bright lights, or touch. He still has the tics when he becomes more fatigued. After night games he stays in bed until noon to get sufficient rest. Driving a car often tires him, so he leaves the driving to Leann.

Jim has joined in the battle against Tourette's. He has been a guest on Geraldo Rivera's show, he has been the center of nationally aired public service announcements, and each year he hosts some of the victims and their families at a ballgame in Royal Stadium. Perhaps most importantly, he is cited as a role model in the literature distributed to T.S. victims all over the United States. The families are urged to tell their children about successful adults who have T.S., like former Louisiana State University basketball star Chris Jackson, now a professional basketball player for the Denver Nuggets, and Jim Eisenreich.

Mike Lauer is still Jim's closest friend. He lives in North Dakota. Jim hasn't forgotten Mike's unswerving loyalty during the bad times. Jim recently gave him a new $16,000 pick-up truck as a token of their friendship.

At the Boston Baseball Writers Association Banquet in 1991, the shy and reserved Eisenreich began to speak. The 1,200-seat banquet hall went stone silent. People wanted to hear every word he had to say. Jim characteristically minimized his accomplishments by attributing them to certain gifts with which he had been blessed. As he got more comfortable, he spoke of the difficulties he had encountered both before and after the discovery that he had Tourette's Syndrome. He ended by promising that he would play baseball as long and as hard as he could, and he would stop playing only when he was dragged off the field.

The Boston fans stood and applauded with great gusto when Jim finished. It was an emotional moment—a warm welcome back from some of the same fans who had hooted him off the Fenway outfield in the difficult days before his condition was discovered.

His story is about the triumph of the human spirit. He offers hope to every victim of Tourette's Syndrome. In his darkest days he never gave up his dream, and now he lives it every day.

12

BASEBALL, PAST,
PRESENT, AND
FUTURE

JIM KAAT, GREG OLSON, AND CHRIS WEINKE ARE
three clients who represent the past, present, and future of baseball.

Kaat won 283 games in the big leagues. In 1966 he won 25 and lost 13, with a
2.74 ERA for Minnesota. After a long battle with owner Calvin Griffith, he ended up
with a one-year contract for $54,000. After the 1992 season, free agent pitcher David
Cone (won 13 and lost 7 with a 2.88 ERA) signed with Kansas City for three years at
$18 million, and free agent pitcher John Smiley (won 16 and lost 9 with a 3.21 ERA)
signed with Cincinnati for four years at $18.5 million. The most money Kaat made in
a season was $285,000, a salary he negotiated for himself at age 42 in 1983, his last year
in the majors. Clearly, Kaat was born 25 years too early.

Olson, an All Star catcher in 1990, plays for one of the best teams in baseball,
the Atlanta Braves. He labored in the minors for seven and a half seasons before
making it to the big leagues at the age of 29. In his first three major league seasons, his
team twice made it to the seventh game of the World Series. He is coming back from
an injury sustained in a home-plate collision and hopes to be part of the Atlanta Braves
dynasty of the 1990s. It is happening right now for Greg.

In 1990, Weinke had to choose between college football and pro baseball. A
second-round pick in the baseball draft, he dropped out of Florida State and signed a
$375,000 contract with the Toronto Blue Jays. We don't know if he'll be as successful

on the field as Kaat and Olson, nor do we know where the economics of baseball are going, but Weinke is off to a great start.

JIM KAAT

Kaat certainly could tell Weinke some stories. Jim Kaat pitched in the majors in four different decades. He was a Washington Senator when John F. Kennedy and Lyndon Johnson were senators in Washington. Kaat won a record 16 Gold Gloves, ranks as the fourth winningest lefty in baseball history, and is a candidate for the Hall of Fame.

Mickey Mantle, Roger Maris, Frank Robinson, Al Kaline; Kaat faced 'em all. But year in and year out, his toughest opponent was Calvin Griffith, the tightwad owner of the Senators and the Twins. Kaat played in an era when players negotiated their own contracts and woe to the player who tried to squeeze a nickel out of Calvin. After winning 25 games for the Minnesota Twins and being named American League Pitcher of the Year in 1966, Kaat got his $54,000 contract. In 1967, Kaat went 16 and 13, and the Twins missed winning the American League Championship by only one game. Kaat was given a $6,000 raise to $60,000, but only after he held out for part of spring training. It was downhill from there. In 1968, he went 14 and 10 for the seventh-place club, so Calvin cut his salary back to $55,000. In 1969, he won 14 and lost 12 for a division winner, and Calvin again cut his salary to $50,000. In 1970, he won 14 and lost 13 for a division winner, and Calvin cut his salary again to $48,000. In 1971, Kaat went 13 and 14, and Calvin cut his salary yet again, this time to $47,750. At this rate, Kaat was going to wind up paying Calvin for the honor of pitching for the Twins. Unfortunately, Kaat's only choice was to accept a pay cut or hold out the entire season with no pay.

Each year, Calvin offered a different excuse. If the team's record was good, he pointed to reduced club revenue. If it was bad, he complained about the record. If both were good, he complained about Kaat's performance. Calvin would say, "I pay you to win 20 games." That was that.

In 1972, Kaat won 10 games and lost 2 during the first half of the season, leading the American League in most of the pitching stats, but he then broke his left wrist and was out for the rest of the season. After the season, when Griffith offered again to cut his salary for a fifth straight year, Kaat exploded. He was mad as hell and he was not going to take it anymore. Kaat insisted that his salary be restored to the $60,000 he had earned six years earlier. He refused to go to spring training. Griffith finally relented a short time before the regular season started, but when it was time to sign the contract,

Calvin would neither look at Kaat nor shake his hand.

After signing the papers, Kaat told his roommate, Phil Roof, that he expected to be traded before the end of the season. After the '72 All Star break, the Twins "waived" Kaat. When Gentleman Jim heard he'd been waived, he went to the Twins manager Frank Quilici to say good-bye. Quilici volunteered, "Jim, I was opposed to your waiver but Calvin didn't think you could pitch any more." Kaat went to Griffith to say good-bye, and Calvin said, "Jim, I didn't want to put you on the waiver list, but Quilici didn't think you could pitch any more." The White Sox picked him up for $20,000. The Twins got nothing in return. Kaat won 20 for Chicago in both 1974 and 1975. Calvin probably would have found a reason to cut his pay.

Calvin always found ways to save nickels. Major league players in the mid-60s got a $10-a-day meal money allowance while on the road. Kaat discovered that on some occasions the Twins were only giving him $6.50 a day. When Kaat inquired about the discrepancy, he was informed that $3.50 was deducted whenever players were served meals on the airplane. Kaat responded, "I don't usually eat the meals on the airplane." Too bad, he was told. Club policy. A player had no recourse. Is it any wonder that Kaat was involved in organizing the baseball union in 1966?

The articulate Kaat in 1986 made a smooth transition from the pitching mound to the television booth, but his unpleasant and sometimes bitter experiences as his own negotiator led him to me. In 1986, he'd done the "color" for New York Yankee's baseball games with play-by-play announcers Bill White and Phil Rizzuto. Although Kaat was green, his obvious talent as an analyst was overlooked by Yankee boss George Steinbrenner, who replaced him with the oft-fired Yankee manager Billy Martin. Kaat had displeased his boss because he was not "pro-Yankee" enough on the air. Because Steinbrenner canned Kaat so late in the year, Jim didn't have time to catch on with another team for the 1987 season. He did some work for ESPN in '87, then got a break when he was asked to return to Minnesota as a TV analyst for Twins games in 1988. In 1989, another local television station, the CBS affiliate, acquired the rights to do the Twins games and tapped Kaat to be the TV color analyst. At the same time, ESPN wanted to renew Kaat's contract to do college baseball games. Kaat asked me to handle the local TV contract, and although the amount of pay and other fringes on the new ESPN contract had already been agreed upon, Kaat wanted me to work out the "fine print." Most people erroneously assume that the fine print is sacred, especially if it is part of a printed form contract. If any of these so-called boiler plate clauses significantly affects my client's rights, I'm not bashful about insisting on changes—printed form or not.

Too often the fine print is overlooked and then it comes back to bite you later.

Recently, a major radio station drove one of its talents, who had a three-hour mid-morning show, to me for advice. The station manager apparently wanted to fire the personality in question. As there was no legal basis to do so under the contract, the station manager reassigned the individual to the graveyard shift from 1:00 A.M. to 4:00 A.M. The fine print permitted the reassignment, and the talent had no recourse. He resigned with some modest severance pay. Sometimes the "fine print" turns out to be more important than the money.

Kaat informed me that NBC's contract with major league baseball would be expiring after the 1989 season, and that if CBS should obtain the new rights to televise the games, there was a remote possibility that he would be selected as one of the two "color analysts" for the major league baseball Game of the Week, the All Star Game, the playoffs, and the World Series. This would be a major plum for Jim, who had been in the booth for a short time. He wanted me to preserve his right to accept such an opportunity in the event it became available. ESPN, too, had its eye on major league baseball and contemplated that if it acquired any rights to televise games, it wanted Kaat as part of its team. Kaat didn't want to be tied down to ESPN in the event he was offered a CBS job, but he did want the two-year ESPN contract. ESPN insisted upon a clause in the agreement providing that it could elect to have Kaat cover major league baseball for ESPN exclusively if it obtained any rights to televise any games.

My objective was to negotiate wording that would be acceptable to the other side but would leave us with a loophole in case CBS came calling. We got it. The clause provided that if ESPN wanted Kaat to work major league baseball games, Jim would be paid a supplemental fee to be determined by negotiations between the parties. When ESPN and CBS each acquired rights to televise certain major league baseball games starting in the 1990 season, ESPN wanted Kaat on its team. CBS had already hired Tim McCarver as their lead baseball TV "color" man, but the network needed two pairs to do the games and selected Kaat over a number of other outstanding candidates. Both ESPN and CBS offered contracts, but at this point, ESPN realized that it couldn't legally stop Kaat from joining CBS, because an agreement to negotiate an agreement is unenforceable. Kaat opted for CBS, and ended up with an opportunity to work the big games for a major network on national TV with a salary that was higher because of the competing bid from the cable network. It sure beat haggling for $3.50 meal money with Calvin Griffith.

GREG OLSON

Greg Olson was an outstanding catcher for the University of Minnesota baseball team when he was drafted on the seventh round by the New York Mets in 1982. I helped him with his rookie contract, and we stayed in touch. The Mets gave up on him after six and a half unspectacular seasons in the minors. Before the 1989 season, Olson signed a $21,000 Triple A contract with the Twins' minor league team in Portland. It was his biggest payday yet.

The Twins promoted Olson to the big leagues in June, but he played in only three games, was shipped back to Triple A, and then dumped at the end of the season. One Twins official was overheard saying, "He'll never be anything more than a third-string catcher."

Olson refused to hang up the spikes and catching gear. Though he was 29 years old and recently married, he survived financially by living with his parents during the offseason. This is the side of baseball most fans don't think about. For every guy you see making an "easy" million to sit on the bench as a backup shortstop, there are hundreds of young men hanging on the fringe of the majors, just trying to make ends meet.

There was interest in Greg, but only as a Triple A catcher. He and I sorted through the several proposals from major league clubs, one of which was from Atlanta offering Greg $5,200 per month. We scanned the rosters, analyzing the strengths and weaknesses of catchers on the other clubs. We gave no consideration to the amount of money offered. We were looking for opportunity. The money was marginally better elsewhere, but we grabbed the Braves' proposal because in our judgment, Atlanta offered Greg the quickest route to the "bigs."

After Olson signed the contract, we walked out into the reception area of my office, where autographed pictures of major leaguers I have represented adorn the walls. A determined Olson pointed to the pictures on the wall, turned to me, and said, "Simon, next year my picture is going to be hanging on that wall."

Greg was sent to the minors at the end of spring training, but the day before the regular season started, the Braves' third-string catcher, Phil Lombardi, quit baseball. Olson was called up as the 27th and last player on the Braves' roster. (Two players had been added temporarily because of a labor dispute.) He would backup 36-year-old Jody Davis and 37-year-old Ernie Whitt, and figured to go back to the minors at the end of April. Then things started to happen. First baseman Nick Esasky came down with a career-ending vertigo condition. Davis was moved to first base, and Olson, a right-handed hitter, was used to spell Whitt against left-handed pitchers.

Olson made the most of his break. He hit a pair of homers in one game and belted a grand slam homer in another. When club officials saw that he could hit left-handed pitching, the aging Davis was released. Olson platooned with the left-handed-hitting Whitt. In mid-May, Whitt was injured in a game against Montreal, and Olson inherited the regular catcher's job.

By the All Star break, Olson (whose career average in the minors was .248) was batting .289 with 6 homers and 25 RBIs. Johnny Bench described Olson as the best catcher in the majors at blocking balls. Several days before the All Star Game, Olson encountered Atlanta sports reporter Bill Zack as he walked across a stadium parking lot. Zack called out, "How's it going, All Star catcher?" Olson was speechless.

"I wanted to cry," Greg said later. "I took a minute to say a prayer and then I called Lisa.

"She said, 'You stud!'"

In the history of baseball, only Don Newcombe (1949, Dodgers), Don Schwall (1961, Red Sox), and Alvin Davis (1984, Mariners) had been selected All Stars after starting the season in the minors.

A day after Greg's selection, I was in Atlanta sharing the excitement with him and his wife. I marveled at his perseverance. He told me, "I never considered quitting baseball, even though I spent all my time in the minor leagues, because baseball is a kids' game and I love it." Like many baseball fans, I was also curious about the suddenness of his success. How did he explain his impressive record at the plate in the major leagues, when he was a career .248 hitter in the minors? "When you are desperate to stay in the major leagues, your concentration is at its peak," he said. "Also, when you have an opportunity to play regularly, your timing is much better. Once I began to hit well in the majors this year, my confidence began to build."

Everyone, it seemed, found something to admire in Greg's tenacity. A day before the All Star Game, Olson was even approached by then–Baseball Commissioner Fay Vincent during practice at Wrigley Field. Vincent, who has a bad leg, spotted Olson while riding around the field in a golf cart. The commissioner drove up to Olson for a chat. "Greg," he said, "to have something like this happen is great for baseball. It's the American Dream to play major league baseball and suddenly, after seven and a half years in the minor leagues, to play in the major league All Star Game. It's incredible."

After the season, Olson was selected as a catcher for a U.S. All Star team that was to play in Japan against Japanese teams during a two-week period in November. He didn't want to leave Lisa, who was expecting their first child in November, but he so desperately needed the $50,000 stipend that he consented. You would too, if you'd been making $26,000 a year just a few months earlier. Greg's lucky streak continued when he arrived home three and a half hours before Lisa went into labor. He was there when Ryan arrived.

After Olson returned from Japan, he stopped by my office to say hello. As he walked in the door, he immediately peered to the wall on the left. He saw his picture proudly displayed, among the other major leaguers on my office wall, just as he had earlier predicted.

The story doesn't end here.

The Braves marched to the National League West Championship in 1991, and Olson found himself in the middle of a pennant race, a playoff, and a World Series. He caught 32 consecutive games in the autumn stretch drive, then smacked the winning hit in the ninth inning of the sixth game of the National League Championship series against Pittsburgh. The win avoided elimination for Atlanta. After the game, Jane Fonda—the wife of Braves' owner Ted Turner—was so happy that she promised Greg she would name her next dog "Olie" after him.

Olson is not the type to carry a grudge, but it had to feel good to come back to the Twin Cities as starting catcher for the NL champs in the 1991 World Series. The Twins had given up on their hometown product less than two years earlier. In the memorable '91 series, Greg started every game, and in Game 1 he was on the receiving end of one of the most violent home-plate collisions in series' history. Greg was catching when Dan Gladden, another client, attempted to score from third on a fly to left field. Gladden slid into Olson hard, Olson went airborne, involuntarily making a perfect somersault, and then diving straight to the ground head first. Olson didn't drop the ball, Gladden was out, and neither player was injured. A photo of the crash adorned the cover of *Sports Illustrated* and now hangs in the waiting room of my office.

It was a less dramatic home-plate collision that took Olson out of the 1992 World Series. Late in the regular season, after the Braves had clinched the NL West, Greg suffered a broken leg and tore ankle ligaments in a home-plate crash with Houston's Ken Caminiti. Olson was in excruciating pain and lay motionless on the ground for ten minutes. When the team physician placed him in a neck brace for precautionary reasons, Olson became concerned about the reaction of his wife, who was watching the game on TV. As he was carried off the edge of the field to the applause of the fans, he raised his right arm from his side and gave the "Tomahawk Chop." The gesture was intended to signal to his wife that he was okay. He ended up in a cast and was out for the playoffs and the World Series.

During the National League Championship series with Pittsburgh, Greg's team-mates rubbed his cast for good luck. When it was removed, Atlanta was playing the World Series in Toronto, down three games to one. The cast was shipped to Toronto and at the beginning of Game 5, the Braves rubbed it again for good luck. The Braves won, forcing the series back to Atlanta for Game 6. Doctors told Greg he would be out of baseball for about eight months. His career was in jeopardy. We were all holding our breath. Fortunately, Greg is back behind the plate, sharing catching duties with Damon Berryhill for the best pitching staff in baseball.

Don Sutton, who pitched 23 years in the major leagues, says, "There are catchers who can throw better than Greg. There are catchers who can hit for a higher average and more power. No doubt. All Greg Olson is is the best 'receiver' in the National League. And nobody knows it. He makes the pitchers' jobs easier. He frames the strike zone, he has soft hands, so he can steal a strike for you. He knows how to work inside and out. He knows the strengths and weaknesses of all of his pitchers. That's all he does. If I were pitching, I'd want Greg Olson to catch me."

CHRIS WEINKE

As a high school senior, Chris Weinke had to look no farther than pictures on the corridor walls of his school to find perfect role models. St. Paul's Cretin–Derham Hall High School was the home of football's Steve Walsh and baseball's Paul Molitor. In the school season of 1989–90, Weinke was everything Walsh and Molitor had been. He was a high school All American in both sports and wanted to play both at a major university.

In two seasons at quarterback, Weinke passed for almost 4,000 yards and 24 touchdowns, completing 57 percent of his passes. He was rated the number-one high school quarterback in the country by USA Today. In his junior year, he led the team to the State Championship Finals. In baseball, during his senior year the first baseman/third baseman hit .450, setting a school record with 11 homers and 43 RBIs. During his junior year, his Raiders won the State Baseball Championship, and that summer he helped the U.S. Junior Team win the World Tournament in Quebec. In the summer following his senior year, he was honored by the U.S. Baseball Federation as the Junior Player of the Year.

Weinke always had a simple answer to the question of which sport he preferred: "During football, I like football, and during baseball, I like baseball."

The recruiting process began early. Chris received over 500 telephone calls from college recruiters around the nation. "It was a pattern," he remembered. "I would receive calls every night, Sunday through Thursday—maybe four to six calls a night—from college recruiters. Every Saturday I'd hear from three or four by cellular telephone from the sidelines of games in progress. I think they wanted to impress me with the crowd noise in the background."

More than 1,000 letters, brochures, and other materials from college recruiters filled six large boxes. Two of the top prep football rating reports in the country named Chris as one of the two most heavily recruited quarterbacks in the nation.

Weinke and his family narrowed the field to Alabama, Illinois, Florida State, Arizona State, Miami, and Minnesota. All promised he could play both sports in college. He visited all six campuses.

At Florida State, Chris was impressed with both Bobby Bowden and his staff, as well as with baseball coach Mike Martin. Football coach Bowden had just signed a lifetime contract, which gave the program stability. Coach Bowden made him no promises but was very genuine. During the visit, each of the 27 cheerleaders came up to Chris individually, introduced herself, and told him how much she would like to see him come to Florida State. Weinke picked Florida State.

At a news conference in St. Paul, he explained his decision: "Florida State gives me the opportunity to contend nationally, both in football and baseball, year in and year out. And the opportunity to play for Bobby Bowden is something I have always dreamed of. There have been athletes [at FSU] who have played both sports, and that swayed me a little bit that way. At present they have three football players who play both."

Weinke had settled on his future for at least the next four or five years. And then came the baseball draft. In early June 1990, Weinke was drafted in the middle of the second round (the 53rd pick) by the Toronto Blue Jays. Chris was now facing another major decision. When asked about the likelihood of turning to pro baseball, Weinke said, "I don't think anyone would offer me enough money to pass up four years of college. I wouldn't sign for $100,000."

Under baseball rules, if Weinke did not sign a pro baseball contract before the first day of his college classes, he could no longer turn pro for three years, when he would next be eligible for the pro baseball draft. In that event, Toronto would also lose its right to sign him. Under NCAA rules, Weinke could forfeit his college eligibility if he retained an agent to help him negotiate the baseball contract. Unlike most draftees, Chris had the option of playing football and baseball for a college powerhouse and turning pro in baseball three years later, or possibly signing a pro baseball contract immediately but also playing college football.

Ron and Betty Weinke faced a dilemma. The stakes were high and the negotiations with the Blue Jays would be extremely complicated. The Weinkes did not have the experience or skill to handle the matter. Yet if Chris agreed to have an agent, he could lose his college eligibility. He would then no longer have a choice and would be forced to turn pro in baseball. Without the option of playing in college, the signing bonus would be a lot smaller. Steve Walsh's father, Bill, and Chris's high school football coach, Mal Scanlan, urged Ron Weinke to consult with me.

I was well aware of a couple of horror stories about baseball executives "snitching" to the NCAA on drafted players who had had agents in similar circumstances. When present Seattle pitcher Bill Swift was drafted high by the Minnesota Twins in the early 1980s, Swift was represented by an agent during the negotiations. After Swift rejected the Twins' final offer and returned to college for his final year of eligibility, an irate Calvin Griffith "blew the whistle." Swift was punished by the NCAA, although fortunately he didn't lose the entire year of eligibility. I have always found it contemptible for agents to sign up athletes with remaining college eligibility when the athlete and his family are not fully aware of the possible consequences of loss of eligibility. The NCAA has left us one loophole. It allows a student-athlete to receive "advice from a lawyer concerning a proposed professional sports contract," but it is a rule violation if the lawyer represents the student in negotiations.

When I first met with Ron Weinke in June to discuss the matter, I took great precautions to inform him fully of all the risks of my involvement. It was finally agreed that to reduce the risk of a rule infraction, I would remain in the background and would serve as their legal advisor. I would prep them before each meeting, and they would then report back to me regarding the progress.

At the first meeting at the Weinke home, the Toronto scouts told Weinke and his wife, Betty, that they would not lowball them but implied that they would be making their best offer immediately.

Although the amount of the signing bonuses paid to the top draft picks is not available as the major league salaries are, through several contacts I had been able to determine that most of the first-round picks who had already signed had received signing bonuses in the range of $175,000 to $250,000. Toronto offered $250,000, a very generous offer, especially for a second-rounder. However, it was not clear if Chris would also have to give up college football.

When I met with the Weinkes the next day, I suggested a counterproposal at $500,000 on condition Chris could also play college football. That signing bonus would be the largest ever for a baseball draftee at the time. It sounded outrageous to Ron Weinke. When he gulped, I suggested he jot the number and the conditions on a piece of paper, and hand it to the Toronto scouts. I knew he wouldn't be able to look them straight in the eye and verbalize the counteroffer. His facial expressions and body language would give him away. I prepared Mr. Weinke for the negative reaction I anticipated, told him not to bring Chris to the meeting (although the Toronto people had requested it), and suggested that he tell the Toronto people that his figure was based upon the judgment of his "baseball people" so he wouldn't have to justify it. I emphasized Chris was not to be present because he would be so impressed that he wouldn't be able to hide his enthusiasm. He followed my instructions.

The Toronto people responded predictably. The counterproposal was way out of line; in any event, Chris would have to give up college football, and they wanted to talk with his "baseball people." Weinke apologetically responded, "I had to start somewhere." The negotiations stalled. It was mid-July and Chris was leaving for Tallahassee for the beginning of football practice on August 9.

As the reporting date approached, it became obvious to me that these negotiations could not be completed successfully unless I became directly involved. The charade had to be abandoned. Only personal, candid discussions could produce a deal. However, I was now clearly moving from the safety of a "legal advisor" to a lawyer representing the player. To minimize the risk, I decided to call upon Andy MacPhail, the Minnesota Twins' general manager whom I knew and trusted. I explained the situation to MacPhail and asked him in early August if he could contact his counterpart, Pat Gillick of the Toronto Blue Jays, whom I had never met. I asked Andy to pass on to Gillick the message that I would become personally involved in the negotiations on condition that neither Gillick nor any other member of the Toronto organization would at any time blow the whistle on me. MacPhail called Gillick, and Gillick agreed. I again informed the Weinkes of the risk. They decided to take a gamble.

By this time, Chris had told me he would like to play college football and pro baseball if possible. Toronto had ruled this option out because it wanted Chris to focus all of his energy on baseball. The club was also concerned about the risk of injury and the development of muscles in football that are harmful to a baseball player's coordination.

I encouraged Chris to try college football because he would have the benefit of a college education, on which I placed a high premium, the normal social development which college life offers, and the thrills and the excitement of probably playing quarterback for one of the top college teams in the country. In addition, if Chris changed his mind, this move could create the kind of leverage that could produce a giant contract, worthwhile enough to lure Chris away from college.

Chris was leaving for Tallahassee on August 9 to report for football practice. Time was running out. For the first time on August 5 I met personally with Toronto representatives Don Welke and Emil Belick at the Weinke home. The Toronto people insisted that they would not meet with us unless Chris was present, so I had no choice.

Chris was well prepped, and he said very little. No progress was made because I insisted that Chris be permitted to play college football if he turned pro in baseball; the Toronto people said that was "not negotiable."

It appeared that Toronto would make its final run the day before Chris was to leave. The Weinkes and I met again at their home with Don Welke and another Toronto scout, Bob Engel. The offer was increased to $275,000, but we rejected it because Chris would not be permitted to play college football as well. Chris was leaving for Florida State the next day. At Mr. Engel's request, I contacted him from a pay telephone booth that evening at the Metrodome between late innings of a Minnesota Twins game. At this point, I made a proposal of $550,000 but conceded for the first time that Chris would give up football. The hour was late; it was almost 10:30 P.M. Engel pushed for a late-night meeting at the Weinke home, but I rejected the suggestion.

There is a time and place for important negotiations. I try to avoid negotiations when I'm tired because my judgment is not as keen. President Clinton agrees. In the January 25, 1993, edition of *U.S. News and World Report* he is reported to have said, "Every major error in my life I have made when I was tired." Daily levels of alertness vary with each individual. I am most alert in the morning and mid- to late afternoon. My decision-making ability is better when I'm more alert, so whenever possible I schedule negotiating sessions during these periods.

Another factor in my decision was that Chris was leaving the next morning, and it would have been very unsettling for him. It was not the right environment or time for making a sound decision.

I was, however, willing to listen to another offer by telephone. Engel complied. He offered $360,000, but it was "funny money." The signing bonus would be $110,000, and then Chris would be paid $50,000 a year without interest for the next five years. Nevertheless, I figured the offer had a value of close to $300,000, not exactly chicken feed and higher than most of the first-round draft choices had received. I reduced my offer to $500,000. It was rejected. Engel indicated that he and his people would have to "regroup." Sometimes, only one word is enough to tip your hand. To me, this implied the negotiations were not dead, and there was still a "crack in the door." The deadline was now 19 days away.

I saw several advantages to Chris's departure to Florida State. First, Chris would have the important advantage of actually seeing the campus as a student, meeting the people, getting involved in the football program, and making a more informed judgment on how well he liked it. Second, if Chris did turn pro in baseball, he would not be haunted the rest of his life about what it would have been like at Florida State. He would at least have had a sample of college football. Third, it was a good negotiating ploy because it appeared that Chris had irrevocably cast his lot with college football. Perhaps a better offer would come before the deadline. Finally, Chris would be escaping from the Twin Cities area—the "pressure cooker"—where he was becoming confused by the different advice he was receiving from all of his well-meaning friends and relatives. Each one put in their "two cents' worth." Chris would be safely tucked away in Florida concentrating on football, insulated from the pressure.

A confused and nervous Chris Weinke was going off to college for the first time, leaving behind his family and friends, and a lucrative offer worth almost $300,000 that he might never see again. Chris was so shook up at the airport early the next morning, where friends and family gathered to bid him farewell, that he forgot to say good-bye to his mother.

Reporting to football practice for the first time at Florida State, he learned a great deal. Coach Bowden pulled him aside and told him in all honesty it would be tough for Chris to play both football and baseball. He explained that the quarterbacks were expected to stay in Tallahassee during the summer to work with the receivers. This would conflict with baseball, pro or amateur. It was clear that for the FSU quarterbacks, football was a 12-month proposition.

My client Steve Walsh, the All American quarterback from Miami who now plays for the New Orleans Saints, was right after all. I had asked his opinion as to whether or not Chris would be allowed to play both football and baseball at any major college football power. He said, "Every school will tell him he can, but when push comes to shove if he is going to be the starting quarterback, the football people won't allow it."

Chris discovered that the players practiced all day, and then in the evenings, when the other players were resting, the five or six quarterbacks studied film and playbooks together for another four hours. Chris also quickly found out that Florida State was loaded with four other great quarterback candidates. He had been led to believe there were only two.

When Chris reported for football practice, the Tallahassee newspaper reported that he had turned down a baseball offer of over $200,000. One of the other quarterback prospects confided in Weinke. "Chris," he said, "I was in the same boat a year ago, and I regret not turning pro in baseball. Now I have to wait two more years before I can be drafted again. I envy you. You should turn pro."

Chris was calling home every other day telling his dad about the newest revelations. With each additional story, Chris was leaning more toward a pro baseball career only. In several days, the players would be wearing pads and would begin to have "contact." Chris was concerned about an injury.

On August 13 after football practice, Weinke grabbed a bite to eat with one of the trainers, who asked him, "Do you know what you are going to have to put up with if you stay here and play football?" He said the intensity was unbelievable, and if he were Chris, he would turn pro in baseball. Chris Weinke had seen and heard enough. He had made up his mind.

That evening, he called his father and advised him of his decision to turn pro in baseball. His father agreed. The problem, of course, was that the negotiations had stalled with no new talks set, the deadline was 14 days away, and the players were going to start scrimmaging. I called Chris to sort out the facts, and to assure myself that he had made a final, irrevocable decision. I was convinced. The Weinkes wanted me to take the initiative and wrap up the negotiations at once. They were quite satisfied with the last offer from Toronto, which had a value of about $300,000. I suspected, however, that if I was the one who resurrected the talks, there was no way I would be able to improve on this offer and it might even be reduced. I definitely wanted to avoid initiating any new discussions. A negotiator should avoid negotiating with himself, that is to say, making a proposal that is rejected without a counteroffer and then making a less attractive proposal. I had one last idea.

The Toronto Blue Jays were scheduled to come to Minneapolis to play the Minnesota Twins in a four-game series starting the following Thursday evening, August 16. My hope was that Gillick would join the club in Minneapolis and contact Ron Weinke while he was here. I asked the Weinkes to give me six more days, until Sunday, August 19, 1990. They agreed. If Gillick called, I had a chance to negotiate a substantially larger signing bonus. It would suggest to me the club was still interested—even though their last offer had been rejected—and it would then follow that they would up the ante.

Gillick accompanied his team to the Twin Cities and did call Ron Weinke upon his arrival. He suggested the Weinkes and I meet with him and Chris Bourjos, a young Toronto scout, to talk about the contract.

Gillick is a personable, outgoing, and open guy. He had put together the expansion Blue Jays' first team in 1977, now the blueprint for expansion franchises, and was the dean of general managers in major league baseball. Because he made very few trades over the years, he was stuck with the nickname "Stand Pat." We had a constructive discussion, during which Gillick made it very clear that Toronto would not sign Chris under any circumstances if he played college football. Unlike some general managers I had dealt with in the past, he knew how to disagree without being disagreeable. With college football clearly out, I wanted to turn a lemon into lemonade.

I had to provide Gillick with the ammunition for justifying a signing bonus in excess of $300,000. Several first-round draft choices had signed for $175,000, and most had signed for less than $300,000. Signing bonuses for second-rounders were running $125,000 to $150,000. I suggested that Chris deserved a substantial premium over and above the amounts paid to other first-and second-round draft choices because, unlike the others, he was giving up the opportunity to become a college football star. The argument was good, but my leverage—the upcoming deadline for signing or losing Chris—was more important.

Gillick went to work. He was an exceptional "people person"—a master diplomat. He offered to drive 75 miles with Bourjos to my lake cabin to talk with me because it was his policy to always "talk in person rather than by telephone" during negotiations. Upon his arrival he presented my wife with a dozen roses and apologized for disturbing our weekend. He increased the offer to $350,000 and threw in some "sweeteners": Chris would be allowed to travel with the Toronto Blue Jays as a non-roster player during their pennant race until he had to report to the instructional league in Florida on September 9; Chris's family would have an all-expense-paid trip for three days the following week when Toronto played Boston at Toronto in a key series; the family would also have an all-expenses-paid week in Florida during the 1991 spring training, and another week that year in the area where Chris was playing minor league ball. Chris would also be invited to the major league camp as a non-roster player in 1991. Gillick did point out, however, that he would be reluctant to exceed this offer because the club's first-round draft choice, Steve Karsay, had just signed for $350,000. I understood this barrier. In order to get more than $350,000, I would have to come up with a novel approach.

I proposed that some part of the $350,000 signing bonus be paid in such a way that it would be tax-free to Chris. Chris would in effect end up receiving a higher signing bonus, but the gross amount would still be $350,000 and Karsay would not be offended.

On the following day (Sunday, August 19) we met again at my office. Gillick reported that the club's "bean counters" were opposed to this accommodation, but instead he would offer $375,000, which we accepted. It was a win/win negotiation. Chris got the big signing bonus, and Toronto got a potential star who almost slipped away. The only loser was Bobby Bowden.

Although we had reached an agreement, Gillick was not finished with his touches of class. On Sunday evening, he and Bourjos drove to the Weinke home to congratulate Mr. and Mrs. Weinke personally. On Monday, he presented my secretary, Gail, with a dozen roses in appreciation for her help. At the press conference that followed, he insisted that the seat next to mine and Chris Weinke's be occupied by his young scout, Chris Bourjos. He stood in the background, giving the credit to Bourjos. At the end of the press conference, when he was asked to say a few words, he emphasized, "We never could have reached this agreement without the help of Ron Simon." He had touched every base and had created enormous goodwill and trust with Chris Weinke, his family, and me.

The $375,000 signing bonus was the highest ever paid to a second-round draft choice and the fourth highest ever paid to any draft choice in the history of baseball at the time. The other three were

Todd Van Poppel—$500,000 (1990, Oakland)

John Olerud—$500,000 (1989, Toronto)

Tony Clark—$500,000 (1990, Detroit).

The average signing bonus for first-rounders skyrocketed from $243,000 in 1990, to $355,000 in 1991, and to $477,000 in 1992. The average signing bonus for second-rounders in 1992 was $153,000. Jamie Howard, who signed with Atlanta for $400,000, was the only second-rounder who received more than $200,000. Nevertheless, Weinke's contract package, which included other benefits, still stands as the best ever received by a second-rounder.

Weinke still had one difficult task remaining. He had to break the news to Coach Bowden. He later told me, "As I dialed the telephone number I was literally shaking. It was the worst experience I ever had. I was so nervous I could hardly talk."

Weinke barely got the words out: "Coach, I settled on a contract with the Blue Jays."

Bowden responded: "Is that right?"

Weinke said: "Yes. Thanks for everything."

Bowden was understanding and generous. He said: "Chris, you could have been a great quarterback, and if you have any problems with baseball, if it doesn't work out, give me a call." Bowden added: "I've never seen a freshman come in and throw like that. God bless you. I wish you the best."

Weinke remains a top prospect, developing in the Toronto minor league organization.

Since 1991, "Stand Pat" Gillick has done a masterful job of improving his team. He traded for Joe Carter and Roberto Alomar, and added Candy Maldonado in 1991, picked up free agents Jack Morris and Dave Winfield before the 1992 season, and traded for David Cone during the 1992 stretch drive. It all paid off. In 1992, Toronto beat Oakland in the American League playoffs and went on to triumph over the Atlanta Braves in the 1992 World Series. Pat lost his nickname. I wasn't surprised.

EPILOGUE

My experiences over the last 22 years as a sports attorney have been unique, exciting, and enjoyable. In addition I was paid handsomely for the work. I am indeed fortunate, because much of the time I didn't consider it work. Apparently word has leaked out. On average, I get two inquiries a week from strangers who want to enter the field. I point out to them that the main problem with wanting to be a sports attorney is that you can't get your first client until you have been in the business and you can't be in the business until you get your first client. It's a Catch 22.

When I think back to my start, I am certain that if Lou Nanne had not introduced me to his North Star teammates and if George Thomas had not dragged Paul Molitor and Kent Hrbek into my office, I would still be laboring in the court rooms today. Although I like to think that I seized opportunity when it presented itself and that I did the job at the highest level when I had the chance, I don't ever want to forget that luck, not skill, was the door-opener for me.

I am well aware that I owe much of any success I may have had to Nanne and Thomas and to the four athletes who gambled with me when I was a rookie with no client list, and who stuck with me as they settled into long and successful careers. Reed Larson, Keith Fahnhorst, Paul Molitor, and Kent Hrbek all defied the odds by becoming All Stars in their respective sports. Not even the most skillful negotiator can get a big contract for a mediocre player. When these four clients excelled consistently over the years, it gave me the opportunity to get them attention-grabbing contract settlements that established my reputation. We grew together.

Although I love what I do, as with any profession, there are times when I get frustrated. Once, after a particularly trying set of circumstances, I complained to a senior partner about actions and words of clients that seemed careless, stupid, or irresponsible and that made my job of representing them more difficult. He pointed out the obvious to me. If people could do it right themselves, I would be out of business.

As collective bargaining agreements become more complex and as tax laws change more frequently, the industry is becoming more of a business than a sport and the need for agents is definitely growing. Unfortunately, the current statutes and regulations governing agents are toothless and don't prevent inexperienced, unqualified, or dishonest people from entering the field. I look forward to the time when agents will be regulated in much the same way as doctors and lawyers are. In the meantime, if anyone asks, I'm a sports attorney.

Athletes come and go. Their careers are short in comparison with the careers of others; however, I hope the close friendships I have developed with many of the athletes over the years will endure long past the day when they "hang it up" and move on to other things. When all is said and done, of all the experiences I have had, the richest and most enduring are these friendships.

ACKNOWLEDGMENTS

Many people have helped me with the book over the past three years. Without their assistance, *The Game Behind the Game*, never would have been published. Unfortunately, the constraints of space and the lengthy list of contributors will not permit me to identify each individual.

I wish to thank David Shama for his helpful research and his many critical suggestions, which improved the manuscript.

My deepest gratitude goes to Francie Paper and Jack Caravella, who together found me the right publisher at the right time. Francie also kept me on course whenever I veered.

Thanks to Bob DuBois and Tom Lebovsky of Voyageur Press for their confidence in me and their belief that my experiences would be interesting and informative to others.

Harvey Mackay provided me with invaluable advice, steered me through the rough spots, and helped me in countless other ways. I will forever be grateful to him for his most important contributions.

My special thanks to my editor, Jane McHughen, whose professional expertise, sound judgment, skillful guidance, and way with a word improved the book immeasurably. She encouraged me when I needed encouragement, and pushed me when I needed a push.

I also want to acknowledge all the other people at Voyageur Press, who were so helpful and enthusiastic.

The burden of the day-to-day work on the book fell upon Gail Hyster, my secretary and assistant for the past 12 years. She labored longer and harder than anyone. I thank her not only for all of the grunt work, but also for providing me with many valuable insights based on her long-standing knowledge of me and of the clients. Without her, I would still be stuck on chapter 1.

My heartfelt thanks to my family: to my wife, Schatzi, a voracious reader who helped me in numerous ways, and who tolerated and supported me over this three-year marathon; to my son, Stephen, my 1993 MVP during crunch time down the home stretch, his writing and research skills, coupled with his keen judgment and his willingness to do the leg work, helped me immeasurably when I needed it the most; to my daughter, Andrea, who has consistently out-negotiated me, for her constant long-distance inquiries and unflagging interest that kept me motivated to the end.

Last, but certainly not least, I want to thank the wonderful group of clients about whom I have written in this book. Each of them provided unfailing support of the endeavor, gave generously of their time for interviews and chapter reviews, and permitted me to write about sometimes sensitive or intimate details of their private lives and their professional careers. These people are the ones who provided me with the opportunity to play the game behind the game, and to them I will be eternally grateful.

ABOUT THE AUTHOR

Beginning as a trial lawyer, Ron Simon has been a practicing attorney in Minneapolis since 1959. During the 1970s and 1980s, he gradually developed a practice as a sports and media attorney. He is one of only a few sports attorneys who have represented and negotiated contracts for first-round draft choices in football, basketball, baseball, and hockey.

Ron presents lectures on his representation of professional athletes and the various negotiating techniques he has found to be helpful. He has been mentioned in a number of newspapers and magazines, including *USA Today*, *Sports Illustrated*, the *Wall Street Journal*, and the *New York Times*.

Simon was born in St. Paul, Minnesota. He and his wife have two children and live in Minneapolis.